ISBN: 9781313432221

Published by:
HardPress Publishing
8345 NW 66TH ST #2561
MIAMI FL 33166-2626

Email: info@hardpress.net
Web: http://www.hardpress.net

All books are subject to recall after two weeks.
Olin/Kroch Library

DATE DUE

	JUN 1	
GAYLORD		PRINTED IN U.S.A.

THE POEMS OF
EDGAR ALLAN POE

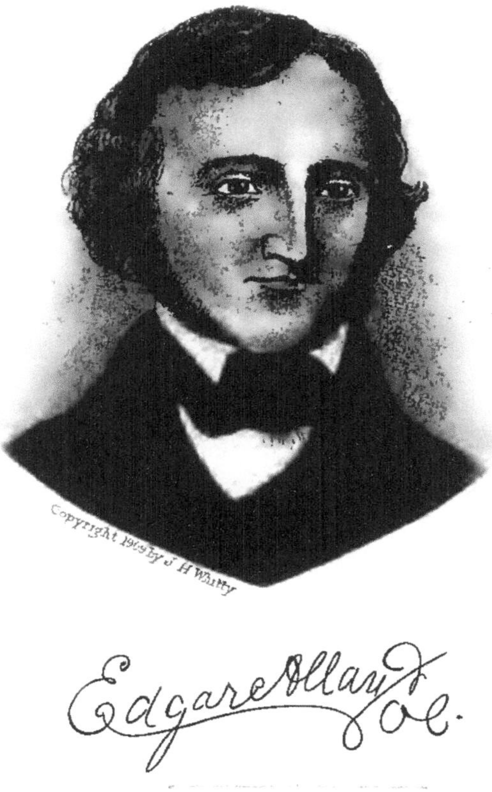
Copyright 1909 by J H Whitty
Edgar Allan Poe.

THE COMPLETE POEMS

OF

EDGAR ALLAN POE

COLLECTED, EDITED, AND ARRANGED
WITH MEMOIR, TEXTUAL NOTES
AND BIBLIOGRAPHY

BY

J. H. WHITTY

WITH ILLUSTRATIONS

BOSTON AND NEW YORK
HOUGHTON MIFFLIN COMPANY
The Riverside Press Cambridge

ERB

Published May 1911

THIRD EDITION, REVISED, 1919

TO
GEORGE EDWARD WOODBERRY

PREFACE

POE showed the utmost solicitude for the final text of his poems. He constantly revised and reprinted them. Professor G. E. Woodberry in his revised Life of Poe says: "There is no such example in literature of poetic elaboration as is contained in the successive issues of these poems." His revisions were minute — sometimes a mere word, and again only a punctuation mark or two. But even the mere matter of punctuation in the text, to an artistic poet like Poe, was of more than passing moment. Poe himself more fully explains this in *Graham's Magazine* for February, 1848, where he wrote: "That punctuation is important all agree; but how few comprehend the extent of its importance! The writer who neglects punctuation, or mis-punctuates, is liable to be misunderstood. It does not seem to be known that, even when the sense is perfectly clear, a sentence may be deprived of half its force — its spirit — its point — by improper punctuation."

Under these circumstances there is no difficulty in deciding upon Poe's last revision as the authoritative· and final text of his poems. Indeed in the preface to the Stedman-Woodberry edition of Poe's poems it is said, "The claim of his latest revision to be accepted as the authorized text seems to the Editors irresistible." The text of the poems adopted by them was that of the so - called J. Lorimer Graham copy of the 1845 edition of Poe's poems, revised by marginal corrections in Poe's hand which were long regarded as his final revisions. They were not, however, his last corrections. Poe not only made later revisions of his poems, but reprinted them, and also while on his last visit to Richmond prepared his writings for a new edition. John M. Daniel stated in the Richmond *Examiner* of October 12, 1849, that the last time he saw Poe he was just starting for the North to have them published.

As was Poe's habit when associated with various journals [1] he sent into the composing room of the Richmond *Examiner* a number of his revised poems and tales for publication in that newspaper. The space being crowded at that time, his copy was used by the printers as "stop matter," to keep them employed, and was typeset for later publication. Fortunately the revised proofs of these poems were retained by one of the printers, and they eventually fell into the hands of his old-time associate, F. W. Thomas, who was afterwards connected with the Richmond *Enquirer* at Richmond, Virginia. These poems were: "The Bridal Ballad," "The Sleeper," "Lenore," "Israfel," "Dream-Land," "The Conqueror Worm," "The Haunted Palace," "The Bells," "For Annie," "Sonnet to My Mother,"

---

[1] Authority of Judge Robert W. Hughes and other employees of the *Examiner*. *The Richmond Examiner During the War, Or the Writings of John M. Daniel*, With a Memoir of his Life by his Brother, Frederick S. Daniel (New York. Printed for the Author. 1868), p. 220, states: "Edgar A. Poe was induced to revise his principal poems for special publication in the *Examiner*, and at the time of his death was under engagement to furnish literary articles to its editor, who regarded him as the poet of America."

While John M. Daniel was Minister to Italy, his brother F. S. Daniel was his secretary, and was familiar with his life and his association with Edgar A. Poe.

"Annabel Lee," "Ulalume," and "To —— (A Dream Within A Dream)."

One of the poems, "Dream-Land," appeared in the *Examiner* shortly after Poe's death. His well-known tale, "MS. Found in a Bottle" as from "The late Edgar A. Poe's tales of the Grotesque and Arabesque," printed from the *Examiner* type and in that office, is now in my possession. The reason more of the poems did not appear is explained in the *Examiner* of October 19, 1849, which stated: "We do not quote them ('The Bells') here because they are too long. We have already published, with his own corrections, 'The Raven,' which is a beautiful specimen of the more solemn and elevated of his verse. We wish to give a sample of his still more delicate style — the *epicureanism* of language which was an art of his own. 'Ulalume' and 'Annabel Lee,' the last thing he ever wrote, are samples of this, but they have both been too much in the newspapers of late. We therefore choose and will publish in our next one from his collected poems which we do not think has been properly appreciated. It is a fanciful picture of dreams — and the broken fantastic images which cross the mind's eye — when the senses and judgment are enveloped in sleep."

This poem was "Dream-Land," and appeared as revised by Poe in the *Examiner* of October 29, 1849. The editor promised to give further reviews of Poe's writings when he had more space for them.

An important contribution of Poe's to the *Examiner* was his final revision of "The Raven." It was given as the only correct copy published, and now appears here for the first time since its appearance in that newspaper. The poems from proof sheets of the *Examiner* were compiled by F. W. Thomas with the intention of publishing a volume of Poe's poems. He wrote his *Recollections of Edgar A. Poe* for this, but his death ended the project. Judge Hughes afterwards placed the manuscript in my hands for publication in the Richmond, Virginia, Sunday *Times*, with which newspaper I was associated at the time, but it was found unavailable. A copy, however, was retained, and all the important facts and changes are incorporated in this volume.

The final text of "Lenore" left by Poe, which now appears here, is of inestimable value, and forever sets at rest the discussion as to Poe's intention of what should constitute his final revision of that poem. His corrections of this poem in the J. Lorimer Graham copy of his 1845 poems were misunderstood by his later editors and incorrectly printed. The final revision of the other poems, in particular "Ulalume," "The Bells," and "Annabel Lee," now determines the state in which Poe wished them all to rest. The text of the poems from the Baltimore *Saturday Morning Visiter* and the *Flag of Our Union* appears for the first time since Poe's death. It is now established that "A Dream Within A Dream" and "Eldorado" first appeared in the latter newspaper. The supposed lost first part of the manuscript of Poe's "The Haunted Palace" has been found, as well as new and unpublished manuscripts of "The Sleeper," "To M. L. S.," and others. Besides the eight poems now first collected, will be found two poems among the "Additional Poems," never before printed with Poe's poems. The revisions made by Poe in the J. Lorimer Graham edition of the 1845 poems have never been fully published, but they are now recorded here in the notes as Poe left them. The changes

made by Poe in the presentation copy of his 1829 poems
to his cousin Elizabeth Herring have been carefully
examined, and also appear here for the first time.

In the textual notes I have aimed to present an ex-
haustive "variorum" edition, while the Bibliography is,
I believe, the latest and most complete yet published.

With this new and authoritative text of Poe's poems,
there is presented in the Memoir a new, and I hope,
faithful life of the poet. It is the fruit of researches
extending over a period of thirty years which began in
Baltimore, Maryland, when I was associated with the
late Edward Spencer, who edited the Poe-Snodgrass letters. The finding of the F. W. Thomas *Recollections of
E. A. Poe* was a most fortunate discovery. With the
other important facts connected with Poe's history
which have been obtained, they have made it possible
to present a comprehensive story of the poet's career
with much new light upon certain disputed points.

J. H. W.

RICHMOND, VA., *March* 1, 1911.

PREFACE TO SECOND EDITION

SINCE the first edition of this volume, further new
Poe discoveries have been made. The most important
are five additional poems. There have also been found
hitherto unknown manuscript versions of three of Poe's
poems; also an introduction to the poem "For Annie."

The new verse has been brought into Poe's newly
collected poems, and other later matters incorporated
under the different headings, with a view of continuing
the volume, as the one final, complete, comprehensive,
and definite edition of Poe's poems.

RICHMOND, VA., *March* 1, 1917.   **J. H. W.**

CONTENTS

POEMS WRITTEN IN YOUTH

CONTENTS

ILLUSTRATIONS

MEMOIR

EDGAR ALLAN POE was born at Boston, Massachusetts, January 19, 1809. This was the date entered for him in the matriculation book at the University of Virginia in 1826. Other evidence exists to establish the date as true, although Poe himself has given the year of his birth as both 1811 and 1813. His age as recorded at the United States War Department and at West Point Military Academy is also at variance with the accepted date of his birth.

The question of correct age did not seem to give Poe much concern. In *Burton's Gentleman's Magazine* for April, 1840, he wrote: "The infirmity of falsifying our age is at least as old as the time of Cicero, who, hearing one of his contemporaries attempting to make out that he was ten years younger than he really was, very drily remarked, 'Then, at the time you and I were at school together, you were not born.'"

Poe also called himself both a "Bostonian" and a "Virginian." His mother, Elizabeth Arnold, arrived at Boston early in 1796, accompanied by her mother, an actress from the Theatre Royal, Covent Garden. Mrs. Arnold soon afterwards married a Mr. Tubbs, but their history is unknown. The daughter followed a theatrical career, and *Carr's Musical Repository* for 1800 published, among the popular songs of the day — "Tink a Tink," and "Chica cho," as sung by Miss Arnold in "Blue Beard." She married C. D. Hopkins, an actor, about May, 1802. He died October 26, 1805, and shortly afterwards she married another member cf her theatrical company named David Poe. He came from Baltimore, Maryland, where his family connections stood well. The first child, William Henry Leonard Poe, was probably born in 1807. He was afterwards taken in charge by his father's family at Baltimore. The Boston tax office shows that David Poe, actor, was assessed in May, 1808, with three hundred dollars, personal property, which represented at least double that amount. The Poe family left Boston in the fall of 1809, and joined the New York Company, playing with them until the end of the following season in July. In New York all definite traces of David Poe seem lost. Mrs. Poe joined her old company and appeared with them without her husband, at Richmond, Virginia, August 18, 1810. The notice in the Richmond *Enquirer* of that date announcing the play, "Castle Spectre," has, — "Mrs. Poe as Angela (From the Theatre, New York)." She also took the part of "Maria" in the afterpiece called, "Of Age To-morrow." All the names of the company were printed, but that of David Poe did not appear. A benefit was given Mrs. Poe September 21, when she sang and danced. The company left Richmond November 14, 1810. The fact that the company with Mrs. Poe were in Norfolk, Virginia, in December, and that she did not appear upon the stage, would indicate that her third child, Rosalie, was born there about that date. This event probably occurred at the Forrest Mansion, in that city, and has led to the supposition by some, that it was Edgar's birth, instead of his sister's.

E. A. Poe stated that his father died within a few weeks of his mother at Richmond, Virginia, which cannot be verified. Strong evidence to the contrary tends to show that David Poe was dead, or had deserted his family, prior to Mrs. Poe's last visit to Richmond. F. W. Thomas in his manuscript *Recollections of E. A. Poe* states:[1] "I was intimate with Poe's brother in Baltimore during the year 1828. He was a slim, feeble young man, with dark inexpressive eyes, and his forehead had nothing like the expansion of his brother's. His manners were fastidious. We visited lady acquaintances together, and he wrote Byron poetry in albums, which had little originality. He recited in private and was proud of his oratorical powers. He often deplored the early death of his mother, but pretended not to know what had become of his father. I was told by a lawyer intimate with the family that his father had deserted his mother in New York. Both his parents had visited Baltimore when he was a child, and they sent money from Boston to pay for his support."

Mrs. Poe went to Charleston, South Carolina, after leaving Norfolk, and the *Courier* of that city printed the following, April 28, 1811: "For the benefit of Mrs. Poe on Monday evening April 29th, will be presented, 'The Wonder,' or 'A Woman Keeps a Secret'; after the play a comic pantomimical ballet called 'Hurry Scurry, or the Devil among the Mechanics,' to which will be added, the much admired entertainment called 'The Highland Reel.'" Mrs. Poe and her company returned to Norfolk, Virginia, the following July. In a notice of Mrs. Poe's benefit, July 26, 1811, the Norfolk *Herald* printed a communication stating: "Misfortunes have pressed heavily upon Mrs. Poe, who has been left alone, the

---

[1] All statements from F. W. Thomas are from the same source.

support of herself and several young children." This, printed under Mrs. Poe's own eye, while she was in Norfolk, strongly indicates that her husband had in some manner left the family. No record of his death can be found at Norfolk or Richmond.[1]

From Norfolk Mrs. Poe went to Richmond in August, 1811, and there she made her last appearance on the stage October 11. It is a coincidence that Poe also made his last public appearance in Richmond. A benefit for Mrs. Poe was repeated in Richmond, and an appeal for charity for her published in a daily paper. She died December 8, as recorded in the Richmond *Enquirer*, December 10; and a notice that her funeral would take place on Tuesday, December 10, appeared in the Richmond *Virginia Patriot* of that date. No record of her burial place has been found in Richmond. I have made careful search, and only find an entry of a burial by the city corresponding with the date of her death, in old St. John's Churchyard, but no name is given.

Edgar Poe was taken in charge by Mrs. John Allan, and his sister by Mrs. William MacKenzie, both Richmond families. Mrs. Allan's husband reluctantly acquiesced in the quasi-adoption of Edgar.[2] Although John Allan's financial affairs were not prosperous, the family lived in modest, but comfortable circumstances. It is said that Edgar was baptized December 11, 1811,

---

[1] The statements by Poe himself, and his biographers, that David Poe died in Richmond, also the recent claim as to Norfolk, Virginia, have no foundation of fact.

[2] This, with other direct early information concerning Poe and the Allan family, is derived from Judge R. W. Hughes, Dabney Dandridge, a colored servant of the Allans, and other old Richmond residents. (The Allans also had another old servant named "Jim.")

but I am unable to find the church record. The family,
with Edgar and a sister of Mrs. Allan's, Miss Ann
Moore Valentine, went to London, England, in the
summer of 1815. There Edgar was sent to the Academy of Rev. Dr. Bransby, in Stoke Newington, near
London. This school is well portrayed by Poe in his
story called "William Wilson." He also attended the
Misses Dubourg's boarding-school in London. F. W.
Thomas states that Poe told him that his school days
in London were sad, lonely and unhappy. In *Burton's
Gentleman's Magazine* for April, 1840, Poe wrote: "Since
the sad experience of my schoolboy days to this present
writing, I have seen little to sustain the notion held
by some folks, that schoolboys are the happiest of all
mortals." Poe visited Scotland, stopping with members of the Allan family, at Irvine and Kilmarnock.
He attended school at Irvine. He wrote A. Ramsey,
of Stonehaven, Scotland, December 30, 1846, asking
about the Allans.

Allan's business affairs in London were unsuccessful,
and after five years' absence the family returned to
Richmond, Virginia, in the summer of 1820. They settled
down again to economical living, and Poe was sent to
the school of J. H. Clarke. Allan wished to give him
an education, but otherwise was cold and formal,
while his wife was the reverse. Edgar was of an effemi-
nate disposition, and although he indulged in boyish
sports, preferred girls for playmates. In one of his
early magazine notes he speaks of using roller skates
in his boyhood, to show that they were not a more
modern invention. He also had more than the usual
boy's yearning for reading matter. Allan's library was
scant, and he had peculiar notions of what Edgar

should read. Mrs. Allan, a consistent member of the Episcopal Church, was mainly seeking to instill in his mind the fear of God.

Among the intimate church acquaintances of Mrs. Allan were the families of Chief Justice John Marshall and J. H. Strobia, both mentioned by Poe in later life. Edgar always accompanied Mrs. Allan to church meetings, and here was likely laid the foundation of his knowledge of the Bible and Christian religion. John Allan was not much of a church attendant, and rather a liberal thinker. The germ out of which Poe's later materialism evolved may have come from this source. There seems an autobiographical hint of this in his tale "The Domain of Arnheim," which he has said contains "much of his soul." Here he wrote: "Some peculiarities, either in his early education, or in the nature of his intellect, had tinged with what is termed materialism all his ethical speculations; and it was this bias, perhaps, which led him to believe that the most advantageous at least, if not the sole legitimate field for the poetic exercise, lies in the creation of novel moods of purely *physical* loveliness." Mrs. Allan also had a god-child named Catherine Elizabeth Poitiaux, who was Poe's early playmate and child-love. At church Poe met the early companion of his boyhood, Ebenezer Burling, the son of a widowed mother, who lived in a house on Bank Street, in which Poe was afterwards married and resided with his wife and Mrs. Clemm.

There Poe also caught the first glimpse of his sweetheart, Sarah Elmira Royster, who was to inspire so much of his youthful verse. In early boyhood Burling and Poe were often together. When matters went wrong at Allan's,[1] Edgar hastened to Burling's home, and spent the night there, in opposition to the Allans' wishes. It was Burling who taught Poe to swim, and also engaged with him in other manly sports. Dr. Rawlings, who lived near Burling and attended him, said that he was rough in his manner and of a different disposition to Poe. He was fond of light literature, and most likely Poe derived some of his early ideas of adventure from him, and there obtained his reading matter on such subjects.

Poe's own statement of his first reading of "Robinson Crusoe," in the *Southern Literary Messenger* for January, 1836, is interesting. He wrote: "How fondly do we recur in memory to those enchanted days of our boyhood when we first learned to grow serious over Robinson Crusoe!—when we first found the spirit of wild adventure enkindling within us; as by the dim firelight, we labored out, line by line, the marvellous import of those pages, and hung breathless and trembling with eagerness over their absorbing — over their enchanting interest! Alas! the days of desolate islands are no more!"

These sad words, with the plaintive, "no more," were written from a window with a view of his boyhood haunts, while adjoining was the old warehouse of Ellis & Allan, where he spent many hours of his youth. That he frequented this place early is shown by a power of attorney given by the firm November 17, 1823, which has Edgar Allan Poe as a witness.[2] It was in the spring of the year 1825 that John Allan inherited money from

[1] Mrs. Clemm said this was not infrequent.

[2] This with his name in an early school book in my possession are his earliest known autographs.

an uncle. And soon after this he surrounded his
home with luxuries — purchased costly draperies, and,
besides the foundation for a library, added works of
art, including a marble bust of Mary Magdalen by
Canova, and another of Dante. This sudden change
in the mode of living must have had its effect upon
Edgar's mind. Here might be found the germ for
some tastes displayed in after years, — his minute descriptions of draperies and of furniture. About this
same period another change took place in the family
affairs tending to leave a greater impress upon the
discerning mind of the boy Edgar. The marital relations of the Allans became unhappy. The reasons
that caused the second Mrs. Allan to renounce her
husband's will, May 26, 1834, began to trouble the
first wife. John Allan stated in his will made April 17,
1832, and recorded at Richmond, Virginia, that he
had confessed his fault, before marriage to his second
wife.[1]

A letter of the second Mrs. Allan's, written to Colonel
T. H. Ellis, is on record, very damaging to Poe. The
Valentine Museum at Richmond, Virginia, has numerous unpublished letters, written by Poe to John Allan,
with the latter's notations on them, which were read
to a small select audience in Richmond, some years
ago. The letters taken with the notations are said to

[1] He also left several legacies to provide for the maintenance
of the results of this fault. The Richmond court records with
the original entry of this will were destroyed by fire. It was also
recorded in another court, but was not accessible to Poe's previous biographers. I have a copy of the will, as well as the full
proceedings of the lengthy legal contest made to break the will
of the second Mrs. Allan, which was finally decided by the
Supreme Court.

give an impression that Poe was ungrateful to his patron. They also contain references to other people, which has hindered their early publication. They are said to date from 1826 to 1830, referring mainly to his college career, and represent Poe in a sincere, but sad mood.

All these circumstances, as well as the importance of showing the influences surrounding Poe's early bringing up, make it necessary for this memoir not to ignore the existing documents in the matters, which are also public records. With Mrs. Allan suspicious and jealous of her husband, the natural disposition of Poe was to side with her in family matters, which made Allan anxious to have him out of the way. The educational solution was the best that offered itself and the easiest to arrange with both Poe and Mrs. Allan. It was decided to send Edgar to the University of Virginia, but he seems to have been reluctant in going there. He had been making desperate love to Miss Royster, and his pleadings had not been in vain. The old colored servitor, who assisted Poe in getting away, has left a statement that Edgar and Mrs. Allan were sad at heart the day he left for the University, and on the way Poe intimated a desire to break away from Allan, and seek his own living. He intrusted the servant with a letter to be handed in person to Miss Royster, which was the last she was to see for some time. For with the ardent lover away her parents intercepted Poe's letters and soon substituted another suitor, to whom she was married. All his letters to Miss Royster were destroyed but one, and this the newly wedded found when it was too late. Without response to his letters, Poe felt that his first and only love had proven untrue to her vows to him. His relations with Allan were uncongenial and his money allowances rather meagre. In the company of gay companions he became reckless, indulged in liquor, played cards for money, and became involved in debt. He stood well in his studies at the University, but left at the end of the session, December 15, 1826, under a financial cloud, with lawyers trying to force Allan into paying his gambling debts.[1]

Upon Poe's return to Richmond, Mrs. Allan greeted him with oldtime endearments, which her husband resented. He made Poe feel in the way, and put him to work in his firm's counting-house. Here Poe chewed the cud of bitter discontent. He first wrote a letter to The Mills Nursery of Philadelphia, Pennsylvania, with whom the Allan firm had dealings, asking for employment. That firm sent the letter to Allan, and the matter ended in a war of warm words. Poe, with a determined will, had made up his mind to leave Richmond. Besides the discontent at home, he had learned of the deceit shown in his love affair with Miss Royster, and is reported to have upbraided her parents after his return. There is also a current story that Mrs. Shelton, formerly Miss Royster, created a scene in her household after finding out that Poe's letters had been kept from her. In a matter-of-fact story written by Poe early in 1835 he mentioned that after leaving college he went down to his guardian's country place, and also dipped into the study of the law. He also made a reference to "E—— P——, who swam from Mayo's Bridge to Warwick wharf some years ago." This swimming feat has been frequently mentioned.

In a letter to a Richmond editor in May, 1835, Poe

---

[1] The attorneys' letters are still preserved in Richmond.

wrote: "The writer seems to compare my swim with that of Lord Byron, whereas there can be no comparison between them. Any swimmer 'in the falls' in my days, would have swum the Hellespont, and thought nothing of the matter. I swam from Ludlam's wharf to Warwick (six miles), in a hot June sun, against one of the strongest tides ever known in the river. It would have been a feat comparatively easy to swim twenty miles in still water. I would not think much of attempting to swim the British Channel from Dover to Calais."

The Allans had a country place in Goochland County, Virginia, called "The Lower Byrd Plantations," which Poe may have visited at some time. But he did not linger long about Virginia. The supposition is that he concluded that London was his "Eldorado," and that whatever literary dreams he had, were beginning to shape themselves. Judge Hughes had the statement from the owner of a vessel trading with Allan's firm that Poe had made an arrangement to work his way to England in his vessel. Allan is said to have been fully aware of this. However, when the time came for Poe to tell his designs to Mrs. Allan, she went into hysterics and would not allow the subject to be mentioned again. Through her entreaty the vessel owner was seen by Allan and the plans abandoned. But it seems that Poe meant to carry out his adventure at all hazards. He is said to have talked the matter over with his companion, Burling, who became enthusiastic and consented to join him in the trip abroad. Burling had become addicted to drink, and a favorite resort of his was an inn kept by Mrs. E. C. Richardson. They both quietly arranged to work their way in a vessel bound for England. The old colored servant, who knew the secret, told Judge Hughes that he wanted to tell Mrs. Allan, but fear kept him from it. He carried a small bundle of Poe's personal effects from his room to Mrs. Richardson's. Poe and Burling afterwards went there in a hack, spending the night, and leaving early the next morning for the vessel, lying at the dock. During his short stay in Richmond Poe paid some attention to a young lady stopping with Mrs. Juliet J. Drew. The colored servant remembered carrying notes to her there but did not recall her name. After sobering up, Burling deserted at the first stopping point the vessel reached and returned to Richmond. Mrs. Allan had frequent fainting spells after Poe left, and when she learned from Burling that he had gone abroad, she was for weeks inconsolable. She tried to have her husband take steps to have him return, but he never seemed to trouble himself again in the matter. Mrs. Allan wrote Poe two letters, begging him to return and absolving him from all blame in the Allan family matters. Poe's wife guarded these letters with jealous care during her life. When she was about to die she asked that they be read to her. Eliza White, daughter of the founder of the *Southern Literary Messenger*, remembered the incident, and her impression was that the letters had been sent to Poe abroad. She recalled the matter more readily, because she had seen the letters some years previously in Richmond, where Poe's wife had shown them to her family. Mrs. Smith, formerly Miss Herring, Poe's Baltimore cousin and early love, who was about the Poe house at the time Virginia died, told Miss White afterwards that she had the letters.[1]

[1] I have made repeated efforts to locate the papers of Mrs. Smith, who died about 1887, but her nearest relative could give

While it is generally admitted that Poe left Richmond in a sailing vessel, it is disputed that he ever reached England. An argument is that the time, from March to May 26, was insufficient for the events. The "Florida" had a record of a trip in twenty-five days, while other vessels made much quicker time. If the ocean trips had consumed as much time as the "Florida's" records, which is unlikely, there would still have been time for further events. The time to me seems ample. Burling, who left Richmond in the vessel with Poe, told Dr. George W. Rawlings that their destination was England. Judge Hughes is the authority that Burling also informed Mrs. Allan that Poe had gone abroad. Miss Eliza White was of the opinion that the two letters written to Poe by Mrs. Allan were sent to him abroad. Miss Ann Valentine has stated that Poe corresponded with Mrs. Allan while he was in Europe. The second Mrs. Allan has stated in her letter to Colonel T. H. Ellis that Poe's letters were scarce and dated from St. Petersburg, Russia. They may have had other European dates, and being probably familiar with Poe's own legend of his visit to Russia, she was in error.

F. W. Thomas states: "Henry Poe visited his brother in Richmond twice, the last time in 1825. He said Edgar had quarrelled with Mr. Allan after coming from college, about the small allowance of money he was receiving, and left him. He worked his own passage abroad in a vessel, reaching the metropolis of England

me no information. Some poetry written by Poe to Miss Herring, also a copy of his early poems presented to her, were sold some years since. It is likely that the original possessor of this material holds these letters.

after a rough voyage. There he met with disappointment in finding employment, and his funds being low proceeded to Paris, still hoping to find work. What money he had left was taken from him, with the exception of a sum sufficient to pay his passage back to London. Thus left without money and without friends he hurried back to England, where he took passage in a vessel for America, bound for a New England port."

Wherever he sailed in these days, he afterwards displayed in his writings considerable nautical knowledge, and like Camoëns, the poet, he also held on to his manuscript verses, through all his vicissitudes. He met with C. F. S. Thomas in Boston, who published them in his first volume of poems, — "Tamerlane, By A Bostonian. Boston, 1827." The book could not have brought him any money, and only found slight notice. Poe determined to try the army, and enlisted May 26, 1827, at Boston under the name of Edgar A. Perry. He was assigned to Charleston, South Carolina, and one year later transferred to Fortress Monroe, Virginia, where he was appointed Sergeant Major.[1] While at Fortress Monroe, Poe was identified by a relative of Mrs. Allan, who communicated the fact to her. She was ill, and pleaded to see Edgar again. She interested her husband in aiding Poe to secure a discharge. In doing this, however, Allan made sure that Poe was to enter West Point and that he would not trouble him again.

---

[1] A peculiar fact connected with his army career was an appointment at Charleston, May 1, 1828, as "artificer." The office called for "military mechanics," of some kind, which Poe was never known to possess. The records do not show what duties he performed, or whether he actually displayed mechanical skill in any way.

Mrs. Allan died February 28, 1829, which made a change in Poe's future dreams. In one of the many sadly written letters in the Valentine Museum, Richmond, he refers to his foster mother in the most affectionate terms, and intimates that matters would have taken a different course if she had lived.

While awaiting entry to West Point, Poe still carried his manuscript verses and had begun to revise them. His mind seemed bent on a literary career. After his discharge from the army he went to Baltimore in 1829, and there published his second volume of poems, — "Al Aaraaf, Tamerlane and Minor Poems." When editing them he sent a notice with some of his verses to the *Yankee* of Boston. He presented his cousin, Elizabeth Herring of Baltimore, with a copy of these poems, which he afterwards used to make the revision of his 1845 edition. He entered West Point in July, 1830, and while there spent a part of his time in again revising his poems. He sent his fourth known publication, "Sonnet — To Science," in October to the Philadelphia *Casket*. He tired of soldier life and obtained his dismissal in March, 1831, by giving offense against discipline. A letter written by him to the Superintendent is on file at the Academy, dated March 10, 1831, asking for a certificate of his standing in his class, and intimating an intention of joining the Polish army. Shortly afterwards he published his third volume of poems, which was not a financial success. He visited Baltimore, and May 6, 1831, wrote a letter to W. Gwynn asking employment.

F. W. Thomas says: "I removed to the country in 1829 and lost sight of Poe's brother. In 1831 I emigrated to Cincinnati, and for some years afterwards

travelled through the West, along the Ohio and Missis-
sippi. On one of these trips of pleasure from Pittsburg
to New Orleans in a first-rate steamer, I made the
acquaintance of an interesting character named James
Tuhey, belonging to the steamer's crew. He possessed
more than ordinary musical ability and was especially
proficient with the flute. I would sit with him for hours
in a quiet corner and listen to his sailor-lore. He observed my manuscript as I was writing to a Cincinnati
newspaper and wanted to know if I was writing poetry.
I told him no. He replied that so much manuscript
reminded him of a Baltimore acquaintance named
Poe. I thought at once that he had reference to Henry
Poe, but soon found that it was Edgar A. Poe he knew.
I also learned that Tuhey lived at Fells Point in Baltimore, when I left there, and had only recently come out
to the West. He was a native of Ireland. In Baltimore
he had an acquaintance with a family named Cairnes.
They were some connection of Poe's. At their house
he often met Poe.

"Tuhey spoke of him as stopping alternately with
one relative, and then another, but later on spending all
his time with the widow, Mrs. Clemm. He wrote for the
newspapers, but earned small pay. While living with
the Cairnes, Poe made the acquaintance of Miss De-
veraux, a dark-eyed beauty, whose parents came from
Ireland. The family lived near the Cairnes residence
and were intimate. They were often seen together and
Poe wanted her to marry him at once. She was young
and told her parents, who, with the Cairnes, interfered
and broke off the affair. Poe became despondent after
this and went with Tuhey in a sailing vessel to the coast
of Wexford, Ireland, and back. It was on this trip that

Tuhey had seen Poe's manuscript, which mine had recalled to his memory. Before leaving Baltimore in 1834,
Tuhey said that he often met Poe at a house on Caro-
line Street near Wilkes, Fells Point. There Poe would
sit in silence for hours listening to sailor stories of the
sea, the only interruption being now and then a tune
from Tuhey's musical flute."

The Richmond court records show that John Allan
was putting his earthly affairs in order, and making
his will April 17, 1832. The will was prepared by an
able lawyer, but Allan was so fearful that the clauses
troubling his conscience might not be carried out, that
he rewrote and repeated them himself a second time in
the will. It is also said that about this time he occasionally intimated a desire to see Poe, before he died.
The supposition is that he had made promises to his
first wife concerning Poe, which had not been fulfilled.
Poe was in communication with Miss Valentine, sister
of the first Mrs. Allan; also had messages from the old
Allan servants, and in other ways kept informed of what
was going on in the Allan household.

An old printer told me that he carried letters for Poe
from Baltimore to Richmond prior to 1835. Poe had
heard the rumor that Allan was ill and wanted to see
him. He stated to Judge Hughes that with the understanding that Allan wished to see him, and a view
of a possible reconciliation, he had gone to Richmond
about June, 1832. He had no feeling against Mrs.
Allan, and thought that all that was necessary was to
go to the old home, and, in any event, find a cordial
reception. Instead, he stated, Mrs. Allan refused him
admittance, and hindered a meeting between himself
and Mr. Allan. He returned to Baltimore without seeing

Allan. The Richmond court records, in the lawsuit to break the will of the second Mrs. Allan, say: "Mrs. Allan was a woman of vigorous intellect and will, remarkable for her self reliance—a woman with likes and dislikes — attachments and resentments — loves and hates — one so self reliant and high spirited that no one dared approach her with any testamentary suggestions." John Allan died March 27, 1834. The terms of his will were not agreeable to his wife, and she rejected them. The second marriage of Allan took place October 5, 1830; Mrs. Allan died April 24, 1881.

Poe took up occasional newspaper work on his return to Baltimore. During these years he also wrote for New York and Philadelphia papers. The supposition is, that in New York he wrote for a newspaper with which Major Noah was associated. In Philadelphia he wrote for Poulson's *American Daily Advertiser* and the Sunday *Mercury.*

In Baltimore there were also days of love-making with his cousin Miss Herring. He read to her, and wrote verses in her album; and his wife Virginia, then a little girl, carried the love letters. The tales Poe sent to the Baltimore *Saturday Morning Visiter*, and his drama, "Politian," were probably prepared during these years. One of them, "Morella," was given by Poe in Baltimore to a neighbor, Mrs. Samuel F. Simmons. The manuscript had been in the possession of her daughter, living in Howard County, Maryland, for many years. It was recently sold by a New York book-auction house. The manuscript is written in the same style, and corresponds with the introduction to "The Tales of the Folio Club," as reproduced in facsimile in Professor G. E. Woodberry's revised Life of Poe. This tale, it is claimed, was written by Poe some time between 1832 and 1833 in Baltimore, while a frequent visitor at the Simmons house.

On October 12, 1833, Poe was awarded fifty dollars for his prize tale, " MS. Found in a Bottle," by the Baltimore *Saturday Morning Visiter*. His poem "The Coliseum" was well considered, but as he had received the largest prize, the next was given to J. H. Hewitt, editor of the paper. It had been the supposition that Poe sent previous contributions to the *Visiter*, which proved correct, as his poem "Serenade" appeared April 20th, after L. A. Wilmer was editor. Hewitt states that he wrote an unfavorable criticism on Poe's 1829 volume in the *Minerva*, a Baltimore publication he edited, for which Poe assailed him on the street. They were not friendly while he edited the *Visiter*, but afterwards met in Washington on good terms. Wilmer and Poe took long walks together and were intimate in Baltimore and afterwards in Philadelphia. Hewitt also seems to have been unfriendly with Wilmer, who, he says, "measured poetry as he would type, and judged its quality as a gauger would the proof of whiskey."

Hewitt gives an intelligent description of Poe's appearance in the early days. He said that he knew Poe as "a thin, handsome, spare young man. He had a broad forehead, a large magnificent eye, dark brown and rather curly hair; well formed, about five feet seven in height. He dressed neatly in his palmy days — wore Byron collars and a black neckerchief, looking the poet all over. The expression of his face was thoughtful, melancholy, and rather stern. In disposition he was somewhat overbearing and spiteful. He often vented his spleen on poor Dr. Loffin, who styled himself the 'Milford Bard,' and who outstripped Poe in the quantity of his poetry, if not the quality. I never saw him under the influence of drink or a narcotic but once, and cannot endorse such stories."

The circumstances indicate that Poe was about the newspaper offices in Baltimore at this period and acquainted with the literary characters of the city. Among them was J. P. Kennedy, who introduced him to Carey & Lea of Philadelphia. They were given the first opportunity to publish Poe's tales, but declined them. The tale of "The Visionary," which was among them, was afterwards published in *Godey's Lady's Book* for January, 1834. He contributed tales to the *Southern Literary Messenger* of Richmond, Virginia, early in 1835. His letters to the proprietor of that periodical show that he had sufficient influence with the Baltimore newspapers to have notices of the *Messenger* published which he wrote himself. In a notice of the *Messenger* in the *Broadway Journal* for March 22, 1845, Poe states: "At the beginning of the seventh month (1835), one of the present editors of the *Broadway Journal* made an arrangement to edit the *Messenger*, and by systematic exertion on the part of both publisher and editor the circulation was increased by the end of the subsequent year to nearly five thousand — a success quite unparalleled in the history of our five-dollar Magazines. After the secession of Mr. Poe, Mr. White took the editorial conduct upon his own shoulders and sustained it remarkably well." Poe made another attempt to have his tales published by Harper & Brothers in March, 1836.

On May 16, 1836, Poe was married at Richmond to

his cousin Virginia Eliza Clemm, who was not quite fourteen years old, by Rev. A. Converse, a Presbyterian minister. A previous marriage license was obtained in Baltimore September 22, 1835. His marriage bond is recorded in Richmond. The contributions of Poe to the *Southern Literary Messenger* show that he was an industrious editor, although at the start occasionally over-indulging in drink. J. W. Fergusson, an apprentice on the *Messenger*, who lived to a ripe old age, and who was afterwards one of the proprietors, has left with me his written recollections of Poe. He says that "like others in his day Poe was addicted to periodical sprees, but they did not interfere to any extent with his writings." Mr. Fergusson, who visited the residence of T. W. White, also Mrs. Bernard, a daughter of White's, both in a position to know, stated that they never knew of any flirtation between Poe and Eliza White, as has been intimated. They were never more than friends. This has also been confirmed by Mrs. Clemm.

In the December, 1835, *Messenger*, Poe in a notice of Chief Justice Marshall, whom he met in the early days at church with Mrs. Allan, spoke of him as: "Our great and lamented countryman, fellow-townsman, neighbor, and friend — for by all these names did a fortuitous conjuncture of circumstances, including his own kind and prideless heart, entitle us to call him." While Poe labored at the editorial desk of the *Messenger*, White the proprietor travelled about Virginia for subscriptions. The list of subscribers increased, but likewise the expense account. Poe was ambitious, and thought that he was entitled to more salary, or a proprietary interest in the journal, but White did not feel inclined to offer either. Poe was also becoming very solicitous for the publication of his tales, and anxious to be nearer the larger publication houses.

After the Harpers returned the manuscript of his tales he began a correspondence with Saunders & Otley of New York.[1] They read his manuscript and seemed disposed to become his publishers here and in England, but at the moment could not take upon themselves to decide for their paternal house abroad. They were also anxious to have the finished manuscript of the tales in order to send out by the next packet. Poe sent his friend Edward W. Johnson of the South Carolina College, who was in New York, to see the firm. His letter of October 4, 1836, stated that he had informed the firm "that the writing of the tales in their final form had yet made too little progress to render so speedy a transmission of the copy possible, and that as the months of November and December are the most advantageous in European publication they had better send back the MS. in their hands, which may be found important in the rapid finishing of the work. This the firm promised to do at once through Smith the bookseller, or the regular mode of conveyance." Johnson advised Poe to send back the finished MS. with all possible expedition, in time for one of the earliest packets. This matter is important as showing that at so late a date Poe's tales in hand were far from being considered finished or complete.

At this time Poe was in correspondence with Dr. F. L. Hawks, who held out some prospects for employment on the *New York Review,* to which Poe afterwards made one contribution.[2]

[1] MS. from Poe's *Southern Literary Messenger* desk.

[2] I have copies of the *Southern Literary Messenger* from the Hawks library with the address in Poe's autograph.

Poe seceded from the *Messenger* in January, 1837, and went to New York. Here the financial panic of the time changed his plans. The family were compelled to take boarders, and Poe eked out a living doing literary hack work. In the *American Monthly Magazine* for June, 1837, he published the tale "Mystification," as "Von Jung, the Mystific." He completed his tale, begun in the *Messenger*, the "Narrative of Arthur Gordon Pym," which the Harpers published in July, 1838, but it brought him no financial help. He had made the acquaintance of an English writer of juvenile books, James Pedder, who interested himself in his welfare and arranged for the family to go to Philadelphia. Pedder edited the *Farmer's Cabinet* of Philadelphia, in the making up of which Poe is thought to have rendered some assistance. It is stated that the family resided with the Pedders for a brief period. That Poe felt grateful to them is evident from the fact that one of the first copies of his *Tales of the Grotesque and Arabesque* from the press of Lea & Blanchard, Philadelphia, 1840, was given to the "Misses Pedders with his grateful acknowledgments." The volumes were recently sold at a book-auction sale. It is also stated that Pedder arranged with Poe to get out *The Conchologist's First Book ; or, a System of Testaceous Malacology*, published by Haswell, Barrington & Haswell, Philadelphia, 1839. It was charged that this was largely a reprint of Captain Thomas Brown's *Conchology*, which Poe denied. A second edition, with a new preface, additions, and alterations, was issued by Poe in 1840, and a third, without his name on the title-page, in 1845. In his criticisms in the *Messenger* Poe shows early knowledge on this subject. The Baltimore *Museum* for September, 1838, contained "Ligeia," followed by "How to Write a Blackwood Article (The Signora Psyche Zenobia)" and "A Predicament (The Scythe of Time)," in December; "Literary Small Talk," in January and February, and the poem "The Haunted Palace" in April. The *Baltimore Book* for 1839 printed "Siope (Silence)." "The Devil in the Belfry" appeared in the Philadelphia *Saturday Evening Chronicle and Mirror of the Times*, May 8. He had also contributed one short article to the Pittsburg *Literary Examiner and Western Monthly Review.*

In July, 1839, Poe began to edit *Burton's Gentleman's Magazine*, and to this magazine he contributed many of his writings, including "The Journal of Julius Rodman." He made numerous compilations of various articles, Field sports, and published "The Philosophy of Furniture." As was his habit in making up "Marginalia" for the *Messenger*, he arranged matter here under the heading:

"OMNIANA.

Every thing by starts, but nothing *long*.

Dryden.

    various; that the mind
Of desultory man, studious of change,
And pleased with novelty, may be indulged.

Cowper."

His correspondence with Dr. J. E. Snodgrass while editing the magazine gives an intimate view of his life for this period. The Philadelphia *Saturday Evening Chronicle and Mirror of the Times*, June 13, 1840, announced that Poe would publish, the following January, a new magazine, — *The Penn Magazine*. His illness was mentioned as the reason for the postponement of this publication until March, 1841.

In the December *Casket* Poe published "The Man of the Crowd." The *Saturday Evening Post*, February 20, 1841, announced that on account of the disturbance in money matters *The Penn Magazine* would not be published, but that Poe would assume the editorial chair of *Graham's Magazine*, which he did in April. He however continued to cherish hopes of getting out his *Penn Magazine*, which he considered "only scotched, not killed." He gave much earnest work to *Graham's*, and contributed to the magazine some of his best writings. He wrote on the subject of cryptography, which attracted attention, and began to show his analytical powers. In a letter from F. W. Thomas in May, 1841, some possibilities of a government position at a good salary, with leisure for literary labors, was hinted to Poe. The idea haunted him for several years, but nothing ever materialized.

In August, 1841, Poe made a proposition to Lea & Blanchard to publish a second edition of his tales of 1840, which they rejected. Poe resigned from *Graham's Magazine* in May, 1842, and was succeeded by R. W. Griswold.

F. W. Thomas states: "I met Poe in Philadelphia during September, 1842. He lived in a rural home on the outskirts of the city. His house was small, but comfortable inside for one of the kind. The rooms looked neat and orderly, but everything about the place wore an air of pecuniary want. Although I arrived late in the morning Mrs. Clemm, Poe's mother-in-law, was busy preparing for his breakfast. My presence possibly caused some confusion, but I noticed that there was delay and evident difficulty in procuring the meal. His wife entertained me. Her manners were agreeable and graceful. She had well formed, regular features, with the most expressive and intelligent eyes I ever beheld. Her pale complexion, the deep lines in her face and a consumptive cough made me regard her as the victim for an early grave. She and her mother showed much concern about Eddie, as they called Poe, and were anxious to have him secure work. I afterwards learned from Poe that he had been to New York in search of employment and had also made effort to get out an edition of his tales, but was unsuccessful.

"When Poe appeared his dark hair hung carelessly over his high forehead, and his dress was a little slovenly. He met me cordially, but was reserved, and complained of feeling unwell. His pathetic tenderness and loving manners towards his wife greatly impressed me. I was not long in observing with deep regret that he had fallen again into habits of intemperance. I ventured to remonstrate with him. He admitted yielding to temptation to drink while in New York and turned the subject off by telling an amusing dialogue of Lucian, the Greek writer. We visited the city together and had an engagement for the following day. I left him sober, but he did not keep the engagement and wrote me that he was ill."

There are more pleasant reminiscences of his home life in Philadelphia recorded than this. While he edited *Graham's Magazine* the family exercised a simple hospitality. They entertained guests, had sufficient means to live upon, and Poe was temperate in his habits. His wife ruptured a blood vessel later on; he gave up his position, and has told in his letters how during this period he had recourse to drink to drown his sorrows.

Poe had several interviews with Charles Dickens in Philadelphia, and at this time corresponded with Thomas Holley Chivers, James Russell Lowell, and John Tomlin.

After the turn of 1843, Poe became closely associated with the Philadelphia *Saturday Museum*. In this paper he published a severe criticism on Griswold's *Poets and Poetry of America*, for which it is said Griswold never forgave him. F. W. Thomas states: "Poe kept up a continuous warfare upon Griswold in the *Museum*, poking fun at him, and alluding to him as Mr. Driswold of *Graham's Magazine*, in childish humor."

In a letter to Lowell in March, 1843, Poe stated that he was not editing the *Museum*, although an announcement was prematurely made to that effect. This has never been clearly understood, as no file of the *Museum* can be found. F. W. Thomas states that the *Museum* announced: "We have secured at a high salary the services of E. A. Poe, Esq., a gentleman whose high and versatile abilities have always spoken for themselves, and who after the first of May will aid us in the editorial conduct of the journal." In a letter written to Thomas by Poe, February 25, 1843, it is stated that a copy of the *Museum* containing his Biography was also forwarded. As the only copy of this Biography known, presumed to have been Poe's own, and made up of pasted clippings, is of March 4, 1843, it has puzzled Poe's editors to understand how Poe sent a copy of the paper of a week earlier, as the letter indicated.

Mr. Thomas states that the biography of Poe in the *Museum* had a second edition, which that paper announced as follows: "*The Spirit of the Times* of Friday says, 'The Saturday *Museum* of this week contains a very fair likeness of our friend Edgar A. Poe, Esq., with a full account of his truly eventful life. We look upon Mr. Poe as one of the most powerful, chaste, and erudite writers of the day, and it gives us pleasure to see him placed through the public press in his proper position before the world.'

"We are glad to hear so good a paper as the *Times* speak thus highly of Mr. Poe, not only from the justice which it renders that powerful writer, but because we have been so fortunate as to secure his services as associate editor of the Saturday *Museum*, where we intend it shall be placed beyond the reach of competition. So great was the interest excited by the biography and poems of Mr. Poe published in the *Museum* of last week, that to supply those who were disappointed in obtaining copies we shall be at the expense of an extra edition, which will be printed with corrections and additions. Of this extra we shall publish an edition on fine white paper. It will be ready for delivery at the office Saturday morning."

In a later *Museum* sent to Thomas by Poe it was stated under the heading, "Quick Perception": "We have published in the biographical sketch of Mr. Poe some evidences of the wonderful power which his mind possesses in deciphering the most complicated and difficult questions. We have another striking instance of the exercise of this power. *The Spirit of the Times* copied the following puzzle a few days since. A Nice Puzzle. The Baltimore *Sun* gives the following oddity and asks for its solution. [Here follows an array of mixed words and letters.] The moment it met our eye happening to be in company with Mr. Poe we pointed out the article, when he immediately gave us the solution."

The prospectus of the *Stylus*, another magazine, was issued through the columns of the *Museum*. With a view of securing subscribers to the magazine, and with some hopes of hearing something further about the government position, Poe went to Washington in March, 1843. F. W. Thomas states: "Poe sent me the notes for the *Museum* biography, but I evaded writing them. I told him afterwards that I knew more of his history than he had sent me. He was amused, and laughed the matter off by confessing that the story was intended to help the magazine project. I was confined to my room by sickness when Poe came to Washington early in 1843. He was sober when I saw him, but afterward in the company of old friends he drank to excess. My physician attended him for several days, and he suffered much from his indiscretion." Poe wrote a letter March 16, 1843, that he arrived home in Philadelphia "in safety and sober." In June he won the hundred-dollar prize with his tale "The Gold-Bug" from the *Dollar Newspaper*. He asked Griswold to send him five dollars and to come to see him June 11, as stated in Griswold's memoir. With a view of raising funds he contemplated the publication of his tales in serial form, but only one number was issued.

This was published about the last of August, 1843, — "The Prose Romances of Edgar A. Poe. No. 1. The Murders of the Rue Morgue and The Man that was Used Up, 1843. Philadelphia: Published by William H. Graham." Poe sent a notice of this to a New York magazine early in September, with the latter tale included. It was about this time that he made an attempt upon the lecture platform, which proved a failure. After Griswold withdrew from *Graham's*, Poe began to contribute to the critical department. He had a review of " Orion " in the March, 1844, number, and after that had a correspondence with the author R. H. Horne, to whom he sent his tale " The Spectacles " with a view of publication in England.

Poe went to New York early in April, 1844. On his arrival he wrote to Mrs. Clemm a letter dated " April 7, (just after breakfast)," which shows interesting characteristics of his domestic life. In this letter he mentions the "Duane" *Southern Literary Messengers*. He used them in preparing his tales of 1840. I found the volumes some years ago in an old Boston second-hand book-shop. His "Balloon Hoax" appeared in the New York *Sun* April 13, 1844. He corresponded with Lowell in May regarding the writing of his biography for *Graham's*. In June he wrote a letter to Charles Anthon asking his influence to induce the Harpers to publish his tales in five volumes. This matter was delayed until the fall, and Anthon replied that he was unable to assist him. The *Columbian Magazine* for August had a paper by Poe on "Mesmeric Revelation." Shortly afterwards he was engaged as an assistant by N. P. Willis, who was converting the *New Mirror* into a daily, the *Evening Mirror*. He had been contributing to *Godey's*, *Graham's*, and the *Southern Literary Messenger* and *Democratic Review*

" The Raven " first appeared in the *Evening Mirror* of January 29, 1845. F. W. Thomas says: "Poe stated that ' The Raven ' was written in a day. The idea of having it appear anonymously was a whim of his, like Coleridge's publication of his 'Raven.' He afterwards thought it a mistake, and conceived the idea of having it introduced in Willis's paper with his name. Poe read all the older English poets with fondness, and his name of Quarles merely had reference in his mind to the old English poet." It has been stated that "The Raven" was printed from advance sheets of the *American Whig Review*, which may have been the case, but in such an event Poe handled the proof and made corrections. The two publications show a number of deviations. On May 4, 1845, Poe wrote F. W. Thomas that "The Raven" was copied into the *Broadway Journal* by Briggs, his associate, before he joined the paper. Poe had some idea of having his poems published by Clarke of London, which were to be introduced by Griswold. He made an announcement in the *Mirror* of February 15, 1845, that the poems would shortly appear in the series, with other American poets. The sketch of Poe written by Lowell, with a portrait, appeared in the February *Graham's Magazine*. On February 28 Poe lectured in New York on the subject of "American Poetry." He resigned from the *Mirror* March 8, and in the issue of that journal for the same date appeared the answer to Poe's Longfellow criticisms signed, "Outis." On this date C. F. Briggs also wrote in a letter that Poe was his assistant on the *Broadway Journal*. The *Southern Literary Messenger* for April, 1845, announced: "Literary Criticisms: E. A. Poe, Esq. We have engaged the services of Mr. Poe; who will contribute monthly a *critique raisonnée* of the most important forthcoming works in this Country and in Europe." Poe had contributed "The Raven" in a revised form to the *Messenger* in March. B. B. Minor, editor of the *Messenger*, stated to me that he had an arrangement with John Biscoe, publisher of the *Broadway Journal*, to take subscriptions in New York; that there had been some dispute about the amount due Poe by the *Messenger*, and

Biscoe paid Poe without authority, never making the
Messenger any returns. Poe did not contribute to the
Messenger again until J. R. Thompson became editor.

The *Mirror* of July 19, 1845, gave seven entire pages
to an event in New York City, which must have been
considered of importance, in which Poe figured promi-
nently. He had at some time previously had a disagree-
ment with H. T. Tuckerman, but they met again on
this occasion and renewed their friendship.[1] It was the
commencement exercises of Rutgers Female Institute,
which took place July 11, when the Rutgers Street
Church was crowded. The committee on the composition of the First Department consisted of Edgar A. Poe,
Chairman, W. D. Snodgrass, and Henry T. Tuckerman.
The first award in poetry was given to a poem, of a little
over one hundred lines, beginning, —

> "Deep in a glade by trees o'erhung."

This poem was afterwards read to the audience by
Poe. On the stage with Poe were Professor Tellkampf,
Professor Lewis, Professor Elias Loomis, Dr. J. W.
Francis, and other men of eminence. His "Tales" (By
Edgar A. Poe. New York: Wiley & Putnam. 1845)
were published the latter part of June.

In the *Broadway Journal* of October 11, in answer
to some comments by Willis regarding the Tales, Poe
replied "that he was not preparing another edition
for England; that his 'Tales' had been reproduced in
England — long ago, but he had nothing to do with
the reproduction; that if he was to issue another edition,

[1] Mentioned in a letter of Charles Fenno Hoffman to Griswold,
July 11, 1845: *Passages from the Correspondence and other Papers
of R. W. Griswold* (Cambridge, Mass., 1898), p. 186.

instead of 'Tales' he would style them 'The Gold-Bug and Other Tales.'" Poe's habit of apologizing for errors committed was not confined to his letters. In the *Broadway Journal* for August 30, 1845, he wrote: "We thank the New-York correspondent of the *Cincinnati Gazette* for the gentlemanly tone of his reply to some late pettish comments of our own. We saw only a portion of one of his letters. Had we seen more, we should at once, through the precision and purity of his style, have recognized a friend." R. H. Stoddard, one of Poe's later biographers, sent a poem, "The Grecian Flute," to the *Broadway Journal*. In the issue of July 26, Poe stated: "We fear we have mislaid the poem," and August 2: "We doubt the originality of 'The Grecian Flute' for the reason that it is too good at some points to be so bad at others. Unless the author can reassure us we decline it." This is not in full accord with statements of the affair afterwards published by Stoddard, who also failed to tell that on another occasion he wrote to Poe for his autograph. On October 16, Poe read his boyish poem, "Al Aaraaf," before the Boston Lyceum, which incident provoked much comment and criticism at the time.

In the *Broadway Journal* Poe revised and published most of his tales and poems. His romantic acquaintance with Mrs. Frances Sargent Osgood began while he edited this journal. He had eulogized her in his New York lecture and sent her by Willis a copy of "The Raven," with a desire for her opinion and a personal introduction. A few days after this he called at the Astor House with Willis to meet her. In a letter written to Griswold she said: "I shall never forget the morning when I was summoned to the drawing room by Mr. Willis to receive him. With his proud and beautiful head erect, his dark eyes flashing with the electric light of feeling and of thought, a peculiar, an inimitable blending of sweetness and hauteur in his manner, he greeted me, calmly, gravely, almost coldly, yet with so marked an earnestness that I could not help being deeply impressed by it. From that moment until his death we were friends; although we met only during the first year of our acquaintance."

Previous biographies of Poe state that Mrs. Osgood sent some lines in the character of "Israfel" addressed to Poe, which appeared in the *Broadway Journal* April 5, 1845, to which he responded, April 26, with his lines "To F——," and signed "E." The "Israfel" verses by Mrs. Osgood did not appear in the *Broadway Journal* until November 29. In that journal's issue of April 5 is printed a poem, "The Rivulet's Dream" (From the German of Somebody), signed Kate Carol, preceded by a Poe note stating: "We might *guess* who is the fair author of the following lines, which have been sent us in a MS., evidently disguised — but we are not satisfied with guessing and would give the world to *know*." In the following week's issue appeared a poem signed by Mrs. Osgood, — "Love's Reply," concluding "write from your *heart to me*." She used the pseudonym of "Kate Carol," and also included this poem of "The Rivulet's Dream" in her later publications. Poe published, April 26, his lines "To F——," signed "E.," conjecturally to Mrs. Osgood. In the Editorial Miscellany of the same number Poe printed "Impromptu. To Kate Carol."

"When from your gems of thought I turn
To those pure orbs, your heart to learn,
I scarce know which to prize most high —
The bright *i-dea*, or bright *dear-eye*."

On May 31 is published a poem, "Lenore," signed "Clarice," which Poe attributed to Mrs. Osgood December 13. This was followed by a signed poem by Mrs. Osgood, August 30, "Slander," referring to the "breaking of somebody's heart." She sent another poem, September 6, "Echo Song," commencing, —

> "I know a noble heart that beats
> For one it loves how 'wildly well!'"

It was to this that Poe evidently responded, September 13, with his short lines "To F——," afterwards addressed in his poems of 1845 "To F——s S. O——d." She wrote again November 22, with lines beginning, —

> "O! they never can know that heart of thine,
> Who dare accuse *thee* of flirtation!"

The following week's issue contained her "Israfel" verses. Her contributions after this take a more serious turn. On December 13 she has "A Shipwreck," followed in the next by some scolding verses commencing, —

> "Though friends had warned me all the while,
>   And blamed my willing blindness,
> I did not once mistrust your smiles,
>   Or doubt your tones of kindness.
>
> "I sought you not — you came to me —
>   With words of friendly greeting:
> Alas! how different now I see
>   That ill-starred moment's meeting."

These were her last verses in the *Broadway Journal*, but she sent some lines to the *Metropolitan* about Poe in January, 1849, and published others, in her volume of poems, prior to her death.

The *Broadway Journal* also contains contributions

from Anne C. Lynch, Mary E. Hewett, Mary L. Lawson, and Elizabeth Fries Ellet.

Poe afterwards met Mrs. Osgood at the weekly receptions of Anne Charlotte Lynch in Waverley Place, and his lines "A Valentine" were addressed to her. She has intimated that her influence over Poe was for his good, and that she corresponded with him at his wife's request. Mrs. E. F. Ellet while visiting the Poe home saw one of these letters couched in rather endearing terms. She consulted with Mrs. Osgood and some of her friends, and a committee of Margaret Fuller and one other was deputized to recall all her letters. Poe was surprised when they called and stated their errand, and in the flush of excitement remarked that "Mrs. Ellet should look after her own letters," which only added fuel to the flame of scandal. Mrs. Ellet's brother demanded her letters from Poe, who in the mean time had left them at her door. Mrs. Osgood was on her deathbed when she wrote Griswold: "I think no one could know him — no one has known him personally — certainly no woman — without feeling the same interest. I can sincerely say that, although I have frequently heard of aberrations on his part from 'the straight and narrow path,' I have never seen him other-wise than gentle, generous, well bred, and fastidiously refined. To a sensitive and delicately-nurtured woman there was a peculiar and irresistible charm in the chivalric, graceful, and almost tender reverence with which he invariably approached all women who won his respect. It was this that first commanded and always retained my regard for him."

From October, when Poe borrowed fifty dollars from Horace Greeley on a promissory note, with which to purchase the full control of the *Broadway Journal*, he had a hard struggle to sustain the paper. He was harassed for ready funds, and compelled to discontinue December 26, 1845. About this time his volume of poems, *The Raven and Other Poems*, was issued. During the latter part of this year he also worked getting out books, among them *The Literary Emporium* and the third edition of his *Conchologist's First Book*. At the turn of the year 1846, Poe had little in sight to cheer him, except his literary reputation. The publication of "The Raven," his connection with the *Broadway Journal*, followed by the publication of the two volumes of his writings, had made him much sought after in certain social and literary circles of New York. He was for a time a literary lion. At an earlier period in his career he wrote in the *Messenger* how he arrived at a "Lionship," by his attention to " Nosology." Then his experiences were published as "Some Passages in the Life of a Lion." He had not forgotten this, and being in need of funds, as one of his recent biographers has facetiously implied, he began to "make copy out of his friends." "The Literati of New York" was published in *Godey's Lady's Book* from May to October, attracting much attention and comment. In the introduction Poe stated: "My design is, in giving my unbiased opinion of the *literati* (male and female) of New York, to give at the same time very closely, if not with absolute accuracy, that of conversational society in literary circles. It must be expected, of course, that, in innumerable particulars, I shall differ from the voice, that is to say, what appears to be the voice, of the public; but this is a matter of no consequence whatever." The papers numbered thirty-eight and were thought to complete the series. Another number not mentioned by Poe's editors appeared in the *Democratic Review* for August, 1848, on S. Anna Lewis. The criticisms made while the papers were being published in *Godey's* apparently caused Poe to be cautious. An examination of the original manuscript he sent to *Godey's* shows that he made many changes in his proofs. In some instances entire pages are erased and omitted from the printed text. The passages struck out have mainly an irreligious tone.

An installment of " Marginalia " printed in the *Democratic Review* for July, 1846, has also been overlooked by most of Poe's editors. This deals with a French translation of Lady Morgan's *Letters on Italy ; Decline of the Drama ; The Alphadelphia Tocsin ;* Simms's *Areytos ;* Goethe's *Sorrows of Werther,* and Cranch's poems. In view of the discussion as to Poe's knowledge of German, it is of interest that in his notice of the *Sorrows of Werther,* he said : " The title is mistranslated:— *Lieden* does not mean *Sorrows,* but *Sufferings.*" [1]

While Poe sent occasional contributions to other magazines, his main source of revenue at this period was *Godey's*. The number of drafts drawn on *Godey's* by Poe, which now turn up as autographic mementoes of the poet, indicate that he drew his pay punctually. In Griswold's volume of *The Literati,* 1850, appears an interesting Poe notice of Henry B. Hirst. It contains lines quoted from both "Lenore" and "Ulalume." The text of this has eluded search until recently, when the manuscript was called to my attention among the papers of the late E. C. Stedman. It had been sent to *Graham's Magazine,* but was not published.

[1] Poe's spelling of "Leiden" is incorrect. He also has "Werter " for Werther.

Miss Sarah F. Miller, long a resident of the Bronx, New York, gives the following recollections of the Poe family at this time: —

"One of the most cherished memories of my earliest childhood is the recollection of having often seen Edgar Allan Poe. When I was a little girl we lived in a house facing Turtle Bay, on the East River, near the present 47th Street. Among our nearest neighbors was a charming family trio consisting of Mr. Poe, his wife Virginia, and his mother-in-law, Mrs. Clemm. Poor Virginia Poe was very ill at the time, and I never saw her leave her home.

"Poe and Mrs. Clemm would very frequently call on us. He would also run over every little while to ask my father to lend him our rowboat, and then how he would enjoy himself pulling at the oars over to the little islands just south of Blackwell's Island, for his afternoon swim.

"Mrs. Clemm and my mother soon became the best of friends, and she found mother a sympathetic listener to all her sad tales of poverty and want. I would often see her shedding tears as she talked. In the midst of this friendship they came and told us they were going to move to a distant place called Fordham, where they had rented a little cottage, feeling sure the pure country air would do Mrs. Poe a world of good."

It was very late in the spring when Poe and his family retired to the cottage at Fordham. Mrs. Gove-Nichols wrote to the *Sixpenny Magazine*, February, 1863, of a visit made to Poe about this time, as follows: —

"We found him, and his wife, and his wife's mother — who was his aunt — living in a little cottage at the top of a hill. There was an acre or two of greensward, fenced in about the house, as smooth as velvet and as clean as the best kept carpet. There were some grand old cherry trees in the yard, that threw a massive shade around them. The house had three rooms — a kitchen, a sitting-room, and a bed-chamber over the sitting-room. There was a piazza in front of the house. The sitting-room was laid out with check matting; four chairs, a light stand and a hanging book-shelf completed the furniture. On the book-shelf there lay a volume of Poe's poems. He took it down, wrote my name in it, and gave it to me."

Poe appears to have kept a supply of his poems of 1845 on hand, and made many presentation copies. They have frequently turned up at book-auction sales and in other ways since his death. He presented Mrs. Shew with one at Fordham, which was sold by a London bookseller some years ago. This was said to have slight changes made in the text by Poe, which is an error. Poe tore out a leaf from a volume of the poems to send Mrs. Whitman the early poem of "Helen," and also presented her with a volume which is now in a New York private library. He also sent a copy of his poems to Miss Elizabeth Barrett Barrett (afterwards Mrs. Browning), who wrote him a letter in April, 1846, in which she stated: "Your 'Raven' has produced a sensation, a 'fit horror,' here in England. Some of my friends are taken by the fear of it and some by the music. I hear of persons haunted by the 'Nevermore,' and one acquaintance of mine who has the misfortune of possessing a 'bust of Pallas' never can bear to look at it in the twilight. I think you will like to be told that our great poet Mr. Browning, the author of 'Paracelsus' and the 'Bells and Pomegranates,' was struck much by the rhythm of that poem. Then there is a tale of yours, which is going the rounds of the newspapers, about mesmerism, throwing us all into 'most admired disorder,' and dreadful doubts as to whether 'it can be true,' as the children say of ghost stories. The certain thing in the tale in question is the power of the writer, and the faculty he has of making horrible improbabilities seem near and familiar." Very many associations of the poet cling around the Fordham cottage. Although he struggled here with poverty, and both he and his wife were ill, the quiet retreat gave him much pleasure. He was in communication in August with P. P. Cooke about his biography, which appeared in the *Southern Literary Messenger* for January, 1848. It was styled "Edgar A. Poe. An estimate of his literary merits. By P. P. Cooke," and stated: "The following paper is a sequel to Mr. Lowell's memoir (so called), of Mr. Poe, published two or three years since in *Graham's Magazine*. Mr. P. edited the *Messenger* for several years, and the pages of that Magazine would seem therefore a proper place for the few hurried observations which I have made upon his writings and genius." The article was largely a review of the "Raven," the "Valdemar Case," "Ligeia," "The Fall of the House of Usher," and "Lenore." The concluding remarks, probably inspired by Poe, were as follows: "As regards Wiley & Putnam's tales — I think the book in some respects does him injustice. It contains twelve tales out of more than seventy; and it is made up almost wholly of what may be called his analytic tales. This is not *representing* the author's mind in its various phases. A reader gathering his knowledge of Mr. Poe from this Wiley & Putnam issue would perceive nothing of the diversity and variety for which his writings are in fact remarkable. Only the publication of all his stories, at one issue, in one book, would show this diversity in their *full* force; but much more might have been done to represent his mind by a judicious and not wholly one-toned selection."

Poe was also in correspondence at this time with William Gilmore Simms and Hawthorne. His letters show his great solicitude for his wife, who was slowly dying. It was while the *Literati Papers* were running that Poe made some facetious remarks about the poet, Thomas Dunn English, referring to him as Thomas Done Brown. English retaliated in a newspaper article. Poe replied and finally brought suit for damages, and on February 17, 1847, recovered damages of $225.[1] It was Poe's intention eventually to publish his *Literati Papers;* and the original memoranda for the prospectus of the *Living Writers of America*, entirely in his autograph, were in the library of the late Bishop Hurst, which was dispersed at auction in March, 1905. They were written on four pages of folio paper and on four pages of smaller size, with many alterations and erasures by Poe. The title on the first page was: "The Living Writers of America. Some Honest Opinions about their Literary Merits, with Occasional Words of Personality. By Edgar A. Poe. With Notices of the Author by James Russell Lowell & P. P. Cooke." He commenced with a reference to the Godey publications, and said the publisher was badgered into giving

---

[1] An unpublished letter written by Poe to J. M. Fields, editor of the St. Louis *Reveille*, dated June 15, 1846, giving an account of the English matter in the New York *Mirror* was among the papers of the late E. C. Stedman.

it up. He speaks of the English attack and says: "Success induced me to extend the plan . . . discard petty animosities — it will be seen that where through petulance or neglect, or underestimate of the impression the papers were to make, I have done injustice, I have not scrupled to repair the wrong, even at the expense of consistency. . . . Political sectional animosities . . . result a depreciation of Southern and Western talent, which upon the whole is greater, more vivid, fresher, than that of the North, less conventional, less conservative — want of centralisation gives birth to a peculiar cliquism whose separate penchants render it nearly impossible to get at the truth — Instance the Humanity clique — to which belong Emerson, Lowell, Hawthorne, Godwin, Fuller, Mrs. Child, Whittier — and who judge all literature in accordance with its hobby." There is much of the matter personal and about his literary work; also notes on prominent literary characters of his day, with trenchant criticisms.

In some correspondence with E. A. Duyckinck in November, 1845, Poe mentions his *American Parnassus*, and the supposition is that he had made a work along this same line at that time, or this may have been the same work revised. Mrs. Gove, who visited the Poe family in October, found them in destitute circumstances, and with a view of rendering aid introduced Mrs. M. L. Shew. Some notice of the family's condition was published in the newspapers, and a contribution of sixty dollars was raised. Poe wrote an open letter December 30, 1846, endeavoring to modify the humiliating publications. With the turn of the year 1847 his wife began to sink. Mrs. Shew had proven the ministering angel to the household. She was in constant attendance, and Poe in his gratitude wrote her a number of letters. He also wrote her two poems. Mrs. William Wiley, a daughter of Mrs. Shew now residing at Long Island, remembers many pleasant reminiscences of Poe told her by her mother. It was at her house that he wrote an early draft of the "Bells," the manuscript of which, it is claimed, Mrs. Shew sent to England, with other material as a loan. This was afterwards sold, but is now in this country. When Mrs. Wiley was a schoolgirl and was given some lessons on Poe by her teacher, her mother gave her this manuscript to show to her teacher.

Poe's wife died January 30, 1847. She was buried at Fordham, but her remains were afterwards reinterred in the same plot with Poe at Baltimore. After his wife's death Poe was very ill, which was mentioned by Cooke in the *Messenger* for January, 1848. He was cared for by Mrs. Clemm and Mrs. Shew, while other friends raised funds for his support. After some months Poe began to recover, and Mrs. Shew, having other important engagements, took leave of the family and advised Poe to marry a "sensible woman." When he was able to go about again, he spent some time planning his prose poem — "Eureka." In the March *Home Journal* it was announced that Poe would soon publish *The Authors of America, in Prose and Verse*, but nothing more was heard of this. It was probably his *American Parnassus*, which was finally changed to the *Living Writers of America*. His poem "Ulalume" was published at the close of the year. In the early part of 1848 he had some correspondence looking towards the revival of his scheme of publishing the *Stylus*. He delivered a lecture in the hall of the Society Library, New York, in February, on the "Cosmogony of the Universe." His volume *Eureka* was published in New York in the summer. His own copy of this was also in the Bishop Hurst library sale. This volume was sent after Poe's death by a relative to Griswold, who wrote his name and the remark that it was "Poe's private copy" on the first end paper. It is marked throughout with penciled additions and alterations. A note in Poe's hand on the last leaf has caused some comment. It reads: "The pain of the consideration that we shall lose our identity, ceases at once when we further reflect that the process, as above described, is, neither more nor less than that of the absorption, by each individual intelligence, of all other intelligences (that is, of the Universe) into its own. That God may be all in all, each must become God." Poe embodied some of his ideas in *Eureka* in an article in *Burton's Gentleman's Magazine* for August, 1839, which is headed "An Opinion on Dreams." This stated: "Various opinions have been hazarded concerning dreams — whether they have any connection with the invisible and eternal world or not; and it appears to me, the reason why nothing like a definite conclusion has yet been arrived at, is from the circumstance of the arguers never making any distinction between *Mind* and soul, always speaking of them as one and the same. I believe man to be in himself a Trinity, viz. Mind, Body, and Soul; and thus with dreams, some induced by the mind, and some by the soul. Those connected with the mind, I think proceed partly from supernatural and partly from natural causes; those of the soul I believe are of the immaterial world alone." The remainder of the article endeavors to show how the soul's dream and that of the mind are distinguishable; and whether sometimes, or often, they are not both at the same moment bearing their part in the nocturnal vision. It was early in 1848 when Poe wrote the first draft of the "Bells," which he sent to *Sartain's Union Magazine*, but it did not find publication. He also contributed "Marginalia" and "Fifty Suggestions" to *Graham's*, and a "Sonnet" to the *Union Magazine*.

In July Poe went to Lowell and lectured on the "Poetic Principle." There he made the acquaintance of the Richmond family. Mrs. Richmond was "his Annie." His descriptions in "Landor's Cottage" are said to correspond with his first visit to the Richmond home, and in writing this story he is presumed to have had the Richmond cottage in mind; in fact, he has left a written statement that the tale has something of "Annïe" in it. In the light of Poe's later love affairs this is interesting. He says: "As no bell was discernible, I rapped with my stick against the door, which stood half open. Instantly a figure advanced to the threshold — that of a young woman about twenty-eight years of age — slender, or rather slight, and somewhat above the medium height. As she approached, with a certain *modest decision* of step altogether indescribable, I said to myself, 'Surely here I have found the perfection of natural, in contradiction from artificial *grace*.' The second impression which she made on me, but by far the more vivid of the two, was that of *enthusiasm*. So intense an expression of *Romance*, perhaps I should call it, or of unworldliness, as that which gleamed from her deep-set eyes, had never so sunk into my heart of hearts before. I know not how it is, but this peculiar expression of the eye, wreathing itself occasionally into the lips, is the most powerful, if not absolutely the *sole* spell, which rivets my interest in woman. '*Romance*,' provided my readers fully comprehend what I would here imply by the word 'romance,' and 'womanliness' seem to me convertible terms: and, after all, what man truly *loves* in woman is, simply, her *womanhood*. The eyes of Annie (I heard some one from the interior call her 'Annie, darling!') were 'spiritual gray'; her hair, a light chestnut: this is all I had time to observe of her." It was only a few months afterwards when he published his lines "To ——," giving another romantic description of his first meeting with Mrs. Sarah Helen Whitman, — "His Helen of a thousand dreams."

In July Poe went to Richmond, Virginia, on a lecture tour. It is singular that no newspaper notice of his arrival, his departure, nor mention of this visit can be found in that city. As he wrote to Snodgrass of the earlier days in Richmond, he gave way again "to the temptations held out by the spirit of Southern conviviality." This was Poe's failing, for whenever he listened to the voice of the tempter, he usually succumbed — a glass of wine or cider causing a protracted spree. His visit to the MacKenzie family, where his sister Rosalie resided, was brief, and he spent most of his time among the newspaper fraternity. His early child-love, Miss Poitiaux, has stated that he was refused admittance at her home when he called on this visit, because of his condition. In a letter of John R. Thompson to Patterson, dated November 9, 1849, in reply to inquiries concerning Poe, he wrote "that his acquaintance began in the Spring of 1848. That he had heard of Poe being on a debauch in the lower section of the city for two weeks. The day following Poe called on him." After such a spree as Thompson's letter indicates Poe suffered dreadfully, and it usually took him many days to recover. If, as Thompson states, he was able to call on him in so short a time afterwards, Poe was hardly drinking at his worst, but moderately. This is verified by a statement made to me by the late Charles M. Wallace, Richmond's historian, who had an accurate memory. He saw Poe during this visit several times and knew he was drinking, but never saw him unable to take care of himself. Late one night Mr. Wallace was called out of bed by Richmond's best known newspaper editor in that day, who took him to meet the then famous poet at a nearby resort and hear him declaim "Eureka" and "The Raven," before a select assemblage of Richmond Bohemians. When he arrived Poe was standing among the assemblage discussing matters of the day. His manners were nervous and his countenance was flushed, but he was not drunk. Mr. Wallace was introduced to Poe, who bowed in a dignified way, and in a few moments by request began his discourse, which lasted for about an hour, and was entertaining. It is not thought that Thompson saw much of Poe on this visit, and his information about Poe's habits possibly came second hand. I have another unpublished letter of Thompson's to P. P. Cooke, dated October 17, 1848, in which he states:[1] "Poe is not in Richmond. He remained here about three weeks, horribly drunk, and discoursing 'Eureka' to the audiences of Bar Rooms. His friends tried to get him sober and set him to work, but to no effect, and were com-

[1] John R. Thompson to P. P. Cooke, MS.

pelled at last to *reship* him to New York. I was very anxious for him to write something for me, while he remained here, but his 'lucid intervals' were so brief and infrequent that it was quite impossible. 'The Rationale of Verse' I took, more as an act of charity than anything else, for though exhibiting great acquaintance with the subject, it is altogether too *bizarre*, and too technical for the general reader. Poe is a singular fellow."

Poe's work during this period shows that he was sober long enough to write many columns of matter. Some of his manuscript, given away by Thompson, is still in Richmond, — "a work of manual art." Besides "The Rationale of Verse" and a review of Mrs. Lewis's poems, in the *Messenger*, he also sent a new "Literati" paper on Mrs. Lewis to the *Democratic Review*. He is not thought to have seen Mrs. Shelton, his early love, on this visit. His love affairs were never much of a secret. In her letter to Griswold about Poe in 1850, Mrs. Osgood wrote: "Mrs. Ellet asked an introduction to him and followed him everywhere, Miss Lynch begged me to bring him there and called upon him at his lodgings, Mrs. Whitman besieged him with valentines and letters long before he wrote or took any notice of her, and all the others wrote poetry and letters to him." Very much has been written about Poe's relations with women, and his letters and love affairs have been closely investigated, but many incidents hinted at in this letter of Mrs. Osgood, which might put some matters in a different light, have been lost sight of. Mrs. Lewis, who was anxious for public recognition and advertisement of her poems, also followed him about, and he had an intimate acquaintance with her. He asked her to write his life when he died. Mrs.

Clemm wrote her letters in the latter days, and after Poe's death went to live with her. Her husband wrote Miss S. S. Rice of Baltimore a letter October 11, 1875, which I am permitted to use. He said: "I have resided and practised my profession of the law in Brooklyn for about thirty years. Shortly after I moved here, in 1845, Mr. Poe and I became personal friends. His last residence, and where I visited him oftenest, was in a beautifully secluded cottage at Fordham, fourteen miles above New York. It was there that I often saw his dear wife during her last illness, and attended her funeral. It was from there that he and his 'dear Muddie' (Mrs. Clemm) often visited me at my house, frequently, and at my urgent solicitation, remaining many days. When he finally departed on his last trip south, the kissing and handshaking were at my front door. He was hopeful; we were sad: and tears gushed in torrents as he kissed his dear 'Muddie' and my wife 'good-bye.' Alas, it proved, as Mrs. Clemm feared, a final adieu. I offered Mrs. Clemm a home in my family, where she resided until 1858, when she removed to Baltimore to lay her ashes by the side of her 'darling Eddie.' Mr. Poe was one of the most affectionate, kind-hearted men I ever knew. I never witnessed so much tender affection and devotion as existed in that family of three persons. I have spent weeks in the closest intimacy with him, and never saw him under the slightest influence of any stimulants whatever. In my presence he was the polished gentleman, the profound scholar, the true critic, and the inspired oracular poet — dreamy and spiritual, lofty, but sad. His biographers have not done his virtues or his genius justice; and, to produce a startling effect by contrast, have magnified his errors and attributed to him faults that he never had."

With so many devoted lady admirers as Poe had when he was in Richmond on his first visit, his movements were closely watched. While the "Whitman romance" had just started, still it was talked about in literary circles and mentioned by Poe himself in Richmond. Among the literary characters he met with there was John M. Daniel of the *Examiner*. They did not get along together, and bad feelings existed between them from the start. Daniel had an acquaintance with Mrs. Whitman's family, and, hearing about Poe's attentions, made disparaging remarks, which came to Poe's ears. This with some other dispute about a debt infuriated Poe, who sent a challenge to Daniel to fight a duel.[1] The affair was well remembered by Judge Hughes. The newspaper men arranged to have Poe meet Daniel alone in the *Examiner* office, but the matter was settled without any recourse to arms. Daniel afterwards published an unkind allusion to the reported engagement of Poe and Mrs. Whitman, but became one of his most intimate friends. And yet when Poe died he wrote in the *Messenger* a rather harsh account of his life. Later still he wrote a pleasant and favorable letter about Poe to Mrs. Whitman, which she quoted in her publication, *Edgar Poe and his Critics*.

After Poe's return home he traveled between New York, Lowell, and Providence, lecturing on the "Poetic Principle." In the Richmond *Whig* of August 17, 1849, probably inspired by Poe, it was stated: "This lecture

[1] *The Life of Edgar Allan Poe.* By George E. Woodberry. Houghton Mifflin Co., Boston and New York. 1909. Vol. ii, p. 443, reprints a full account.

on the Poetic Principle is one of the course delivered before the Providence Lyceum last fall, the other lecturers being Rufus Choate, Theodore Parker, Alonzo Potter (Bishop of Pennsylvania), Louis Agassiz, the French savant, and Daniel Webster, who opened the course. Mr. Poe had the largest audience of the season, more than 1600 persons." In another notice in this paper Poe gave some mention of the publication of his tales in France, showing a knowledge of the publications.

Among other incidents in the life of Poe, much has been written about his love entanglements with Mrs. Sarah Helen Whitman. He was to marry her in December. She is said to have heard that Poe was drinking again, and when he called she drenched her handkerchief with ether and threw herself on a sofa, hoping to lose consciousness. She remembered his last words and that she told him that she "loved him." After this Mrs. Whitman mentioned that she playfully sent some verses about him — "Stanzas for Music" — to the *Metropolitan Magazine* for February, 1849. She always would have it that Poe construed these lines as an olive branch, and in return wrote "Annabel Lee." Poe during his last visit to Richmond stated to Judge Hughes that Mrs. Whitman had made repeated efforts towards a reconciliation, which he refused. It seems evident that he paid no attention to her lines in the *Metropolitan*, for Mrs. Whitman again sent other verses to the *Southern Literary Messenger*, where she knew they would come under his eye. So that Poe might not regard them as old stock, she dated them "Isle of Rhodes, March, 1849." They appeared in the June number of the *Messenger*, beginning, —

"I bade thee stay. Too well I knew
The fault was mine, mine only."

Mrs. Whitman forgot to mention these lines in after life, and possibly lived in hopes that they had been forgotten, but she took pains to revise them for the later publication of her poems.

After Poe's death Mrs. Whitman made a fetish of his memory. She gave out portions of his letters written to her, and a fragment of a facsimile. After her own death there appeared *The Last Letters of Edgar Allan Poe to Sarah Helen Whitman*. The matter in the volume appeared in the *Century Magazine* for January, 1909, as "New Light on a Romantic Episode." It was claimed that the letters now appeared without "omissions, garbling or diversion." A comparison with that text and the fragment of the facsimile shows a slight difference in at least one of the letters. There are also some deviations between the marriage and another contract as given in the book and magazine.

After parting with Mrs. Whitman Poe drew closer to "Annie," as his letters show. He also seemed hopeful and made preparations for more active literary labors. In an unpublished letter dated Fordham, Saturday, January 20 (1849), he wrote the *American Whig Review*: [1] "May I trouble you to hand the accompanying brief article to Mr. Whelpley and see if he can give me $10 for it? About four years ago, I think, I wrote a paper on 'The American Drama' for your review. It was printed anonymously — my name not given in the index. The criticism referred chiefly to Willis's 'Tortesa' and Longfellow's 'Spanish Student.' Could you procure me the number containing it?"

[1] Poe to John Priestly, Proprietor, MS.

His later correspondence shows that the article sent in this communication was "Critics and Criticism," which was not accepted, and he sent it to *Graham's*, where it did not find publication until after his death. His income does not appear to have been sufficient for his needs, and he had to resort to his former habit of borrowing, as evidenced by a sixty days' note given by him for sixty-seven dollars, February 3, 1849, to Isaac Cooper, a relative of the novelist. In this same month he wrote in a letter to F. W. Thomas: "Right glad am I to find you once more in a true position — 'in the field of letters.' Depend upon it after all, Thomas, literature is the most noble of professions. In fact, it is about the only one fit for a man. For my own part there is no seducing me from the path. I shall be a *littérateur*, at least, all my life; nor would I abandon the hopes which still lead me on for all the gold in California." He had also remarked to a friend, "One Richard, whom you know is himself again." He sent a review of Griswold's *Female Poets of America* to the *Messenger* for February, which has been overlooked by previous biographers. In the March number he wrote his criticism on Lowell's *A Fable for Critics*. He wrote for *Godey's*, and had also become a regular contributor to the Boston *Flag of Our Union*. His contributions there have never been known with any degree of certainty until now. He contributed: March 3, "A Valentine"; March 17, "Hop Frog"; March 31, "A Dream within a Dream"; April 14, "Von Kempelen and his Discovery"; April 21, "Eldorado"; April 28, "For Annie"; May 12, "Xing a Paragrab"; June 9, "Landor's Cottage," and July 7, "Sonnet — To my Mother." These were mentioned as by Edgar A. Poe, a regular contributor.

In May Poe's hopes for the publication of his *Stylus* were revived by finding a partner in E. H. Patterson. It was with the object of securing subscriptions for this that he started South in June. At Philadelphia he met with his old companions again, with the usual result that he was in the end desperately ill. His friend John Sartain and others took care of him, and he finally arrived in Richmond, Saturday, July 14, 1849. He stopped at the old Swan Tavern, where Dr. George W. Rawlings, the physician who was with his early companion Burling when he died of cholera, attended him.

Dr. Rawlings, who lived in a small frame house on Broad Street adjoining the Swan Tavern, stated that in his delirium Poe drew a pistol and tried to shoot him. Burling, before his death about 1832, lived around the corner from Dr. Rawlings on Ninth Street. When Poe recovered he joined a temperance society. A reference to this from the Philadelphia *Bulletin* was copied in the Richmond *Whig* in September, while Poe was in Richmond. The same paper about this time copied a favorable notice from the Cincinnati *Atlas*, referring to Poe's visit to Richmond and his lecture. A lengthy review of Mrs. Osgood's poems, written by Poe, appeared in the August *Messenger*. He delivered his first lecture August 17 in the Exchange concert rooms. His subject was the "Poetic Principle." The *Whig* had a favorable notice, and urged him to repeat the lecture. Poe has written in his letters of this lecture, and mentioned that all the press notices were favorable except one written by Daniel, whom he had once challenged. This notice, inaccessible until now, is of interest, and appeared in the *Examiner* of August 21, as follows: —

"Poe's subject was the 'Poetic Principle,' and he treated it with all the acuteness and imagination that we had expected from him. We were glad to hear the lecturer explode what he properly pronounced to be the poetic 'heresy of modern times,' to wit: that poetry should have a purpose, an end to accomplish beyond that of ministering to our sense of the beautiful. We have in these days poets of humanity and poets of universal suffrage, poets whose mission it is to break down corn laws and poets to build up workhouses. The idea infects half the criticism and all the poetry of this utilitarian country. But no idea can be more false, as we have elementary faculties in our minds whose end is to reason, others to perceive colors and forms, and others to construct, and as argument, painting, and mechanics are the products of those faculties and are only intended for them; as we have nerves to be pleased with perfumes; others with gay colors and others with the contact of soft bodies — so have we an elementary faculty for perceiving beauty with ends of its own and means of its own — Poetry is the product of this faculty, and of no other; it is addressed to the sense of the beautiful and to no other sense. It is ever injured when subjected to the criterion of other faculties, and was never intended to fulfill any other objects than those peculiar to the organ of the mind from which it received its birth. Mr. Poe made good his distinction with a great deal of acuteness and in a very clever manner. His various pieces of criticism upon the popular poets of the country were for the most part just, and were very entertaining. But we were disappointed in Mr. Poe's recitations. We had heard a good deal of his manner, but it does not answer our wants. His voice is soft and distinct, but neither clear nor sonorous. He does not make rhyme effective; he reads all verse like blank verse ; and yet he gives it a sing song of his own more monotonous than any versification. On the two last syllables of every sentence he invariably falls a fifth. He did not make his own 'Raven' an effective piece of reading. At this we would not be surprised were any other than the author its reader. The chief charm perhaps of that extraordinary composition is the strange and subtle music of the versification. As in Mr. Longfellow's rhythm we can hear it with our mind's ear while we read it ourselves, but no human organs are sufficiently delicate to weave it into articulate sounds. For this reason we are not surprised at ordinary failures in reading these pieces. But we anticipated some peculiar charm in their utterances by the lips of him who created the verse, and in this case we were disappointed. A large audience was in attendance. Indeed the concert room was completely filled. Mr. Poe commenced his career in this city, and those who had not seen him since the days of his obscurity of course felt no little curiosity to behold so famous a townsman. Mr. Poe is a small thin man, slightly formed, keen visaged, with dark complexion, dark hair, and we believe dark eyes. His face is not an ordinary one. The forehead is well developed and the nose somewhat more prominent than usual. Mr. Poe is a man of very decided genius. Indeed we know of no other writer in the United States who has half the chance to be remembered in the history of literature. But his reputation will rest on a very small minority of his compositions. Among all his poems there are only two pieces which are not execrably bad, —

'The Raven' and 'Dream-Land.' The majority of his prose compositions are the children of want and dyspepsia, of the printer's devils and the blue devils — had he possessed the power of applying his creative faculty, — as have the Miltons, the Shakespeares, and all the other *demiurgi,* — he would have been a great man. But there is not one trace of that power in any of his compositions that we have read; and if rumor is to be credited his career has been that of the Marlowes, the Jonsons, the Dekkers, and the Websters, the old dramatists and translunary rowdies of the Elizabethan age. Had Mr. Poe possessed talent in the place of genius, he might have been a popular and money-making author. He would have written a great many more good things than he has; but his title to immortality would not and could not be surer than it is — For the few things that the author has written which are at all tolerable are coins stamped with the unmistakable die. They are of themselves, *sui generis,* unlike any diagrams in Time's kaleidoscope, either past, present, or to come — and gleam with the diamond hues of Eternity."

Poe afterwards called to see Daniel to disabuse his mind of the unfavorable portions of this criticism. He succeeded in so far as to effect an arrangement to become an associate with Daniel on the *Examiner* newspaper. It was arranged that he was to do the book reviewing and other literary work. He was also to revise and republish his writings, especially his poems, and the principal poems were to be published in the *Examiner.* He was shown a desk by Daniel and asked to commence work. This was Daniel's way, and it was also his habit not to say much in his paper about his associates. He always liked Daniel to be kept fully in the foreground. The connection of Poe, however, was talked about in newspaper circles and well understood at the time.

The late Bishop O. P. Fitzgerald wrote: —

"I was in Richmond in 1849, and remember Mr. Poe, with his white linen coat and trousers, black velvet vest, and broad Panama hat. He was the most notable figure among the group of specialists that gathered around John M. Daniel, editor of the Richmond *Examiner*. Daniel was an electric battery, fully charged, whose touches shocked the staid and lofty-minded leaders in Virginia politics. There was about him that indefinable charm that draws men of genius towards one another, though differing in the quality and measure of their endowment. There was Robert W. Hughes, with his strong judicial brain, just starting on his path of distinction. There was Patrick Henry Aylett, a descendant of the great orator, and a rising young lawyer. There was Arthur Petticolas, who had an æsthetic touch that gave his dissertations on Art a special charm and value. The *Examiner* under Daniel was a free lance: it made things lively for all sorts of readers.

"Mr. Poe naturally found his way thereto as literary editor. He had already attained celebrity as a writer whose prose and poetry were unlike those of all other persons. The reading public was watching him expectantly, looking for greater things. There was about him something that drew especial notice. His face was one of the saddest ever seen. His step was gentle, his voice soft, yet clear; his presence altogether winning. Though unlike in most particulars, Poe and Daniel affiliated in dealing with a world in which sin and folly on the one hand provoked their wrath and scorn, and on the other appealed to their pity and helpfulness.

"That Mr. Poe was battling with tragic threatenings at this time, now seems pretty clear. The literary public of Richmond knew enough of him to elicit a profound interest in his behalf. They wished to express their good will and invited him to deliver a lecture. The whole transaction was unique and gave a touch of the Old South. The lecture was delivered, and by special request the lecturer then and there recited his own poem, 'The Raven,' the remembrance of which is a pleasure to one of his hearers — unto this day."

Judge Hughes and others of the *Examiner* have also told of his work done in that office. He sent many of his best known poems revised into the composing room, where they were typeset for future use, but only "The Raven" and "Dream-Land" appeared. The others, however, were preserved in proof sheets and used by F. W. Thomas, who was afterwards connected with the Richmond *Enquirer* as literary editor, to prepare a new edition of Poe's poems. These are now published for the first time.

After his first lecture Poe went to Norfolk, Virginia. Miss Susan Ingram in the New York *Herald* of February 19, 1905, tells of meeting him with a Virginia party at Old Point Comfort, Sunday, September 9. She said: —

"That Sunday evening in early September at Old Point stands out like a lovely picture. I cannot describe it fitly. There was more in it than may be expressed in mere words. There were several of us girls, all friends, and all of us knew Mr. Poe. I can see just how we looked, sitting about there in our white dresses. There was a young collegian, too, who was my particular friend. He is gone long years since, and all the others in that little group have passed away except Sister and myself.

"Mr. Poe sat there in that quiet way of his which made you feel his presence. After a while my aunt, who was nearer his age, said: 'This seems to be just the time and place for poetry, Mr. Poe.' And it was. We all felt it. The old Hygeia stood some distance from the water, but with nothing between it and the ocean. It was moonlight, and the light shone over everything with that undimmed light that it has in the South. There were many persons on the long verandas that surrounded the hotel, but they seemed remote and far away. Our little party was absolutely cut off from everything except that lovely view of the water shining in the moonlight, and its gentle music borne to us on the soft breeze. Poe felt the influence. How could a poet help it? And when we seconded the request that he recite for us he agreed readily. He recited 'The Raven,' 'Annabel Lee,' and last of all 'Ulalume,' with the last stanza of which he remarked that he feared it might not be intelligible to us, as it was scarcely clear to himself, and for that reason it had not been published (*sic*). The next day he sent a copy of the poem with a letter.

" We went from Old Point Comfort to our home near Norfolk, and he called on us there, and again I had the pleasure of talking with him. Although I was only a slip of a girl and he what then seemed to me quite an old man, and a great literary one at that, we got on together beautifully. He was one of the most courteous gentlemen I have ever seen, and that gave a great charm to his manner. None of his pictures that I have ever seen look like the picture of Poe that I keep in my memory. Of course they look like him, so that any one seeing them could have recognized him from them, but there was something in his face that is in none of them. Perhaps it was in the eyes, perhaps in the mouth. I do not know, but any one who ever met him would understand what I mean.

"There were no indications of dissipation apparent when we saw Poe in Virginia at that time. I think he had not been drinking for a long time. If I had not heard or read what had been said about his intemperance I should never have had any idea of it from what I saw in Poe. To me he seemed a good man, as well as a charming one, very sensitive and very high-minded.

"I remember one little incident that illustrates how loyal he was to the memory of those who had been kind to him. I was fond of orris root, and always had the odor of it about my clothes. One day when we were walking together he spoke of it. 'I like it, too,' he said. 'Do you know what it makes me think of? My adopted mother. Whenever the bureau drawers in her room were opened there came from them a whiff of orris root, and ever since when I smell it I go back to the time when I was a little boy, and it brings back thoughts of my mother.'"

Poe lectured in the Norfolk Academy on the "Poetic Principle" Friday, September 14, and it was noticed in the *American Beacon* of that city. He returned to Richmond, where he lectured again on the same subject September 24, which was his last public appearance. During this visit Poe made many social calls, often in the company of his sister Rosalie, who still resided in Richmond. He visited the Bernards, relatives of Whïte of the *Messenger;* the Strobias, who were old church friends of the first Mrs. Allan as well as the Poitiaux family. His child-love Miss Poitiaux was alive, and she has left her statement of this last visit. She published some lines on the death of Poe in Richmond in August, 1852, with the following introduction : —

"The writer of these lines was in early life a playmate of the unfortunate Edgar A. Poe, and the god-daughter of the lady by whom he was adopted. He even then gave promise of the talent which has since made his name one long to be remembered as a writer — I will not say unequaled, but not surpassed by any poet of his time. Some few weeks preceding his sorrowful demise he visited our city and read before the public his 'Raven,' and others of his own and Hood's beautiful verses. I was at that time too unwell to venture out, and did not hear him, but a few days afterwards he called on me. His unfortunate propensity had made us refuse to see him on a former occasion, but this time he unexpectedly entered the room in which I was sitting, saying as I rose to meet him: 'Old friend, you see I would not be denied.' He only stayed a few minutes, but in that short time left an impression on my memory which has never since been effaced. He was to be married in a few weeks to a lady of our city, and as he stood upon the steps bidding me farewell, I asked, alluding to his marriage, when I should see him again. It was no fancy, but a strange reality, that a gray shadow such as I had never seen before, save on the face of the dying, passed across his as, gazing gravely in mine, he answered slowly: 'In the words of my Raven, perhaps — nevermore,' and in a moment he had gone. In a few weeks I heard the tidings of his death."

Poe also made a visit to his dear friend, as he called Eliza Lambert, the sister of General Lambert, once Mayor of Richmond and a near relation of the Strobias. There were other friends of his early days there, and, as he wrote in one of his last letters to Mrs. Clemm, he remained until one o'clock in the morning, talking of the olden times. He also visited the family of W. A. R. Nye, connected with the *Whig*, who were friends of long standing. Much more of his time was spent with Mrs. Shelton, his early love, to whom he was again engaged to be married. She was seen with him at church and at his lectures, and he wrote to Mrs. Clemm that all was in readiness for the marriage. In the same letter he showed distress of mind about "Annie" and wished to be near her. Mrs. Shelton has left her recollections of Poe, which are supposed to be in the Valentine Museum, Richmond. They are not thought to differ materially from her other statements. She gave a pleasing description of Poe in his youthful days calling to see her in company with Burling, and how he met and begged her to marry him in 1849. He visited her the night before he left Richmond for Baltimore, when he complained of feeling ill. Richmond's oldest book-dealer, J. W. Randolph, remembered Poe. He told me that in those days he had Sanxey's old book-stand. Poe was a good customer of Sanxey's in olden times. He had been coming in quietly and looking about Randolph's shop, and now and then buying a magazine. "Look here," he said one day; "it makes me sad to come in here and not see Sanxey. When did he die?" Randolph explained that Sanxey was not dead, but had sold out. Poe went to hunt him up, and returning to the store a few days afterwards, told of a pleasant meeting with his former old book friend.

In order to wind up his affairs before his marriage, arranged for October 17, he made preparations to visit the North. He had a commission to edit a volume of poems in Philadelphia, and told Daniel that he would publish his own writings while away. After leaving Mrs. Shelton's on the evening of September 26, he went to Sadler's restaurant, where he met J. M. Blakey and other friends. Both Sadler and Blakey told Judge Hughes that they remembered meeting Poe at the restaurant that night, and did not think that he was drinking. They were quite certain that he was sober when they saw him last, and talking of going North. He left for Baltimore and Philadelphia early the following morning. As he steamed down the James River thoughts of his former journey more than twenty-two years before must have flashed across his memory, as well as the many other strange vicissitudes through which he had passed since his boyhood swims in the same waters.

He had been wandering about Baltimore for some days when he was found, Wednesday, October 3, in an unconscious condition, near Ryan's Fourth Ward Polls. He was taken to the Washington Hospital, where he died October 7, 1849.

A notice of Poe's death was printed in the Richmond *Whig* of October 9, as follows: " It is with profound grief that we give place this morning to the painful intelligence which will be read below. The sad announcement was received in yesterday's evening mail. When we reflect that it was but the other day that the deceased was delighting our citizens with a lecture as beautiful as his own genius was powerful and erratic — that he was walking in our streets in the vigor of manhood and mingling with acquaintances in the sociability of friendship — we would fain believe that it was untrue. The news of the death of Mr. Poe will fall with a heavy and crushing weight upon one in this city who is related to him by the tender tie of sister; and who can hardly have any previous knowledge of his illness; whilst it will be read with profound regret by all who appreciate generous qualities or admire genius. In the beautiful language of his own 'Lenore,' let there be a requiem for the dead — in that he died so young."

Poe was buried in the churchyard of the Westminster Church at Baltimore. Rev. W. T. D. Clemm read the services of the Methodist Episcopal Church. There were but few friends and relatives present at the sad rites. After his death, "Annabel Lee" was published in the New York *Tribune*, and *Sartain's Union Magazine* for November contained "The Bells." The *Messenger* for December contained "To my Mother"; *Graham's*, January, 1850, "Critics and Criticism"; followed in October by the "Poetic Principle," published in *Sartain's Union Magazine*. In the *Examiner* of October 26, Daniel announced: "Edgar Poe's complete works are to be published under the supervision of Willis and Lowell and under the auspices of Rufus Griswold. O! what a triumvirate." The November *Messenger* published a notice of Poe's death, in which the following letter to Thompson from H. W. Longfellow was given: —

"What a melancholy death is that of Mr. Poe — a man so richly endowed with genius! I never knew him personally, but have always entertained a high appreciation of his powers as a prose writer and a poet. His prose is remarkably vigorous, direct and yet affluent; and his verse has a peculiar charm of melody, an atmosphere of true poetry about it, which is very winning. The harshness of his criticisms I have never attributed to anything but the irritation of a sensitive nature, chafed by some indefinite sense of wrong."

Mrs. Clemm died in Baltimore at the Church Home, February 16, 1871. This was the same building in which Poe died. She was buried beside Poe. Rosalie Poe also became a subject for charity, and entered the Epiphany Church Home, Washington, where she died in July, 1874, at the age of sixty-four, which places her birth in 1810.

All that was mortal of Poe rested in a neglected grave in an obscure corner of the Baltimore Churchyard until November 17, 1875, when a monument was erected. I was present at the services of dedication, and remember that it was a raw, chilly, and bleak November day. Among those present who had known him best were J. H. Hewitt, and his old schoolmaster, Professor Clarke; also Drs. Brooks and Snodgrass. A number of letters and poems were read. Among those who sent tributes were Mallarmé, Swinburne, Hayne, Fawcett, Winter, John Neal, Mrs. Whitman, Saxe, Bryant, Longfellow, Tennyson, Whittier, Lowell, Aldrich, and Holmes. Swinburne wrote: "Widely as the fame of Poe has already spread, and deeply as it is already rooted in Europe, it is even now growing wider and striking deeper as time advances; the surest presage that Time, the eternal enemy of small and shallow reputations, will prove in this case also the constant and trusty friend and keeper of a poet's full-grown fame."

The following warm tribute was from O. W. Holmes:
"No one, surely, needs a mausoleum less than the poet.

> 'His monument shall be his gentle verse,
>   Which eyes not yet created shall o'erread;
> And tongues to be, his being shall rehearse
>   When all the breathers of this world are dead.'

Yet we would not leave him without a stone to mark
the spot where the hands that 'waked to ecstasy the
living lyre' were laid in dust. He that can confer an
immortality which will outlast bronze and granite de-
serves this poor tribute, not for his sake so much as ours.
The hearts of all who reverence the inspiration of genius,
who can look tenderly upon the infirmities too often
attending it, who can feel for its misfortunes, will sympathize with you as you gather around the resting-place
of all that was mortal of Edgar Allan Poe, and raise the
stone inscribed with one of the few names which will
outlive the graven record meant to perpetuate its
remembrance."

THE RAVEN
AND OTHER POEMS

DEDICATION TO THE EDITION OF 1845

TO THE NOBLEST OF HER SEX —
TO THE AUTHOR OF
"THE DRAMA OF EXILE"—
TO MISS ELIZABETH BARRETT BARRETT,
OF ENGLAND,
I DEDICATE THIS VOLUME,
WITH THE MOST ENTHUSIASTIC ADMIRATION
AND WITH THE MOST SINCERE ESTEEM.

E. A. P.

PREFACE TO THE POEMS
EDITION OF 1845

THESE trifles are collected and republished chiefly with a view to their redemption from the many improvements to which they have been subjected while going "the rounds of the press." I am naturally anxious that if what I have written is to circulate at all, it should circulate as I wrote it. In defence of my own taste, nevertheless, it is incumbent on me to say that I think nothing in this volume of much value to the public, or very creditable to myself. Events not to be controlled have prevented me from making, at any time, any serious effort in what, under happier circumstances, would have been the field of my choice. With me poetry has been not a purpose, but a passion; and the passions should be held in reverence; they must not — they cannot at will be excited, with an eye to the paltry compensations, or the more paltry commendations, of mankind.

E. A. P.

NOTE. — In the J. Lorimer Graham copy, Poe struck out in the third line after going "at random." He also transposed the sentence, "If what I have written is to circulate at all, I am naturally anxious that it should circulate as I wrote it," to read as above. The word "upon" in the seventh line was changed to "on"; a comma after "say" was erased, and a comma inserted after "excited."

POEMS

THE RAVEN AND OTHER POEMS

THE RAVEN

ONCE upon a midnight dreary, while I pondered, weak
and weary,
Over many a quaint and curious volume of forgotten
lore —
While I nodded, nearly napping, suddenly there came a
tapping,
As of some one gently rapping, rapping at my chamber
door.
"'T is some visiter," I muttered, "tapping at my chamber door —
    Only this and nothing more."

Ah, distinctly I remember it was in the bleak December;
And each separate dying ember wrought its ghost upon
the floor.
Eagerly I wished the morrow; — vainly I had sought to
borrow
From my books surcease of sorrow — sorrow for the
lost Lenore —
For the rare and radiant maiden whom the angels name
Lenore —
    Nameless *here* for evermore.

And the silken, sad, uncertain rustling of each purple
　　　curtain
Thrilled me — filled me with fantastic terrors never
　　　felt before;
So that now, to still the beating of my heart, I stood re-
　　　peating
" 'T is some visiter entreating entrance at my chamber
　　　door —
Some late visiter entreating entrance at my chamber
　　　door; —
　　　　　This it is and nothing more."

Presently my soul grew stronger; hesitating then no
　　　longer,
"Sir," said I, "or Madam, truly your forgiveness I im-
　　　plore;
But the fact is I was napping, and so gently you came
　　　rapping,
And so faintly you came tapping, tapping at my chamber
　　　door,
That I scarce was sure I heard you" — here I opened
　　　wide the door; —
　　　　　Darkness there and nothing more.

Deep into that darkness peering, long I stood there won-
　　　dering, fearing,
Doubting, dreaming dreams no mortal ever dared to
　　　dream before;
But the silence was unbroken, and the stillness gave no
　　　token,
And the only word there spoken was the whispered word,
　　　"Lenore ? "

This I whispered, and an echo murmured back the word,
   "Lenore!"
     Merely this and nothing more.

Back into the chamber turning, all my soul within me
   burning,
Soon again I heard a tapping somewhat louder than
   before.
"Surely," said I, "surely that is something at my window lattice;
Let me see, then, what thereat is, and this mystery
   explore —
Let my heart be still a moment and this mystery explore; —
     'T is the wind and nothing more!"

Open here I flung the shutter, when, with many a flirt
   and flutter,
In there stepped a stately Raven of the saintly days of
   yore;
Not the least obeisance made he; not a minute stopped
   or stayed he;
But, with mien of lord or lady, perched above my
   chamber door —
Perched upon a bust of Pallas just above my chamber
   door —
     Perched, and sat, and nothing more.

Then this ebony bird beguiling my sad fancy into smiling,
By the grave and stern decorum of the countenance it
   wore,
"Though thy crest be shorn and shaven, thou," I said,
   "art sure no craven,

Ghastly grim and ancient Raven wandering from the
    Nightly shore —
Tell me what thy lordly name is on the Night's Plu-
    tonian shore!"
        Quoth the Raven "Nevermore."

Much I marvelled this ungainly fowl to hear discourse
    so plainly,
Though its answer little meaning — little relevancy bore;
For we cannot help agreeing that no living human being
Ever yet was blessed with seeing bird above his cham-
    ber door —
Bird or beast upon the sculptured bust above his
    chamber door,
        With such name as "Nevermore."

But the Raven, sitting lonely on the placid bust, spoke
    only
That one word, as if his soul in that one word he did
    outpour.
Nothing farther then he uttered — not a feather then
    he fluttered —
Till I scarcely more than muttered "Other friends have
    flown before —
On the morrow *he* will leave me, as my Hopes have flown
    before."
        Then the bird said "Nevermore."

Startled at the stillness broken by reply so aptly spoken,
"Doubtless," said I, "what it utters is its only stock
    and store
Caught from some unhappy master whom unmerciful
    Disaster

Followed fast and followed faster till his songs one bur-
    den bore —
Till the dirges of his Hope that melancholy burden bore
    Of 'Never — nevermore.'"

But the Raven still beguiling my sad fancy into smiling,
Straight I wheeled a cushioned seat in front of bird, and
    bust and door;
Then, upon the velvet sinking, I betook myself to link-
    ing
Fancy unto fancy, thinking what this ominous bird of
    yore —
What this grim, ungainly, ghastly, gaunt, and ominous
    bird of yore
        Meant in croaking "Nevermore."

This I sat engaged in guessing, but no syllable express-
    ing
To the fowl whose fiery eyes now burned into my
    bosom's core;
This and more I sat divining, with my head at ease re-
    clining
On the cushion's velvet lining that the lamp-light
    gloated o'er,
But whose velvet-violet lining with the lamp-light
    gloating o'er,
        She shall press, ah, nevermore!

Then, methought, the air grew denser, perfumed from
    an unseen censer
Swung by seraphim whose foot-falls tinkled on the tufted
    floor.
"Wretch," I cried, "thy God hath lent thee — by these
    angels he hath sent thee

Respite — respite and nepenthe from thy memories of
    Lenore;
Quaff, oh quaff this kind nepenthe and forget this lost
    Lenore!"
      Quoth the Raven "Nevermore."

"Prophet!" said I, "thing of evil! — prophet still, if
    bird or devil! —
Whether Tempter sent, or whether tempest tossed thee
    here ashore,
Desolate yet all undaunted, on this desert land en-
    chanted —
On this home by Horror haunted — tell me truly, I im-
    plore —
Is there — *is* there balm in Gilead? — tell me — tell
    me, I implore!"
      Quoth the Raven " Nevermore."

"Prophet!" said I, "thing of evil! — prophet still, if
    bird or devil!
By that Heaven that bends above us — by that God we
    both adore —
Tell this soul with sorrow laden if, within the distant
    Aidenn,
It shall clasp a sainted maiden whom the angels name
    Lenore —
Clasp a rare and radiant maiden whom the angels name
    Lenore."
      Quoth the Raven " Nevermore."

"Be that word our sign of parting, bird or fiend!" I
    shrieked, upstarting —
"Get thee back into the tempest and the Night's
    Plutonian shore!

Leave no black plume as a token of that lie thy soul
 hath spoken!
Leave my loneliness unbroken! — quit the bust above
 my door!
Take thy beak from out my heart, and take thy form
 from off my door!"
  Quoth the Raven "Nevermore."

And the Raven, never flitting, still is sitting, *still* is sitting
On the pallid bust of Pallas just above my chamber
 door;
And his eyes have all the seeming of a demon's that is
 dreaming,
And the lamp-light o'er him streaming throws his
 shadow on the floor;
And my soul from out that shadow that lies floating on
 the floor
  Shall be lifted — nevermore!

THE VALLEY OF UNREST

ONCE it smiled a silent dell
Where the people did not dwell;
They had gone unto the wars,
Trusting to the mild-eyed stars,
Nightly, from their azure towers,
To keep watch above the flowers,
In the midst of which all day
The red sun-light lazily lay.
Now each visiter shall confess
The sad valley's restlessness.
Nothing there is motionless —
Nothing save the airs that brood
Over the magic solitude.
Ah, by no wind are stirred those trees
That palpitate like the chill seas
Around the misty Hebrides!
Ah, by no wind those clouds are driven
That rustle through the unquiet Heaven
Uneasily, from morn till even,
Over the violets there that lie
In myriad types of the human eye —
Over the lilies there that wave
And weep above a nameless grave!
They wave: — from out their fragrant tops
Eternal dews come down in drops.
They weep: — from off their delicate stems
Perennial tears descend in gems.

BRIDAL BALLAD

THE ring is on my hand,
 And the wreath is on my brow;
Satins and jewels grand
Are all at my command,
 And I am happy now.

And my lord he loves me well;
 But, when first he breathed his vow,
I felt my bosom swell —
For the words rang as a knell,
And the voice seemed *his* who fell
In the battle down the dell,
 And who is happy now.

But he spoke to re-assure me,
 And he kissed my pallid brow,
While a reverie came o'er me,
And to the church-yard bore me,
And I sighed to him before me,
(Thinking him dead D'Elormie,)
 "Oh, I am happy now!"

And thus the words were spoken;
 And this the plighted vow;
And, though my faith be broken,
And, though my heart be broken,
Here is a ring, as token
 That I am happy now! —
Behold the golden token
 That *proves* me happy now!

Would God I could awaken!
  For I dream I know not how,
And my soul is sorely shaken
Lest an evil step be taken, —
Lest the dead who is forsaken
  May not be happy now.

THE SLEEPER

At midnight, in the month of June,
I stand beneath the mystic moon.
An opiate vapor, dewy, dim,
Exhales from out her golden rim,
And, softly dripping, drop by drop,
Upon the quiet mountain top,
Steals drowsily and musically
Into the universal valley.
The rosemary nods upon the grave;
The lily lolls upon the wave;
Wrapping the fog about its breast,
The ruin moulders into rest;
Looking like Lethe, see! the lake
A conscious slumber seems to take,
And would not, for the world, awake.
All Beauty sleeps! — and lo! where lies
Irene, with her Destinies!

Oh, lady bright! can it be right —
This window open to the night?
The wanton airs, from the tree-top,
Laughingly through the lattice drop —
The bodiless airs, a wizard rout,
Flit through thy chamber in and out,
And wave the curtain canopy
So fitfully — so fearfully —
Above the closed and fringèd lid
'Neath which thy slumb'ring soul lies hid,
That, o'er the floor and down the wall,
Like ghosts the shadows rise and fall!

Oh, lady dear, hast thou no fear?
Why and what art thou dreaming here?
Sure thou art come o'er far-off seas,
A wonder to these garden trees!
Strange is thy pallor! strange thy dress!
Strange, above all, thy length of tress,
And this all solemn silentness!

The lady sleeps! Oh, may her sleep,
Which is enduring, so be deep!
Heaven have her in its sacred keep!
This chamber changed for one more holy,
This bed for one more melancholy,
I pray to God that she may lie
Forever with unopened eye,
While the pale sheeted ghosts go by!

My love, she sleeps! Oh, may her sleep,
As it is lasting, so be deep!
Soft may the worms about her creep!
Far in the forest, dim and old,
For her may some tall vault unfold —
Some vault that oft hath flung its black
And wingèd panels fluttering back,
Triumphant, o'er the crested palls,
Of her grand family funerals —
Some sepulchre, remote, alone,
Against whose portal she hath thrown,
In childhood, many an idle stone —
Some tomb from out whose sounding door
She ne'er shall force an echo more,
Thrilling to think, poor child of sin!
It was the dead who groaned within.

THE COLISEUM

Type of the antique Rome! Rich reliquary
Of lofty contemplation left to Time
By buried centuries of pomp and power!
At length — at length — after so many days
Of weary pilgrimage and burning thirst,
(Thirst for the springs of lore that in thee lie,)
I kneel, an altered and an humble man,
Amid thy shadows, and so drink within
My very soul thy grandeur, gloom, and glory!

Vastness! and Age! and Memories of Eld!
Silence! and Desolation! and dim Night!
I feel ye now — I feel ye in your strength —
O spells more sure than e'er Judæan king
Taught in the gardens of Gethsemane!
O charms more potent than the rapt Chaldee
Ever drew down from out the quiet stars!

Here, where a hero fell, a column falls!
Here, where the mimic eagle glared in gold,
A midnight vigil holds the swarthy bat!
Here, where the dames of Rome their gilded hair
Waved to the wind, now wave the reed and thistle!
Here, where on golden throne the monarch lolled,
Glides, spectre-like, unto his marble home,
Lit by the wan light of the hornèd moon,
The swift and silent lizard of the stones!

But stay! these walls — these ivy-clad arcades —
These mouldering plinths — these sad and blackened
        shafts —
These vague entablatures — this crumbling frieze —
These shattered cornices — this wreck — this ruin —
These stones — alas! these gray stones — are they all —
All of the famed, and the colossal left
By the corrosive Hours to Fate and me?

"Not all" — the Echoes answer me — "not all!
"Prophetic sounds and loud, arise forever
"From us, and from all Ruin, unto the wise,
"As melody from Memnon to the Sun.
"We rule the hearts of mightiest men — we rule
"With a despotic sway all giant minds.
"We are not impotent — we pallid stones.
"Not all our power is gone — not all our fame —
"Not all the magic of our high renown —
"Not all the wonder that encircles us —
"Not all the mysteries that in us lie —
"Not all the memories that hang upon
"And cling around about us as a garment,
"Clothing us in a robe of more than glory."

LENORE

AH, broken is the golden bowl! — the spirit flown for
ever!

Let the bell toll! — a saintly soul floats on the Stygian
river: —

And, Guy De Vere, hast *thou* no tear? — weep now or
never more!

See! on yon drear and rigid bier low lies thy love,
Lenore!

Come, let the burial rite be read — the funeral song be
sung! —

An anthem for the queenliest dead that ever died so
young —

A dirge for her the doubly dead in that she died so
young.

"Wretches! ye loved her for her wealth and ye hated her
for her pride;

And, when she fell in feeble health, ye blessed her —
that she died: —

How *shall* the ritual then be read — the requiem how be
sung

By you — by yours, the evil eye — by yours the slan-
derous tongue

That did to death the innocence that died and died so
young?"

Peccavimus: — yet rave not thus! but let a Sabbath
song

Go up to God so solemnly the dead may feel no wrong!

The sweet Lenore hath gone before, with Hope that
    flew beside,
Leaving thee wild for the dear child that should have
    ' been thy bride —
For her, the fair and debonair, that now so lowly lies,
The life upon her yellow hair, but not within her eyes —
The life still there upon her hair, the death upon her
    eyes.

"Avaunt! — avaunt! to friends from fiends the in-
    dignant ghost is riven —
From Hell unto a high estate within the utmost
    Heaven —
From moan and groan to a golden throne beside the
    King of Heaven: —
Let *no* bell toll, then, lest her soul, amid its hallowed
    mirth,
Should catch the note as it doth float up from the
    damnèd Earth!
And I — to-night my heart is light: — no dirge will I
    upraise,
But waft the angel on her flight with a pæan of old
    days!"

HYMN

At morn — at noon — at twilight dim —
Maria! thou hast heard my hymn!
In joy and wo — in good and ill —
Mother of God, be with me still!
When the Hours flew brightly by,
And not a cloud obscured the sky,
My soul, lest it should truant be,
Thy grace did guide to thine and thee;
Now, when storms of Fate o'ercast
Darkly my Present and my Past,
Let my Future radiant shine
With sweet hopes of thee and thine!

ISRAFEL [1]

In Heaven a spirit doth dwell
  "Whose heart-strings are a lute;"
None sing so wildly well
As the angel Israfel,
And the giddy stars, (so legends tell)
Ceasing their hymns, attend the spell
  Of his voice, all mute.

Tottering above
  In her highest noon,
  The enamoured Moon
Blushes with love,
  While, to listen, the red levin
  (With the rapid Pleiads, even,
  Which were seven,)
  Pauses in Heaven.

And they say, (the starry choir
  And the other listening things)
That Israfeli's fire
Is owing to that lyre
  By which he sits and sings —
The trembling living wire
Of those unusual strings.

But the skies that angel trod,
  Where deep thoughts are a duty —
Where Love's a grown-up god —

[1] And the angel Israfel, whose heart-strings are a lute, and who
has the sweetest voice of all God's creatures. — *Koran.*

Where the Houri glances are
Imbued with all the beauty
    Which we worship in a star.

Therefore, thou art not wrong,
    'Israfeli, who despisest
An unimpassioned song;
To thee the laurels belong,
    ¿Best bard, because the wisest!
Merrily live, and long!

The ecstasies above
    With thy burning measures suit —
Thy grief, thy joy, thy hate, thy love,
    With the fervor of thy lute —
    Well may the stars be mute!

Yes, Heaven is thine; but this
    Is a world of sweets and sours;
    Our flowers are merely — flowers,
And the shadow of thy perfect bliss.
    Is the sunshine of ours.

If I could dwell
Where Israfel
    Hath dwelt, and he where I,
He might not sing so wildly well
    A mortal melody,
While a bolder note than this might swell
    From my lyre within the sky.

DREAM–LAND

By a route obscure and lonely,
Haunted by ill angels only,
Where an Eidolon, named NIGHT,
On a black throne reigns upright,
I have reached these lands but newly
From an ultimate dim Thule —
From a wild weird clime that lieth, sublime,
   Out of Space — out of Time.

Bottomless vales and boundless floods,
And chasms, and caves, and Titan woods,
With forms that no man can discover
For the dews that drip all over;
Mountains toppling evermore
Into seas without a shore;
Seas that restlessly aspire,
Surging, unto skies of fire;
Lakes that endlessly outspread
Their lone waters — lone and dead, —
Their still waters — still and chilly
With the snows of the lolling lily.

By the lakes that thus outspread
Their lone waters, lone and dead, —
Their sad waters, sad and chilly
With the snows of the lolling lily, —
By the mountains — near the river
Murmuring lowly, murmuring ever, —

By the grey woods, — by the swamp
Where the toad and the newt encamp, —
By the dismal tarns and pools
    Where dwell the ghouls, —
By each spot the most unholy —
In each nook most melancholy, —
There the traveller meets aghast
Sheeted Memories of the Past —
Shrouded forms that start and sigh
As they pass the wanderer by —
White-robed forms of friends long given,
In agony, to the Earth — and Heaven.

For the heart whose woes are legion
'T is a peaceful, soothing region —
For the spirit that walks in shadow
O! it is an Eldorado!
But the traveller, travelling through it,
May not — dare not openly view it;
Never its mysteries are exposed
To the weak human eye unclosed;
So wills its King, who hath forbid
The uplifting of the fringèd lid;
And thus the sad Soul that here passes
Beholds it but through darkened glasses.
By a route obscure and lonely,
Haunted by ill angels only,
Where an Eidolon, named NIGHT,
On a black throne reigns upright,
I have wandered home but newly
From this ultimate dim Thule.

SONNET — TO ZANTE

Fair isle, that from the fairest of all flowers,
    Thy gentlest of all gentle names dost take!
How many memories of what radiant hours
    At sight of thee and thine at once awake!
How many scenes of what departed bliss!
    How many thoughts of what entombèd hopes!
How many visions of a maiden that is
    No more — no more upon thy verdant slopes!
No more! alas, that magical sad sound
    Transforming all! Thy charms shall please *no more* -
Thy memory *no more!* Accursèd ground
    Henceforth I hold thy flower-enamelled shore,
O hyacinthine isle! O purple Zante!
    "Isola d'oro! Fior di Levante!"

THE CITY IN THE SEA

Lo! Death has reared himself a throne
In a strange city lying alone
Far down within the dim West,
Where the good and the bad and the worst and
       the best
Have gone to their eternal rest.
There shrines and palaces and towers
(Time-eaten towers that tremble not!)
Resemble nothing that is ours.
Around, by lifting winds forgot,
Resignedly beneath the sky
The melancholy waters lie.

No rays from the holy heaven come down
On the long night-time of that town;
But light from out the lurid sea
Streams up the turrets silently —
Gleams up the pinnacles far and free —
Up domes — up spires — up kingly halls —
Up·fanes — up Babylon-like walls —
Up shadowy long-forgotten bowers
Of sculptured ivy and stone flowers —
Up many and many a marvellous shrine
Whose wreathéd friezes intertwine
The viol, the violet, and the vine. '
Resignedly beneath the sky
The melancholy waters lie.
So blend the turrets and shadows there
That all seem pendulous in air,

While from a proud tower in the town
Death looks gigantically down.
There open fanes and gaping graves
Yawn level with the luminous waves;
But not the riches there that lie
In each idol's diamond eye —
Not the gayly-jeweled dead
Tempt the waters from their bed;
For no ripples curl, alas!
Along that wilderness of glass —
No swellings tell that winds may be
Upon some far-off happier sea —
No heavings hint that winds have been
On seas less hideously serene.

But lo, a stir is in the air!
The wave — there is a movement there!
As if the towers had thrust aside,
In slightly sinking, the dull tide —
As if their tops had feebly given
A void within the filmy Heaven.
The waves have now a redder glow —
The hours are breathing faint and low —
And when, amid no earthly moans,
Down, down that town shall settle hence,
Hell, rising from a thousand thrones,
Shall do it reverence.

TO ONE IN PARADISE

THOU wast that all to me, love,
    For which my soul did pine —
A green isle in the sea, love,
    A fountain and a shrine,
All wreathed with fairy fruits and flowers,
    And all the flowers were mine.

Ah, dream too bright to last!
    Ah, starry Hope! that didst arise
But to be overcast!
    A voice from out the Future cries,
"On! on!" — but o'er the Past
    (Dim gulf!) my spirit hovering lies
Mute, motionless, aghast!

For, alas! alas! with me
    , The light of Life is o'er!
No more — no more — no more —
(Such language holds the solemn sea
    To the sands upon the shore)
Shall bloom the thunder-blasted tree,
    Or the stricken eagle soar!

And all my days are trances,
    And all my nightly dreams
Are where thy grey eye glances,
    And where thy footstep gleams —
In what ethereal dances,
    By what eternal streams.

EULALIE — A SONG

I DWELT alone
    In a world of moan,
And my soul was a stagnant tide,
Till the fair and gentle Eulalie became my blushing
        bride —
Till the yellow-haired young Eulalie became my smiling
        bride.

    Ah, less — less bright
    The stars of the night
Than the eyes of the radiant girl!
    And never a flake
    That the vapor can make
With the moon-tints of purple and pearl,
Can vie with the modest Eulalie's most unregarded
        curl —
Can compare with the bright-eyed Eulalie's most hum-
        ble and careless curl.

    Now Doubt — now Pain
    Come never again,
For her soul gives me sigh for sigh,
    And all day long
    Shines, bright and strong,
Astarté within the sky,
While ever to her dear Eulalie upturns her matron eye —
While ever to her young Eulalie upturns her violet eye

TO F——s S. O——d

Thou wouldst be loved? — then let thy heart
  From its present pathway part not!
Being everything which now thou art,
  Be nothing which thou art not.
So with the world thy gentle ways,
  Thy grace, thy more than beauty,
Shall be an endless theme of praise,
  And love — a simple duty.

TO F——

BELOVED! amid the earnest woes
   That crowd around my earthly path —
(Drear path, alas! where grows
Not even one lonely rose) ——
   My soul at least a solace hath
In dreams of thee, and therein knows
An Eden of bland repose.

And thus thy memory is to me
   Like some enchanted far-off isle
In some tumultuous sea —
Some ocean throbbing far and free
   With storms — but where meanwhile
Serenest skies continually
   Just o'er that one bright island smile.

SONNET — SILENCE

THERE are some qualities — some incorporate things,
    That have a double life, which thus is made
A type of that twin entity which springs
    From matter and light, evinced in solid and shade.
There is a two-fold *Silence* — sea and shore —
    Body and soul. One dwells in lonely places,
    Newly with grass o'ergrown; some solemn graces,
Some human memories and tearful lore,
Render him terrorless: his name's "No More."
He is the corporate Silence: dread him not!
    No power hath he of evil in himself;
But should some urgent fate (untimely lot!)
    Bring thee to meet his shadow (nameless elf,
That haunteth the lone regions where hath trod
No foot of man,) commend thyself to God!

THE CONQUEROR WORM

Lo! 't is a gala night
  Within the lonesome latter years!
An angel throng, bewinged, bedight
  In veils, and drowned in tears,
Sit in a theatre, to see
  A play of hopes and fears,
While the orchestra breathes fitfully
  The music of the spheres.

Mimes, in the form of God on high,
  Mutter and mumble low,
And hither and thither fly —
  Mere puppets they, who come and go
At bidding of vast formless things
  That shift the scenery to and fro,
Flapping from out their Condor wings
  Invisible wo!

That motley drama — oh, be sure
  It shall not be forgot!
With its phantom chased for evermore,
  By a crowd that seize it not,
Through a circle that ever returneth in
  To the self-same spot,
And much of Madness, and more of Sin,
  And Horror the soul of the plot.

But see, amid the mimic rout
  A crawling shape intrude!

A blood-red thing that writhes from out
  The scenic solitude!
It writhes! — it writhes! — with mortal pangs
  The mimes become its food,
And seraphs sob at vermin fangs
  In human gore imbued.

Out — out are the lights — out all!
  And, over each quivering form,
The curtain, a funeral pall,
  Comes down with the rush of a storm,
While the angels, all pallid and wan,
  Uprising, unveiling, affirm
That the play is the tragedy, "Man,"
  And its hero the Conqueror Worm.

THE HAUNTED PALACE

In the greenest of our valleys
    By good angels tenanted,
Once a fair and stately palace —
    Radiant palace — reared its head.
In the monarch Thought's dominion —
    It stood there!
Never seraph spread a pinion
    Over fabric half so fair!

Banners yellow, glorious, golden,
    On its roof did float and flow,
(This — all this — was in the olden
    Time long ago,)
And every gentle air that dallied,
    In that sweet day,
Along the ramparts plumed and pallid,
    A wingèd odor went away.

Wanderers in that happy valley,
    Through two luminous windows, saw
Spirits moving musically,
    To a lute's well-tunèd law,
Round about a throne where, sitting,
    Porphyrogene,
In state his glory well befitting,
    The ruler of the realm was seen.

And all with pearl and ruby glowing
    Was the fair palace door,

Through which came flowing, flowing, flowing,
    And sparkling evermore,
A troop of Echoes, whose sweet duty
    Was but to sing,
In voices of surpassing beauty,
    The wit and wisdom of their king.

But evil things, in robes of sorrow,
    Assailed the monarch's high estate.
(Ah, let us mourn! — for never morrow
    Shall dawn upon him, desolate!)
And round about his home the glory
    That blushed and bloomed
Is but a dim-remembered story
    Of the old-time entombed.

And travellers, now, within that valley,
    Through the encrimson'd windows see
Vast forms that move fantastically
    To a discordant melody,
While, like a ghastly rapid river,
    Through the pale door
A hideous throng rush out forever
    And laugh — but smile no more.

SCENES FROM "POLITIAN"

AN UNPUBLISHED DRAMA

I

ROME. — A Hall in a Palace.   Alessandra and Castiglione.

Alessandra. Thou art sad, Castiglione.
  Castiglione. Sad! — not I.
Oh, I 'm the happiest, happiest man in Rome!
A few days more, thou knowest, my Alessandra,
Will make thee mine. Oh, I am very happy!
    Aless. Methinks thou hast a singular way of show-
      ing
Thy happiness! — what ails thee, cousin of mine?
Why didst thou sigh so deeply?
    Cas. Did I sigh?
I was not conscious of it. It is a fashion,
A silly — a most silly fashion I have
When I am *very* happy. Did I sigh? (*sighing.*)
    Aless. Thou didst. Thou art not well. Thou hast
      indulged
Too much of late, and I am vexed to see it.
Late hours and wine, Castiglione, — these
Will ruin thee! thou art already altered —
Thy looks are haggard — nothing so wears away
The constitution as late hours and wine.
    Cas. (*musing.*) Nothing, fair cousin, nothing — not
      even deep sorrow —
Wears it away like evil hours and wine.
I will amend.

SOUTHERN LITERARY MESSENGER BUILDING

Aless. Do it! I would have thee drop
Thy riotous company, too — fellows low born —
Ill suit the like with old Di Broglio's heir
And Alessandra's husband.

 Cas. I will drop them.

 Aless. Thou wilt — thou must. Attend thou also
  more
To thy dress and equipage — they are over plain
For thy lofty rank and fashion — much depends
Upon appearances.

 Cas. I 'll see to it.

 Aless. Then see to it! — pay more attention, sir,
To a becoming carriage — much thou wantest
In dignity.

 Cas. Much, much, oh much I want
In proper dignity.

 Aless. (*haughtily.*) Thou mockest me, sir!

 Cas. (*abstractedly.*) Sweet, gentle Lalage!

 Aless. Heard I aright?
I speak to him — he speaks of Lalage!
Sir Count! (*places her hand on his shoulder*) what art
  thou dreaming? he 's not well!
What ails thee, sir?

 Cas. (*starting.*) Cousin! fair cousin! — madam!
I crave thy pardon — indeed I am not well —
Your hand from off my shoulder, if you please.
This air is most oppressive! — Madam — the Duke!

Enter Di Broglio.

Di Broglio. My son, I 've news for thee! — hey? —
  what 's the matter? (*observing Alessandra.*)
I' the pouts? Kiss her, Castiglione! kiss her,
You dog! and make it up, I say, this minute!

I 've news for you both. Politian is expected
Hourly in Rome — Politian, Earl of Leicester!
We 'll have him at the wedding. 'T is his first visit
To the imperial city.
   Aless. What! Politian
Of Britain, Earl of Leicester?
   Di Brog. The same, my love.
We 'll have him at the wedding. A man quite young
In years, but grey in fame. I have not seen him,
But Rumour speaks of him as of a prodigy
Pre-eminent in arts and arms, and wealth,
And high descent. We 'll have him at the wedding.
   Aless. I have heard much of this Politian.
Gay, volatile and giddy — is he not?
And little given to thinking.
   Di Brog. Far from it, love.
No branch, they say, of all philosophy
So deep abstruse he has not mastered it.
Learned as few are learned.
   Aless. 'T is very strange!
I have known men have seen Politian
And sought his company. They speak of him
As of one who entered madly into life,
Drinking the cup of pleasure to the dregs.
   Cas. Ridiculous! Now *I* have seen Politian
And know him well — nor learned nor mirthful he.
He is a dreamer and a man shut out
From common passions.
   Di Brog. Children, we disagree.
Let us go forth and taste the fragrant air
Of the garden. Did I dream, or did I hear
Politian was a *melancholy* man?   (*exeunt.*)

II

A Lady's apartment, with a window open and looking into a garden. Lalage, in deep mourning, reading at a table on which lie some books and a hand mirror. In the back ground Jacinta (a servant maid) leans carelessly upon a chair.

Lalage. Jacinta! is it thou?

Jacinta. (*pertly.*) Yes, Ma'am, I 'm here.

Lal. I did not know, Jacinta, you were in waiting.
Sit down! — let not my presence trouble you —
Sit down! — for I am humble, most humble.

Jac. (*aside.*) 'T is time.

> (*Jacinta seats herself in a side-long manner upon*
> *the chair, resting her elbows upon the back, and*
> *regarding her mistress with a contemptuous look.*
> *Lalage continues to read.*)

Lal. "It in another climate, so he said,
"Bore a bright golden flower, but not i' this soil!"

> (*pauses — turns over some leaves, and resumes.*)

"No lingering winters there, nor snow, nor shower —
"But Ocean ever to refresh mankind
"Breathes the shrill spirit of the western wind."
Oh, beautiful! — most beautiful! — how like
To what my fevered soul doth dream of Heaven!
O happy land! (*pauses.*) She died! — the maiden died!
O still more happy maiden who couldst die!
Jacinta!

> (*Jacinta returns no answer, and Lalage presently re-*
> *sumes.*)

Again ! — a similar tale
Told of a beauteous dame beyond the sea!
Thus speaketh one Ferdinand in the words of the play—
"She died full young" — one Bossola answers him —

"I think not so — her infelicity
"Seemed to have years too many" — Ah luckless lady!
Jacinta! (*still no answer.*)
       Here 's a far sterner story
But like — oh, very like in its despair —
Of that Egyptian queen, winning so easily
A thousand hearts — losing at length her own.
She died. Thus endeth the history — and her maids
Lean over her and weep — two gentle maids
With gentle names — Eiros and Charmion!
Rainbow and Dove! —— Jacinta!
   Jac. (*pettishly.*) Madam, what *is* it?
   Lal. Wilt thou, my good Jacinta, be so kind
As go down in the library and bring me
The Holy Evangelists.
   Jac. Pshaw! (*exit.*)
   Lal. If there be balm
For the wounded spirit in Gilead it is there!
Dew in the night time of my bitter trouble
Will there be found — "dew sweeter far than that
Which hangs like chains of pearl on Hermon Hill."
    (*re-enter Jacinta, and throws a volume on the table.*)
There, ma'am, 's the book. Indeed she is very trouble-
    some. (*aside.*)
   Lal. (*astonished.*)   What didst thou say, Jacinta?
    Have I done aught
To grieve thee or to vex thee? — I am sorry.
For thou hast served me long and ever been
Trust-worthy and respectful. (*resumes her reading.*)
   Jac. I can't believe
She has any more jewels — no — no — she gave me
    all. (*aside.*)
   Lal. What didst thou say, Jacinta? Now I bethink me

Thou hast not spoken lately of thy wedding.
How fares good Ugo? — and when is it to be?
Can I do aught? — is there no farther aid
Thou needest, Jacinta?
    Jac. Is there no *farther* aid!
That 's meant for me. (*aside*) I'm sure, Madam, you need not
Be always throwing those jewels in my teeth.
    Lal. Jewels! Jacinta, — now indeed, Jacinta,
I thought not of the jewels.
    Jac. Oh! perhaps not!
But then I might have sworn it. After all,
There 's Ugo says the ring is only paste,
For he 's sure the Count Castiglione never
Would have given a real diamond to such as you;
And at the best I 'm certain, Madam, you cannot
Have use for jewels *now*. But I might have sworn it.
                        (*exit.*)
    (*Lalage bursts into tears and leans her head upon
       the table — after a short pause raises it.*)
    Lal. Poor Lalage! — and is it come to this?
Thy servant maid! — but courage! — 't is but a viper
Whom thou hast cherished to sting thee to the soul!
                  (*taking up the mirror.*
Ha! here at least 's a friend — too much a friend
In earlier days — a friend will not deceive thee.
Fair mirror and true! now tell me (for thou canst)
A tale — a pretty tale — and heed thou not
Though it be rife with woe. It answers me.
It speaks of sunken eyes, and wasted cheeks,
And Beauty long deceased — remembers me
Of Joy departed — Hope, the Seraph Hope,
Inurned and entombed! — now, in a tone

Low, sad, and solemn, but most audible,
Whispers of early grave untimely yawning
For ruined maid. Fair mirror and true!—thou liest not!
Thou hast no end to gain — no heart to break —
Castiglione lied who said he loved ——
Thou true — he false! — false! — false!
> (*while she speaks, a monk enters her apartment,
> and approaches unobserved.*)

Monk. Refuge thou hast,
Sweet daughter! in Heaven. Think of eternal things!
Give up thy soul to penitence, and pray!
> *Lal.* (*arising hurriedly.*) I *cannot* pray! — My soul
> is at war with God!

The frightful sounds of merriment below
Disturb my senses — go! I cannot pray —
The sweet airs from the garden worry me!
Thy presence grieves me — go! — thy priestly raiment
Fills me with dread — thy ebony crucifix
With horror and awe!

Monk. Think of thy precious soul!

Lal. Think of my early days! — think of my father
And mother in Heaven! think of our quiet home,
And the rivulet that ran before the door!
Think of my little sisters! — think of them!
And think of me! — think of my trusting love
And   confidence — his   vows — my   ruin — think —
> think

Of my unspeakable misery! —— begone!
Yet stay! yet stay! — what was it thou saidst of prayer
And penitence? Didst thou not speak of faith
And vows before the throne?

Monk. I did.

Lal. 'T is well.

There *is* a vow were fitting should be made —
A sacred vow, imperative, and urgent,
A solemn vow!
   Monk. Daughter, this zeal is well!
   Lal. Father, this zeal is anything but well!
Hast thou a crucifix fit for this thing?
A crucifix whereon to register
This sacred vow?   (*he hands her his own.*)
Not that — Oh! no! — no! — no! (*shuddering.*)
Not that! Not that! — I tell thee, holy man.
Thy raiments and thy ebony cross affright me!
Stand back! I have a crucifix myself, —
I have a crucifix! Methinks 't were fitting
The deed — the vow — the symbol of the deed —
And the deed's register should tally, father!
   (*draws a cross-handled dagger and raises it on high.*)
Behold the cross wherewith a vow like mine
Is written in Heaven!
   Monk. Thy words are madness, daughter,
And speak a purpose unholy — thy lips are livid —
Thine eyes are wild — tempt not the wrath divine!
Pause ere too late ! — oh be not — be not rash!
Swear not the oath — oh swear it not!
   Lal. 'T is sworn!

III

An apartment in a palace. Politian and Baldazzar.

   Baldazzar. ——— Arouse thee now, Politian!
Thou must not — nay indéed, indeed, thou shalt not
Give way unto these humours. Be thyself!
Shake off the idle fancies that beset thee,
And live, for now thou diest!

Politian. Not so, Baldazzar!
Surely I live.
 Bal. Politian, it doth grieve me
To see thee thus.
 Pol. Baldazzar, it doth grieve me
To give thee cause for grief, my honoured friend.
Command me, sir! what wouldst thou have me do?
At thy behest I will shake off that nature
Which from my forefathers I did inherit,
Which with my mother's milk I did imbibe,
And be no more Politian, but some other.
Command me, sir!
 Bal. To the field then — to the field —
To the senate or the field.
 Pol. Alas! alas!
There is an imp would follow me even there!
There is an imp *hath* followed me even there!
There is —— what voice was that?
 Bal. I heard it not.
I heard not any voice except thine own,
And the echo of thine own.
 Pol. Then I but dreamed.
 Bal. Give not thy soul to dreams: the camp—the court
Befit thee — Fame awaits thee — Glory calls —
And her the trumpet-tongued thou wilt not hear
In hearkening to imaginary sounds
And phantom voices.
 Pol. It *is* a phantom voice!
Didst thou not hear it *then?*
 Bal. I heard it not.
 Pol. Thou heardst it not! —— Baldazzar, speak no
  more
To me, Politian, of thy camps and courts.

Oh! I am sick, sick, sick, even unto death,
Of the hollow and high-sounding vanities
Of the populous Earth! Bear with me yet awhile!
We have been boys together — school-fellows —
And now are friends — yet shall not be so long —
For in the eternal city thou shalt do me
A kind and gentle office, and a Power —
A Power august, benignant and supreme —
Shall then absolve thee of all farther duties
Unto thy friend.
    Bal. Thou speakest a fearful riddle
I *will* not understand.
    Pol. Yet now as Fate
Approaches, and the Hours are breathing low,
The sands of Time are changed to golden grains,
And dazzle me, Baldazzar. Alas! alas!
I *cannot* die, having within my heart
So keen a relish for the beautiful
As hath been kindled within it. Methinks the air
Is balmier now than it was wont to be —
Rich melodies are floating in the winds —
A rarer loveliness bedecks the earth —
And with a holier lustre the quiet moon
Sitteth in Heaven. — Hist! hist! thou canst not say
Thou hearest not *now*, Baldazzar?
    Bal. Indeed I hear not.
    Pol. Not hear it! — listen now — listen! — the faint·
      est sound
And yet the sweetest that ear ever heard!
A lady's voice! — and sorrow in the tone!
Baldazzar, it oppresses me like a spell!
Again! — again! — how solemnly it falls
Into my heart of hearts! that eloquent voice

Surely I never heard — yet it were well
Had I *but* heard it with its thrilling tones
In earlier days!

   Bal. I myself hear it now.
Be still! — the voice, if I mistake not greatly,
Proceeds from yonder lattice — which you may see
Very plainly through the window — it belongs,
Does it not? unto this palace of the Duke.
The singer is undoubtedly beneath
The roof of his Excellency — and perhaps
Is even that Alessandra of whom he spoke
As the betrothed of Castiglione,
His son and heir.

   Pol. Be still! — it comes again!

   Voice   "And is thy heart so strong
(*very faintly.*) As for to leave me thus
              Who hath loved thee so long
              In wealth and wo among?
              And is thy heart so strong
              As for to leave me thus?
                    Say nay — say nay!"

   Bal. The song is English, and I oft have heard it
In merry England — never so plaintively —
Hist! hist! it comes again!

   Voice   "Is it so strong
(*more loudly.*) As for to leave me thus
              Who hath loved thee so long
              In wealth and wo among?
              And is thy heart so strong
              As for to leave me thus?
                    Say nay — say nay!"

   Bal. 'T is hushed and all is still!
   Pol. All *is not* still.

Bal. Let us go down.

Pol. Go down, Baldazzar, go!

Bal. The hour is growing late — the Duke awaits us, —
Thy presence is expected in the hall
Below. What ails thee, Earl Politian?

    Voice   "Who hath loved thee so long,
(*distinctly*.)   In wealth and wo among,
           And is thy heart so strong?
               Say nay — say nay!"

Bal. Let us descend! — 't is time. Politian, give
These fancies to the wind. Remember, pray,
Your bearing lately savoured much of rudeness
Unto the Duke. Arouse thee! and remember!

Pol. Remember? I do. Lead on! I *do* remember.
                           (*going*.)
Let us descend. Believe me I would give,
Freely would give the broad lands of my earldom
To look upon the face hidden by yon lattice —
"To gaze upon that veiled face, and hear
Once more that silent tongue."

Bal. Let me beg you, sir,
Descend with me — the Duke may be offended.
Let us go down, I pray you.

    (*Voice loudly*.) *Say nay! — say nay!*

Pol. (*aside*.) 'T is strange! — 't is very strange —
    methought the voice
Chimed in with my desires and bade me stay!
              (*approaching the window*.)
Sweet voice! I heed thee, and will surely stay.
Now be this Fancy, by Heaven, or be it Fate,
Still will I not descend. Baldazzar, make
Apology unto the Duke for me;
I go not down to-night.

Bal. Your lordship's pleasure
Shall be attended to. Good night, Politian.
Pol. Good night, my friend, good night.

IV

The gardens of a palace — Moonlight. Lalage and Politian.

Lalage. And dost thou speak of love
To *me*, Politian? — dost thou speak of love
To Lalage? — ah wo — ah wo is me!
This mockery is most cruel — most cruel indeed!
   Politian. Weep not! oh, sob not thus! — thy bitter
      tears
Will madden me. Oh mourn not, Lalage —
Be comforted! I know — I know it all,
And *still* I speak of love. Look at me, brightest,
And beautiful Lalage! — turn here thine eyes!
Thou askest me if I could speak of love,
Knowing what I know, and seeing what I have seen.
Thou askest me that — and thus I answer thee —
Thus on my bended knee I answer thee. (*kneeling.*)
Sweet Lalage, *I love thee — love thee — love thee;*
Thro' good and ill — thro' weal and wo I *love thee.*
Not mother, with her first born on her knee,
Thrills with intenser love than I for thee.
Not on God's altar, in any time or clime,
Burned there a holier fire than burneth now
Within my spirit for *thee.* And do I love? (*arising.*)
Even for thy woes I love thee — even for thy woes —
Thy beauty and thy woes.
   Lal. Alas, proud Earl,
Thou dost forget thyself, remembering me!

How, in thy father's halls, among the maidens
Pure and reproachless of thy princely line,
Could the dishonoured Lalage abide?
Thy wife, and with a tainted memory —
My seared and blighted name, how would it tally
With the ancestral honours of thy house,
And with thy glory?

    Pol. Speak not to me of glory!
I hate — I loathe the name; I do abhor
The unsatisfactory and ideal thing.
Art thou not Lalage and I Politian?
Do I not love — art thou not beautiful —   '
What need we more? Ha! glory! — now speak not of it!
By all I hold most sacred and most solemn —
By all my wishes now — my fears hereafter —
By all I scorn on earth and hope in heaven —
There is no deed I would more glory in,
Than in thy cause to scoff at this same glory
And trample it under foot. What matters it —
What matters it, my fairest, and my best,
That we go down unhonoured and forgotten
Into the dust — so we descend together.
Descend together — and then — and then perchance —

    Lal. Why dost thou pause, Politian?

    Pol. And then perchance
Arise together, Lalage, and roam
The starry and quiet dwellings of the blest,
And still ——

    Lal. Why dost thou pause, Politian?

    Pol. And still *together — together.*

    Lal. Now Earl of Leicester!
Thou *lovest* me, and in my heart of hearts
I feel thou lovest me truly.

Pol. Oh, Lalage! (*throwing himself upon his knee.*)
And lovest thou *me?*

Lal. Hist! hush! within the gloom
Of yonder trees methought a figure past —
A spectral figure, solemn, and slow, and noiseless —
Like the grim shadow Conscience, solemn and noiseless.
                    (*walks across and returns.*)
I was mistaken — 't was but a giant bough
Stirred by the autumn wind. Politian!

Pol. My Lalage — my love! why art thou moved?
Why dost thou turn so pale? Not Conscience' self,
Far less a shadow which thou likenest to it,
Should shake the firm spirit thus. But the night wind
Is chilly — and these melancholy boughs
Throw over all things a gloom.

Lal. Politian!
Thou speakest to me of love. Knowest thou the land
With which all tongues are busy — a land new found —
Miraculously found by one of Genoa —
A thousand leagues within the golden west?
A fairy land of flowers, and fruit, and sunshine,
And crystal lakes, and over-arching forests,
And mountains, around whose towering summits the
          winds
Of Heaven untrammelled flow — which air to breathe
Is Happiness now, and will be Freedom hereafter
In days that are to come?

Pol. O, wilt thou — wilt thou
Fly to that Paradise — my Lalage, wilt thou
Fly thither with me? There Care shall be forgotten,
And Sorrow shall be no more, and Eros be all.
And life shall then be mine, for I will live
For thee, and in thine eyes — and thou shalt be

No more a mourner — but the radiant Joys
Shall wait upon thee, and the angel Hope
Attend thee ever ; and I will kneel to thee
And worship thee, and call thee my beloved,
My own, my beautiful, my love, my wife,
My all; — oh, wilt thou — wilt thou, Lalage,
Fly thither with me?

    Lal. A deed is to be done —
Castiglione lives!

    Pol. And he shall die! (*exit.*)

    Lal. (*after a pause.*) And — he — shall — die!
      ——— alas!
Castiglione die? Who spoke the words?
Where am I? — what was it he said? — Politian!
Thou *art* not gone — thou art not *gone*, Politian!
I *feel* thou art not gone — yet dare not look,
Lest I behold thee not; thou *couldst* not go
With those words upon thy lips — O, speak to me!
And let me hear thy voice — one word — one word,
To say thou art not gone, — one little sentence,
To say how thou dost scorn — how thou dost hate
My womanly weakness. Ha! ha! thou *art* not gone —
O speak to me! I *knew* thou wouldst not go!
I knew thou wouldst not, couldst not, *durst* not go.
Villain, thou *art* not gone — thou mockest me!
And thus I clutch thee — thus! ——— He is gone, he is
    gone —
Gone — gone. Where am I? —— 't is well — 't is very
    well!
So that the blade be keen — the blow be sure,
'T is well, 't is *very* well — alas! alas! (*exit.*)

V

The suburbs. Politian alone.

Politian. This weakness grows upon me. I am faint,
And much I fear me ill — it will not do
To die ere I have lived! Stay — stay thy hand,
O Azrael, yet awhile! — Prince of the Powers
Of Darkness and the Tomb, O pity me!
O pity me! let me not perish now,
In the budding of my Paradisal Hope!
Give me to live yet — yet a little while:
'T is I who pray for life — I who so late
Demanded but to die! — what sayeth the Count?

Enter Baldazzar.

Baldazzar. That knowing no cause of quarrel or of
   feud
Between the Earl Politian and himself,
He doth decline your cartel.
   Pol. What didst thou say?
What answer was it you brought me, good Baldazzar?
With what excessive fragrance the zephyr comes
Laden from yonder bowers! — a fairer day,
Or one more worthy Italy, methinks
No mortal eyes have seen! — *what* said the Count?
   Bal. That he, Castiglione, not being aware
Of any feud existing, or any cause
Of quarrel between your lordship and himself
Cannot accept the challenge.
   Pol. It is most true —
All this is very true. When saw you, sir,
When saw you now, Baldazzar, in the frigid
Ungenial Britain which we left so lately,

A heaven so calm as this — so utterly free
From the evil taint of clouds? — and he did *say?*

   Bal. No more, my lord, than I have told you, sir:
The Count Castiglione will not fight,
Having no cause for quarrel.

   Pol. Now this is true —
All very true. Thou art my friend, Baldazzar,
And I have not forgotten it — thou 'lt do me
A piece of service; wilt thou go back and say
Unto this man, that I, the Earl of Leicester,
Hold him a villain? — thus much, I prythee, say
Unto the Count — it is exceeding just
He should have cause for quarrel.

   Bal. My lord! — my friend! ———

   Pol. (*aside.*) 'T is he — he comes himself! (*aloud.*)
    thou reasonest well.
I know what thou wouldst say — not send the mes-
    sage —
Well! — I will think of it — I will not send it.
Now prythee, leave me — hither doth come a person
With whom affairs of a most private nature
I would adjust.

   Bal. I go — to-morrow we meet,
Do we not? — at the Vatican.

   Pol. At the Vatican.   (*exit Bal.*)

Enter Castiglione.

   Cas. The Earl of Leicester here!

   Pol. I *am* the Earl of Leicester, and thou seest,
Dost thou not? that I am here.

   Cas. My lord, some strange,
Some singular mistake — misunderstanding —
Hath without doubt arisen: thou hast been urged

Thereby, in heat of anger, to address
Some words·most unaccountable, in writing,
To me, Castiglione; the bearer being
Baldazzar, Duke of Surrey. I am aware
Of nothing which might warrant thee in this thing,
Having given thee no offence. Ha! — am I right?
'T was a mistake? — undoubtedly — we all
Do err at times.

   Pol. Draw, villain, and prate no more!
   Cas. Ha! — draw? — and villain? have at thee then
      at once,
Proud Earl!   (*draws.*)
   Pol. (*drawing.*) Thus to the expiatory tomb,
Untimely sepulchre, I do devote thee
In the name of Lalage!
   Cas. (*letting fall his sword and recoiling to the extremity
      of the stage.*)
Of Lalage!
Hold off — thy sacred hand! — avaunt I say!
Avaunt — I will not fight thee — indeed I dare not.
   Pol. Thou wilt not fight with me didst say, Sir Count?
Shall I be baffled thus? — now this is well;
Didst say thou *darest* not? Ha!
   Cas. I dare not — dare not —
Hold off thy hand — with that beloved name
So fresh upon thy lips I will not fight thee —
I cannot — dare not.
   Pol. Now by my halidom
I do believe thee! — coward, I do believe thee!
   Cas. Ha! — coward! — this may not be!
      (*clutches his sword and staggers towards Politian,
       but his purpose is changed before reaching him,
       and he falls upon his knee at the feet of the Earl.*)

Alas! my lord,
It is — it is — most true. In such a cause
I am the veriest coward. O pity me!
  Pol. (*greatly softened.*) Alas! — I do — indeed I pity
    thee.
  Cas. And Lalage ————
  Pol. Scoundrel! — arise and die!
  Cas. It needeth not be — thus — thus — O let me
    die
Thus on my bended knee. It were most fitting
That in this deep humiliation I perish.
For in the fight I will not raise a hand
Against thee, Earl of Leicester. Strike thou home —
                    (*baring his bosom.*)
Here is no let or hindrance to thy weapon —
Strike home. I *will not* fight thee.
  Pol. Now 's Death and Hell!
Am I not — am I not sorely — grievously tempted
To take thee at thy word ? But mark me, sir!
Think not to fly me thus. Do thou prepare
For public insult in the streets — before
The eyes of the citizens. I 'll follow thee —
Like an avenging spirit I 'll follow thee
Even unto death. Before those whom thou lovest —
Before all Rome I 'll taunt thee, villain, — I 'll taunt
      thee,
Dost hear? with *cowardice* — thou *wilt not* fight me?
Thou liest! thou *shalt!*   (*exit.*)
  Cas. Now this indeed is just!
Most righteous, and most just, avenging Heaven!

LATER POEMS

LATER POEMS

THE BELLS

I

Hear the sledges with the bells —
Silver bells!
What a world of merriment their melody foretells!
How they tinkle, tinkle, tinkle,
In the icy air of night!
While the stars that oversprinkle
All the Heavens, seem to twinkle
With a crystalline delight;
Keeping time, time, time,
In a sort of Runic rhyme,
To the tintinnabulation that so musically wells
From the bells, bells, bells, bells,
Bells, bells, bells —
From the jingling and the tinkling of the bells.

II

Hear the mellow wedding bells —
Golden bells!
What a world of happiness their harmony foretells.
Through the balmy air of night
How they ring out their delight! —
From the molten-golden notes,
And all in tune,
What a liquid ditty floats
To the turtle-dove that listens, while she gloats
On the moon!

Oh, from out the sounding cells,
What a gush of euphony voluminously wells!
How it swells!
How it dwells
On the future! — how it tells
Of the rapture that impels
To the swinging and the ringing
Of the bells, bells, bells —
Of the bells, bells, bells, bells,
Bells, bells, bells —
To the rhyming and the chiming of the bells!

III

Hear the loud alarum bells —
Brazen bells!
What a tale of terror, now, their turbulency tells!
In the startled ear of Night
How they scream out their affright!
Too much horrified to speak,
They can only shriek, shriek,
Out of tune,
In a clamorous appealing to the mercy of the fire,
In a mad expostulation with the deaf and frantic
fire
Leaping higher, higher, higher,
With a desperate desire,
And a resolute endeavour
Now — now to sit, or never,
By the side of the pale-faced moon.
Oh, the bells, bells, bells!
What a tale their terror tells
Of despair!

How they clang, and clash, and roar!
What a horror they outpour
On the bosom of the palpitating air!
        Yet the ear, it fully knows,
                By the twanging,
                And the clanging,
        How the danger ebbs and flows;
Yes, the ear distinctly tells,
                In the jangling,
                And the wrangling,
        How the danger sinks and swells,
By the sinking or the swelling in the anger of the
        bells —
                Of the bells —
        Of the bells, bells, bells, bells,
                Bells, bells, bells —
In the clamor and the clangor of the bells!

IV

        Hear the tolling of the bells —
                Iron bells!
What a world of solemn thought their monody
        compels!
        In the silence of the night,
        How we shiver with affright
At the melancholy menace of their tone!
        For every sound that floats
        From the rust within their throats
                Is a groan.
        And the people — ah, the people —
        They that dwell up in the steeple,
                All alone,

And who, tolling, tolling, tolling,
In that muffled monotone,
Feel a glory in so rolling
On the human heart a stone —
They are neither man nor woman —
They are neither brute nor human —
They are Ghouls: —
And their king it is who tolls: —
And he rolls, rolls, rolls,
Rolls
A Pæan from the bells!
And his merry bosom swells
With the Pæan of the bells!
And he dances and he yells;
Keeping time, time, time,
In a sort of Runic rhyme,
To the Pæan of the bells —
Of the bells: —
Keeping time, time, time,
In a sort of Runic rhyme,
To the throbbing of the bells —
Of the bells, bells, bells —
To the sobbing of the bells: —
Keeping time, time, time,
As he knells, knells, knells,
In a happy Runic rhyme,
To the rolling of the bells —
Of the bells, bells, bells: —
To the tolling of the bells —
Of the bells, bells, bells, bells,
Bells, bells, bells —
To the moaning and the groaning of the bells.

TO M. L. S——

Of all who hail thy presence as the morning —
Of all to whom thine absence is the night —
The blotting utterly from out high heaven
The sacred sun — of all who, weeping, bless thee
Hourly for hope — for life — ah, above all,
For the resurrection of deep-buried faith
In truth, in virtue, in humanity —
Of all who, on despair's unhallowed bed
Lying down to die, have suddenly arisen
At thy soft-murmured words, "Let there be light!"
At the soft-murmured words that were fulfilled
In the seraphic glancing of thine eyes —
Of all who owe thee most, whose gratitude
Nearest resembles worship, — oh, remember
The truest, the most fervently devoted,
And think that these weak lines are written by him -
By him, who, as he pens them, thrills to think
His spirit is communing with an angel's.

TO ———— ———— ————

Not long ago, the writer of these lines,
In the mad pride of intellectuality,
Maintained "the power of words" — denied that ever
A thought arose within the human brain
Beyond the utterance of the human tongue;
And now, as if in mockery of that boast,
Two words — two foreign soft dissyllables —
Italian tones made only to be murmured
By angels dreaming in the moonlit "dew
That hangs like chains of pearl on Hermon hill "—
Have stirred from out the abysses of his heart,
Unthought-like thoughts that are the souls of thought,
Richer, far wilder, far diviner visions
Than even the seraph harper, Israfel,
Who has "the sweetest voice of all God's creatures,"
Could hope to utter. And I! my spells are broken.
The pen falls powerless from my shivering hand.
With thy dear name as text, though bidden by thee,
I cannot write — I cannot speak or think,
Alas, I cannot feel; for 't is not feeling,
This standing motionless upon the golden
Threshold of the wide-open gate of dreams,
Gazing, entranced, adown the gorgeous vista,
And thrilling as I see upon the right,
Upon the left, and all the way along
Amid empurpled vapors, far away
To where the prospect terminates — *thee only.*

SONNET [1]

"SELDOM we find," says Solomon Don Dunce,
　　"Half an idea in the profoundest sonnet.
Through all the flimsy things we see at once
　　As easily as through a Naples bonnet —
　　Trash of all trash! — how *can* a lady don it?
Yet heavier far than your Petrarchan stuff —
Owl-downy nonsense that the faintest puff
　　Twirls into trunk-paper the while you con it."
And, veritably, Sol is right enough.
The general Petrarchanities are arrant
Bubbles — ephemeral and *so* transparent —
　　But this is, now, — you may depend upon it —
Stable, opaque, immortal — all by dint
Of the dear names that lie concealed within 't.

[1] The title in all other editions of Poe's poems is, "An Enigma."

TO ——— ——— ———[1]

I saw thee once — once only — years ago:
I must not say *how* many — but *not* many.
It was a July midnight; and from out
A full-orbed moon, that, like thine own soul, soaring,
Sought a precipitant pathway up through heaven,
There fell a silvery-silken veil of light,
With quietude, and sultriness, and slumber,
Upon the upturn'd faces of a thousand
Roses that grew in an enchanted garden,
Where no wind dared to stir, unless on tip-toe —
Fell on the upturn'd faces of these roses
That gave out, in return for the love-light,
Their odorous souls in an ecstatic death —
Fell on the upturn'd faces of these roses
That smiled and died in this parterre, enchanted
By thee and by the poetry of thy presence.

Clad all in white, upon a violet bank
I saw thee half reclining; while the moon
Fell on the upturn'd faces of the roses,
And on thine own, upturn'd — alas! in sorrow!

Was it not Fate that, on this July midnight —
Was it not Fate (whose name is also Sorrow)
That bade me pause before that garden-gate
To breathe the incense of those slumbering roses?
No footstep stirred: the hated world all slept,

[1] The title in all other editions of Poe's poems is, "To
Helen."

Save only thee and me. I paused — I looked —
And in an instant all things disappeared.
(Ah, bear in mind this garden was enchanted!)
The pearly lustre of the moon went out:
The mossy banks and the meandering paths,
The happy flowers and the repining trees,
Were seen no more: the very roses' odors
Died in the arms of the adoring airs.
All — all expired save thee — save less than thou:
Save only the divine light in thine eyes —
Save but the soul in thine uplifted eyes.
I saw but them — they were the world to me.
I saw but them — saw only them for hours —
Saw only them until the moon went down.
What wild heart-histories seemed to lie enwritten
Upon those crystalline, celestial spheres!
How dark a wo! yet how sublime a hope!
How silently serene a sea of pride!
How daring an ambition! yet how deep —
How fathomless a capacity for love!

But now, at length, dear Dian sank from sight,
Into a western couch of thunder-cloud,
And thou, a ghost, amid the entombing trees
Didst glide away. *Only thine eyes remained.*
They *would* not go — they never yet have gone.
Lighting my lonely pathway home that night,
They have not left me (as my hopes have) since.
They follow me — they lead me through the years
They are my ministers — yet I their slave.
Their office is to illumine and enkindle —
My duty *to be saved* by their bright light
And purified in their electric fire —

And sanctified in their elysian fire.
They fill my soul with Beauty (which is Hope)
And are far up in Heaven, the stars I kneel to
In the sad, silent watches of my night;
While even in the meridian glare of day
I see them still — two sweetly scintillant
Venuses, unextinguished by the sun!

A VALENTINE

To —— —— ——

FOR her these lines are penned, whose luminous eyes,
   Brightly expressive as the twins of Lœda,
Shall find her own sweet name that, nestling, lies
   Upon this page, enwrapped from every reader.
Search narrowly this rhyme, which holds a treasure
   Divine — a talisman — an amulet
That must be worn at heart. Search well the measure;
   The words — the letters themselves. Do not forget
The trivialest point, or you may lose your labor.
   And yet there is in this no Gordian knot
Which one might not undo without a sabre,
   If one could merely understand the plot.
Enwritten upon this page whereon are peering
   Such eager eyes, there lies, I say, *perdu,*
A well-known name, oft uttered in the hearing
   Of poets, by poets; as the name is a poet's, too.
Its letters, although naturally lying —
   Like the knight Pinto (Mendez Ferdinando) —
Still form a synonym for truth. Cease trying!
   You will not read the riddle though you do the best
      you *can* do.

FOR ANNIE

THANK Heaven! the crisis —
    The danger is past,
And the lingering illness
    Is over at last —
And the fever called "Living"
    Is conquered at last.

Sadly, I know
    I am shorn of my strength,
And no muscle I move
    As I lie at full length —
But no matter! — I feel
    I am better at length.

And I rest so composedly
    Now, in my bed,
That any beholder
    Might fancy me dead —
Might start at beholding me,
    Thinking me dead.

The moaning and groaning,
    The sighing and sobbing,
Are quieted now,
    With that horrible throbbing
At heart: — Ah that horrible,
    Horrible throbbing!

The sickness — the nausea —
    The pitiless pain —

Have ceased with the fever
   , That maddened my brain —
With the fever called "Living"
   That burned in my brain.

And oh! of all tortures
   That torture the worst
Has abated — the terrible
   Torture of thirst
For the napthaline river
   Of Passion accurst: —
I have drank of a water
   That quenches all thirst: —

Of a water that flows,
   With a lullaby sound,
From a spring but a very few
   Feet under ground —
From a cavern not very far
   Down under ground.

But ah! let it never
   Be foolishly said
That my room it is gloomy
   And narrow my bed;
For man never slept
   In a different bed —
And, to *sleep*, you must slumber
   In just such a bed.

My tantalized spirit
   Here blandly reposes,
Forgetting, or never
   Regretting, its roses —

Its old agitations
    Of myrtles and roses:

For now, while so quietly
    Lying, it fancies
A holier odor
    About it, of pansies —
A rosemary odor,
    Commingled with pansies —
With rue and the beautiful
    Puritan pansies.

And so it lies happily,
    Bathing in many
A dream of the truth
    And the beauty of Annie —
Drowned in a bath
    Of the tresses of Annie.

She tenderly kissed me,
    She fondly caressed,
And then I fell gently
    To sleep on her breast —
Deeply to sleep
    From the heaven of her breast.

When the light was extinguished,
    She covered me warm,
And she prayed to the angels
    To keep me from harm —
To the queen of the angels
    To shield me from harm.

And I lie so composedly,
    Now, in my bed,
(Knowing her love)
    That you fancy me dead —
And I rest so contentedly,
    Now, in my bed,
(With her love at my breast)
    That you fancy me dead —
That you shudder to look at me,
    Thinking me dead: —

But my heart it is brighter
    Than all of the many
Stars in the sky,
    For it sparkles with Annie —
It glows with the light
    Of the love of my Annie —
With the thought of the light
    Of the eyes of my Annie.

SONNET — TO MY MOTHER

BECAUSE the angels in the Heavens above,
  Devoutly singing unto one another,
Can find amid their burning terms of love,
  None so devotional as that of "mother,"
Therefore by that sweet name I long have called you;
  You who are more than mother unto me,
Filling my heart of hearts, where God installed you,
  In setting my Virginia's spirit free.
My mother — my own mother, who died early,
  Was but the mother of myself; but you
Are mother to the dead I loved so dearly,
  Are thus more precious than the one I knew,
By that infinity with which my wife
  Was dearer to my soul than its soul life.

POE'S DESK

Used by him at office of the Southern Literary Messenger

ELDORADO

GAILY bedight,
   A gallant knight,
In sunshine and in shadow,
   Had journeyed long,
   Singing a song,
In search of Eldorado.

   But he grew old —
   This knight so bold —
And o'er his heart a shadow
   Fell, as he found
   No spot of ground
That looked like Eldorado.

   And, as his strength
   Failed him at length,
He met a pilgrim shadow —
   "Shadow," said he,
   " Where can it be —
This land of Eldorado?"

   "Over the Mountains
   Of the Moon,
Down the Valley of the Shadow,
   Ride, boldly ride,"
   The shade replied, —
"If you seek for Eldorado!"

ANNABEL LEE

It was many and many a year ago,
    In a kingdom by the sea,
That a maiden there lived whom you may know
    By the name of Annabel Lee; —
And this maiden she lived with no other thought
    Than to love and be loved by me.

She was a child and *I* was a child,
    In this kingdom by the sea,
But we loved with a love that was more than love
    I and my Annabel Lee —
With a love that the wingèd seraphs of Heaven
    Coveted her and me.

And this was the reason that, long ago,
    In this kingdom by the sea,
A wind blew out of a cloud, by night
    Chilling my Annabel Lee;
So that her high-born kinsmen came
    And bore her away from me,
To shut her up in a sepulchre
    In this kingdom by the sea.

The angels, not half so happy in Heaven,
    Went envying her and me: —
Yes! that was the reason (as all men know,
    In this kingdom by the sea)
That the wind came out of the cloud, chilling
    And killing my Annabel Lee.

But our love it was stronger by far than the love
 Of those who were older than we —
 Of many far wiser than we —
And neither the angels in Heaven above,
 Nor the demons down under the sea,
Can ever dissever my soul from the soul
 Of the beautiful Annabel Lee: —

For the moon never beams without bringing me dreams
 Of the beautiful Annabel Lee;
And the stars never rise but I see the bright eyes
 Of the beautiful Annabel Lee;
And so, all the night-tide, I lie down by the side
Of my darling, my darling, *my life* and my bride
 In her sepulchre there by the sea —
 In her tomb by the sounding sea.

ULALUME — A BALLAD

THE skies they were ashen and sober;
    The leaves they were crispèd and sere —
    The leaves they were withering and sere:
It was night, in the lonesome October
    Of my most immemorial year:
It was hard by the dim lake of Auber,
    In the misty mid region of Weir —
It was down by the dank tarn of Auber,
    In the ghoul-haunted woodland of Weir.

Here once, through an alley Titanic,
    Of cypress, I roamed with my Soul —
    Of cypress, with Psyche, my Soul.
These were days when my heart was volcanic
    As the scoriac rivers that roll —
    As the lavas that restlessly roll
Their sulphurous currents down Yaanek
    In the ultimate climes of the Pole —
That groan as they roll down Mount Yaanck
    In the realms of the Boreal Pole.

Our talk had been serious and sober,
    But our thoughts they were palsied and sere
    Our memories were treacherous and sere;
For we knew not the month was October,
    And we marked not the night of the year —
    (Ah, night of all nights in the year!)
We noted not the dim lake of Auber,
    (Though once we had journeyed down here)

We remembered not the dank tarn of Auber,
    Nor the ghoul-haunted woodland of Weir.

And now, as the night was senescent
    And star-dials pointed to morn —
    As the star-dials hinted of morn —
At the end of our path a liquescent
    And nebulous lustre was born,
Out of which a miraculous crescent
    Arose with a duplicate horn —
Astarte's bediamonded crescent
    Distinct with its duplicate horn.

And I said — "She is warmer than Dian;
    She rolls through an ether of sighs —
    She revels in a region of sighs —
She has seen that the tears are not dry on
    These cheeks, where the worm never dies,
And has come past the stars of the Lion
    To point us the path to the skies —
    To the Lethean peace of the skies —
Come up, in despite of the Lion,
    To shine on us with her bright eyes —
Come up through the lair of the Lion,
    With love in her luminous eyes."

But Psyche, uplifting her finger,
    Said — "Sadly this star I mistrust —
    Her pallor I strangely mistrust —
Ah, hasten! — Ah, let us not linger!
    Ah, fly! — let us fly! — for we must."
In terror she spoke, letting sink her
    Wings till they trailed in the dust —

In agony sobbed; letting sink her
 Plumes till they trailed in the dust —
 Till they sorrowfully trailed in the dust.

I replied — "This is nothing but dreaming:
 Let us on by this tremulous light!
 Let us bathe in this crystalline light!
Its Sybillic splendor is beaming
 With Hope and in Beauty to-night: —
 See! it flickers up the sky through the night!
Ah, we safely may trust to its gleaming,
 And be sure it will lead us aright —
We surely may trust to a gleaming,
 That cannot but guide us aright,
 Since it flickers up to Heaven through the night."

Thus I pacified Psyche and kissed her,
 And tempted her out of her gloom —
 And conquered her scruples and gloom;
And we passed to the end of a vista,
 But were stopped by the door of a tomb —
 By the door of a legended tomb;
And I said — " What is written, sweet sister,
 On the door of this legended tomb?"
 She replied — "Ulalume — Ulalume! —
 'T is the vault of thy lost Ulalume!"

Then my heart it grew ashen and sober
As the leaves that were crispèd and sere —
 As the leaves that were withering and sere;
And I cried — "It was surely October
 On *this* very night of last year
 That I journeyed — I journeyed down here! —

That I brought a dread burden down here —
On this night of all nights in the year,
Ah! what demon hath tempted me here?
Well I know, now, this dim lake of Auber —
This misty mid region of Weir —
Well I know, now, this dank tarn of Auber —
This ghoul-haunted woodland of Weir."

Said *we*, then — the two, then — "Ah, can it
Have been that the woodlandish ghouls—
The pitiful, the Merciful ghouls —
To bar up our way and to ban it
From the secret that lies in these wolds —
From the thing that lies hidden in these wolds —
Have drawn up the spectre of a planet
From the limbo of lunary souls,
This sinfully scintillant planet
From the Hell of the planetary souls?"

POEMS WRITTEN IN YOUTH

PRIVATE reasons — some of which have reference to the sin of plagiarism, and others to the date of Tennyson's first poems — have induced me, after some hesitation, to re-publish these, the crude compositions of my earliest boyhood. They are printed *verbatim* — without alteration from the original edition — the date of which is too remote to be judiciously acknowledged.

E. A. P.

Note by Poe, prefixed to " Poems Written in Youth" in the Edition of 1845.

POEMS WRITTEN IN YOUTH

TAMERLANE

KIND solace in a dying hour!
  Such, father, is not (now) my theme —
I will not madly deem that power
    Of Earth may shrive me of the sin
    Unearthly pride hath revell'd in —
I have no time to dote or dream:
You call it hope — that fire of fire!
It is but agony of desire:
If I *can* hope — Oh God! I can —
  Its fount is holier — more divine —
I would not call thee fool, old man,
  But such is not a gift of thine.

Know thou the secret of a spirit
  Bow'd from its wild pride into shame.
O yearning heart! I did inherit
  Thy withering portion with the fame,
The searing glory which hath shone
Amid the Jewels of my throne,
Halo of Hell! and with a pain
Not hell shall make me fear again —

O craving heart, for the lost flowers
And sunshine of my summer hours!
The undying voice of that dead time,
With its interminable chime,

Rings, in the spirit of a spell,
Upon thy emptiness — a knell.

I have not always been as now:
The fever'd diadem on my brow
    I claim'd and won usurpingly ——
Hath not the same fierce heirdom given
    Rome to the Cæsar — this to me?
    The heritage of a kingly mind,
And a proud spirit which hath striven
    Triumphantly with human kind.

On mountain soil I first drew life:
    The mists of the Taglay have shed
    Nightly their dews upon my head,
And, I believe, the wingèd strife
And tumult of the headlong air
Have nestled in my very hair.

So late from Heaven — that dew — it fell
    ('Mid dreams of an unholy night)
Upon me with the touch of Hell,
    While the red flashing of the light
From clouds that hung, like banners, o'er,
    Appeared to my half-closing eye
    The pageantry of monarchy,
And the deep trumpet-thunder's roar
    Came hurriedly upon me, telling
        Of human battle, where my voice,
    My own voice, silly child! — was swelling
        (O! how my spirit would rejoice,
And leap within me at the cry)
The battle-cry of Victory!

The rain came down upon my head
  Unshelter'd — and the heavy wind
  Rendered me mad and deaf and blind.
It was but man, I thought, who shed
  Laurels upon me: and the rush —
The torrent of the chilly air
Gurgled within my ear the crush
  Of empires — with the captive's prayer —
The hum of suitors — and the tone
Of flattery 'round a sovereign's throne.

My passions, from that hapless hour,
  Usurp'd a tyranny which men
Have deem'd, since I have reach'd to power,
    My innate nature — be it so:
  But, father, there liv'd one who, then,
Then — in my boyhood — when their fire
    Burn'd with a still intenser glow
(For passion must, with youth, expire)
  E'en *then* who knew this iron heart
  In woman's weakness had a part.

I have no words — alas! — to tell
The loveliness of loving well!
Nor would I now attempt to trace
The more than beauty of a face
Whose lineaments, upon my mind,
Are —— shadows on th' unstable wind:
Thus I remember having dwelt
  Some page of early lore upon,
With loitering eye, till I have felt
The letters — with their meaning — melt
  To fantasies — with none.

O, she was worthy of all love!
  Love — as in infancy was mine —
'T was such as angel minds above
  Might envy; her young heart the shrine
On which my every hope and thought
  Were incense — then a goodly gift,
    For they were childish and upright —
Pure —— as her young example taught:
  Why did I leave it, and, adrift,
    Trust to the fire within, for light?

We grew in age — and love — together —
  Roaming the forest, and the wild;
My breast her shield in wintry weather —
  And, when the friendly sunshine smil'd,
And she would mark the opening skies,
I saw no Heaven — but in her eyes.

Young Love's first lesson is —— the heart:
  For 'mid that sunshine, and those smiles,
When, from our little cares apart,
  And laughing at her girlish wiles,
I 'd throw me on her throbbing breast,
  And pour my spirit out in tears —
There was no need to speak the rest —
  No need to quiet any fears
Of her — who ask'd no reason why,
But turn'd on me her quiet eye!

Yet *more* than worthy of the love
My spirit struggled with, and strove,
When, on the mountain peak, alone,
Ambition lent it a new tone —

I had no being — but in thee:
   The world, and all it did contain
In the earth — the air — the sea —
   Its joy — its little lot of pain
That was new pleasure —— the ideal,
   Dim, vanities of dreams by night —
And dimmer nothings which were real —
   (Shadows — and a more shadowy light!)
Parted upon their misty wings,
     And, so, confusedly, became
     Thine image and — a name — a name!
Two separate — yet most intimate things.

I was ambitious — have you known
     The passion, father? You have not:
A cottager, I mark'd a throne
Of half the world as all my own,
     And murmur'd at such lowly lot —
But, just like any other dream,
     Upon the vapor of the dew
My own had past, did not the beam
     Of beauty which did while it thro'
The minute — the hour — the day — oppress
My mind with double loveliness.

We walk'd together on the crown
Of a high mountain which look'd down
Afar from its proud natural towers
   Of rock and forest, on the hills —
The dwindled hills! begirt with bowers
   And shouting with a thousand rills.

I spoke to her of power and pride,
   But mystically — in such guise

That she might deem it nought beside
   The moment's converse; in her eyes
I read, perhaps too carelessly —
   A mingled feeling with my own —
The flush on her bright cheek, to me
   Seem'd to become a queenly throne
Too well that I should let it be
   Light in the wilderness alone.

I wrapp'd myself in grandeur then
   And donn'd a visionary crown ——
     Yet it was not that Fantasy
     Had thrown her mantle over me —
But that, among the rabble — men,
     Lion ambition is chain'd down —
And crouches to a keeper's hand —
Not so in deserts where the grand —
The wild — the terrible conspire
With their own breath to fan his fire.
Look 'round thee now on Samarcand! —
   Is she not queen of Earth? her pride
Above all cities? in her hand
   Their destinies? in all beside
Of glory which the world hath known
Stands she not nobly and alone?
Falling — her veriest stepping-stone
Shall form the pedestal of a throne —
And who her sovereign? Timour — he
   Whom the astonished people saw
Striding o'er empires haughtily
   A diadem'd outlaw!

O, human love! thou spirit given,
On Earth, of all we hope in Heaven!

Which fall'st into the soul like rain
Upon the Siroc-wither'd plain,
And, failing in thy power to bless,
But leav'st the heart a wilderness!
Idea! which bindest life around
With music of so strange a sound
And beauty of so wild a birth —
Farewell! for I have won the Earth.

When Hope, the eagle that tower'd, could see
  No cliff beyond him in the sky,
His pinions were bent droopingly —
  And homeward turn'd his soften'd eye.
'T was sunset: when the sun will part
There comes a sullenness of heart
To him who still would look upon
The glory of the summer sun.
That soul will hate the ev'ning mist
So often lovely, and will list
To the sound of the coming darkness (known
To those whose spirits harken) as one
Who, in a dream of night, *would* fly
But *cannot* from a danger nigh.

What tho' the moon — the white moon
Shed all the splendor of her noon,
Her smile is chilly — and *her* beam,
In that time of dreariness, will seem
(So like you gather in your breath)
A portrait taken after death.

And boyhood is a summer sun
Whose waning is the dreariest one —

For all we live to know is known
And all we seek to keep hath flown —
Let life, then, as the day-flower, fall
With the noon-day beauty — which is all.

I reach'd my home — my home no more ·
   For all had flown who made it so.
I pass'd from out its mossy door,
   And, tho' my tread was soft and low,
A voice came from the threshold stone
Of one whom I had earlier known —
   O, I defy thee, Hell, to show
   On beds of fire that burn below,
   An humbler heart — a deeper wo.

Father, I firmly do believe —
   I *know* — for Death who comes for me
      From regions of the blest afar,
Where there is nothing to deceive,
      Hath left his iron gate ajar,
   And rays of truth you cannot see
   Are flashing thro' Eternity ——
I do believe that Eblis hath
A snare in every human path —
Else how, when in the holy grove
I wandered of the idol, Love,
Who daily scents his snowy wings
With incense of burnt offerings
From the most unpolluted things,
Whose pleasant bowers are yet so riven
Above with trellis'd rays from Heaven
No mote may shun — no tiniest fly —

The light'ning of his eagle eye —
How was it that Ambition crept,
   Unseen, amid the revels there,
Till growing bold, he laughed and leapt
   In the tangles of Love's very hair?

SONNET — TO SCIENCE

Science! true daughter of Old Time thou art!
  Who alterest all things with thy peering eyes.
Why preyest thou thus upon the poet's heart,
  Vulture, whose wings are dull realities?
How should he love thee? or how deem thee wise,
  Who wouldst not leave him in his wandering
To seek for treasure in the jewelled skies,
  Albeit he soared with an undaunted wing?
Hast thou not dragged Diana from her car?
  And driven the Hamadryad from the wood
To seek a shelter in some happier star?
  Hast thou not torn the Naiad from her flood,
The Elfin from the green grass, and from me
The summer dream beneath the tamarind tree?

Copyright J.H.Whitty. May, 1914.

ROSALIE POE

AL AARAAF *

PART I

O! NOTHING earthly save the ray
(Thrown back from flowers) of Beauty's eye,
As in those gardens where the day
Springs from the gems of Circassy —
O! nothing earthly save the thrill
Of melody in woodland rill —
Or (music of the passion-hearted)
Joy's voice so peacefully departed
That like the murmur in the shell,
Its echo dwelleth and will dwell —
Oh, nothing of the dross of ours —
Yet all the beauty — all the flowers
That list our Love, and deck our bowers —
Adorn yon world afar, afar —
The wandering star.

'T was a sweet time for Nesace — for there
Her world lay lolling on the golden air,
Near four bright suns — a temporary rest —
An oasis in desert of the blest.
Away — away — 'mid seas of rays that roll
Empyrean splendor o'er th' unchained soul —
The soul that scarce (the billows are so dense)
Can struggle to its destin'd eminence —

* A star was discovered by Tycho Brahe which appeared suddenly in the heavens — attained, in a few days, a brilliancy surpassing that of Jupiter — then as suddenly disappeared, and has never been seen since.

To distant spheres, from time to time, she rode,
And late to ours, the favour'd one of God —
But, now, the ruler of an anchor'd realm,
She throws aside the sceptre — leaves the helm,
And, amid incense and high spiritual hymns,
Laves in quadruple light her angel limbs.

Now happiest, loveliest in yon lovely Earth,
Whence sprang the "Idea of Beauty" into birth,
(Falling in wreaths thro' many a startled star,
Like woman's hair 'mid pearls, until, afar,
It lit on hills Achaian, and there dwelt)
She look'd into Infinity — and knelt.
Rich clouds, for canopies, about her curled —
Fit emblems of the model of her world —
Seen but in beauty — not impeding sight
Of other beauty glittering thro' the light —
A wreath that twined each starry form around,
And all the opal'd air in color bound.

All hurriedly she knelt upon a bed
Of flowers: of lilies such as rear'd the head
*On the fair Capo Deucato, and sprang
So eagerly around about to hang
Upon the flying footsteps of —— deep pride —
† Of her who lov'd a mortal — and so died.
The Sephalica, budding with young bees,
Uprear'd its purple stem around her knees:
‡ And gemmy flower, of Trebizond misnam'd —

* On Santa Maura — olim Deucadia.
† Sappho.
‡ This flower is much noticed by Lewenboeck and Tournefort.
The bee, feeding upon its blossom, becomes intoxicated.

Inmate of highest stars, where erst it sham'd
All other loveliness: its honied dew
(The fabled nectar that the heathen knew)
Deliriously sweet, was dropp'd from Heaven,
And fell on gardens of the unforgiven
In Trebizond — and on a sunny flower
So like its own above that, to this hour,
It still remaineth, torturing the bee
With madness, and unwonted reverie:
In Heaven, and all its environs, the leaf
And blossom of the fairy plant, in grief
Disconsolate linger — grief that hangs her head,
Repenting follies that full long have fled,
Heaving her white breast to the balmy air,
Like guilty beauty, chasten'd, and more fair:
Nyctanthes too, as sacred as the light
She fears to perfume, perfuming the night:
* And Clytia pondering between many a sun,
While pettish tears adown her petals run:
† And that aspiring flower that sprang on earth —
And died, ere scarce exalted into birth,
Bursting its odorous heart in spirit to wing
Its way to Heaven, from garden of a king:

* Clytia — The Chrysanthemum Peruvianum, or, to employ a better-known term, the turnsol — which turns continually towards the sun, covers itself, like Peru, the country from which it comes, with dewy clouds which cool and refresh its flowers during the most violent heat of the day. — *B. de St. Pierre.*

† There is cultivated in the king's garden at Paris, a species of serpentine aloes without prickles, whose large and beautiful flower exhales a strong odour of the vanilla, during the time of its expansion, which is very short. It does not blow till towards the month of July — you then perceive it gradually open its petals — expand them — fade and die. — *St. Pierre.*

* And Valisnerian lotus thither flown
From struggling with the waters of the Rhone:
† And thy most lovely purple perfume, Zante!
Isola d'oro! — Fior di Levante!
‡ And the Nelumbo bud that floats for ever
With Indian Cupid down the holy river —
Fair flowers, and fairy! to whose care is given
§ To bear the Goddess' song, in odors, up to Heaven:

"Spirit! that dwellest where,
  In the deep sky,
The terrible and fair,
  In beauty vie!
Beyond the line of blue —
  The boundary of the star
Which turneth at the view
  Of thy barrier and thy bar —
Of the barrier overgone
  By the comets who were cast
From their pride, and from their throne
  To be drudges till the last —
To be carriers of fire
  (The red fire of their heart)
With speed that may not tire
  And with pain that shall not part —

* There is found, in the Rhone, a beautiful lily of the Valisnerian kind. Its stem will stretch to the length of three or four feet — thus preserving its head above water in the swellings of the river.

† The Hyacinth.

‡ It is a fiction of the Indians, that Cupid was first seen floating in one of these down the river Ganges — and that he still loves the cradle of his childhood.

§ And golden vials full of odors which are the prayers of the saints. — *Rev. St. John.*

Who livest — *that* we know —
  In Eternity — we feel —
But the shadow of whose brow
  What spirit shall reveal?
Tho' the beings whom thy Nesace,
  Thy messenger hath known
Have dream'd for thy Infinity
  * A model of their own —
Thy will is done, Oh, God!
  The star hath ridden high
Thro' many a tempest, but she rode
  Beneath thy burning eye;
And here, in thought, to thee —
  In thought that can alone

---

* The Humanitarians held that God was to be understood as having really a human form. — *Vide Clarke's Sermons*, vol. 1, page 26, fol. edit.

The drift of Milton's argument, leads him to employ language which would appear, at first sight, to verge upon their doctrine; but it will be seen immediately, that he guards himself against the charge of having adopted one of the most ignorant errors of the dark ages of the church. — *Dr. Sumner's Notes on Milton's Christian Doctrine.*

This opinion, in spite of many testimonies to the contrary, could never have been very general. Andeus, a Syrian of Mesopotamia, was condemned for the opinion, as heretical. He lived in the beginning of the fourth century. His disciples were called Anthropomorphites. — *Vide Du Pin.*

Among Milton's minor poems are these lines: —

Dicite sacrorum præsides nemorum Deæ, &c.
Quis ille primus cujus ex imagine
Natura solers finxit humanum genus?
Eternus, incorruptus, æquævus polo,
Unusque et universus exemplar Dei. — And afterwards,
Non cui profundum Cæcitas lumen dedit
Dircæus augur vidit hunc alto sinu, &c.

Ascend thy empire and so be
A partner of thy throne —
* By winged Fantasy,
My embassy is given,
Till secrecy shall knowledge be
In the environs of Heaven."

She ceas'd — and buried then her burning cheek
Abash'd, amid the lilies there, to seek
A shelter from the fervour of His eye;
For the stars trembled at the Deity.
She stir'd not — breath'd not — for a voice was there
How solemnly pervading the calm air!
A sound of silence on the startled ear
Which dreamy poets name "the music of the sphere."
Ours is a world of words: Quiet we call
"Silence" — which is the merest word of all.
All Nature speaks, and ev'n ideal things
Flap shadowy sounds from visionary wings —
But ah! not so when, thus, in realms on high
The eternal voice of God is passing by,
And the red winds are withering in the sky!

† "What tho' in worlds which sightless cycles run,
Link'd to a little system, and one sun —
Where all my love is folly and the crowd
Still think my terrors but the thunder cloud,
The storm, the earthquake, and the ocean-wrath —
(Ah! will they cross me in my angrier path?)

* Seltsamen Tochter Jovis
Seinem Schosskinde
Der Phantasie. — *Göethe.*

† Sightless — too small to be seen. — *Legge.*

What tho' in worlds which own a single sun
The sands of Time grow dimmer as they run,
Yet thine is my resplendency, so given
To bear my secrets thro' the upper Heaven.
Leave tenantless thy crystal home, and fly,
With all thy train, athwart the moony sky —
* Apart — like fire-flies in Sicilian night,
And wing to other worlds another light!
Divulge the secrets of thy embassy
To the proud orbs that twinkle — and so be
To ev'ry heart a barrier and a ban
Lest the stars totter in the guilt of man!"

Up rose the maiden in the yellow night,
The single-moonèd eve! — on Earth we plight
Our faith to one love — and one moon adore —
The birth-place of young Beauty had no more.
As sprang that yellow star from downy hours
Up rose the maiden from her shrine of flowers,
And bent o'er sheeny mountain and dim plain
†Her way — but left not yet her Therasæan reign.

PART II

HIGH on a mountain of enamell'd head —
Such as the drowsy shepherd on his bed
Of giant pasturage lying at his ease,
Raising his heavy eyelid, starts and sees

* I have often noticed a peculiar movement of the fire-flies; —
they will collect in a body and fly off, from a common centre, into
innumerable radii.

† Therasæa, or Therasea, the island mentioned by Seneca, which,
in a moment, arose from the sea to the eyes of astonished mariners.

With many a mutter'd "hope to be forgiven"
What time the moon is quadrated in Heaven —
Of rosy head, that towering far away
Into the sunlit ether, caught the ray
Of sunken suns at eve — at noon of night,
While the moon danc'd with the fair stranger light
Uprear'd upon such height arose a pile
Of gorgeous columns on th' unburthen'd air,
Flashing from Parian marble that twin smile
Far down upon the wave that sparkled there,
And nursled the young mountain in its lair.
* Of molten stars their pavement, such as fall
Thro' the ebon air, besilvering the pall
Of their own dissolution, while they die —
Adorning then the dwellings of the sky.
A dome, by linkèd light from Heaven let down,
Sat gently on these columns as a crown —
A window of one circular diamond, there,
Look'd out above into the purple air,
And rays from God shot down that meteor chain
And hallow'd all the beauty twice again,
Save when, between th' Empyrean and that ring,
Some eager spirit flapp'd his dusky wing.
But on the pillars Seraph eyes have seen
The dimness of this world: that greyish green
That Nature loves the best for Beauty's grave
Lurk'd in each cornice, round each architrave —
And every sculptur'd cherub thereabout
That from his marble dwelling peerèd out,
Seem'd earthly in the shadow of his niche —
Achaian statues in a world so rich.

* Some star which, from the ruin'd roof
  Of shak'd Olympus, by mischance, did fall. — *Milton*.

* Friezes from Tadmor and Persepolis —
From Balbec, and the stilly, clear abyss
† Of beautiful Gomorrah! O, the wave
Is now upon thee — but too late to save!

Sound loves to revel in a summer night:
Witness the murmur of the grey twilight
‡ That stole upon the ear, in Eyraco,
Of many a wild star-gazer long ago —
That stealeth ever on the ear of him
Who, musing, gazeth on the distance dim,
And sees the darkness coming as a cloud —
§ Is not its form — its voice — most palpable and loud?

But what is this? — it cometh — and it brings
A music with it — 't is the rush of wings —

* Voltaire, in speaking of Persepolis says, "Je connois bien
l'admiration qu'inspirent ces ruines — mais un palais erigé au pied
d'une chaine des rochers sterils — peut il être un chef d'œuvre des
arts!".

† "O, the wave " — Ula Deguisi is the Turkish appellation; but,
on its own shores, it is called Bahar Loth, or Almotanah. There
were undoubtedly more than two cities engulphed in the "dead
sea." In the valley of Siddim were five — Adrah, Zeboin, Zoar,
Sodom and Gomorrah. Stephen of Byzantium mentions eight,
and Strabo thirteen, (engulphed) — but the last is out of all reason.

It is said (Tacitus, Strabo, Josephus, Daniel of St. Saba, Nau,
Maundrell, Troilo, D'Arvieux) that after an excessive drought,
the vestiges of columns, walls, &c. are seen above the surface. At
any season, such remains may be discovered by looking down into
the transparent lake, and at such distances as would argue the existence of many settlements in the space now usurped by the 'As-
phaltites.'

‡ Eyraco — Chaldea.

§ I have often thought I could distinctly hear the sound of the
darkness as it stole over the horizon.

A pause — and then a sweeping, falling strain
And Nesace is in her halls again.
From the wild energy of wanton haste
     Her cheeks were flushing, and her lips apart;
And zone that clung around her gentle waist
     Had burst beneath the heaving of her heart.
Within the centre of that hall to breathe
She paus'd and panted, Zanthe! all beneath,
The fairy light that kiss'd her golden hair
And long'd to rest, yet could but sparkle there!

*Young flowers were whispering in melody
To happy flowers that night — and tree to tree;
Fountains were gushing music as they fell
In many a star-lit grove, or moon-lit dell;   ◂
Yet silence came upon material things —
Fair flowers, bright waterfalls and angel wings —
And sound alone that from the spirit sprang
Bore burthen to the charm the maiden sang:

     "Neath blue-bell or streamer —
       Or tufted wild spray
    That keeps, from the dreamer,
      † The moonbeam away —
    Bright beings! that ponder,
      With half closing eyes,

* Fairies use flowers for their charactery. — *Merry Wives of Windsor.*

† In Scripture is this passage — "The sun shall not harm thee by day, nor the moon by night." It is perhaps not generally known that the moon, in Egypt, has the effect of producing blindness to those who sleep with the face exposed to its rays, to which circumstance the passage evidently alludes.

On the stars which your wonder
  Hath drawn from the skies,
'Till they glance thro' the shade, and
  Come down to your brow
Like —— eyes of the maiden
  Who calls on you now —
Arise! from your dreaming
  : In violet bowers,
To duty beseeming
  These star-litten hours —
And shake from your tresses
  Encumber'd with dew
The breath of those kisses
  That cumber them too —
(O! how, without you, Love!
  Could angels be blest?)
Those kisses of true love
  That lull'd ye to rest!
Up! — shake from your wing
  Each hindering thing:
The dew of the night—
  It would weigh down your flight;
And true love caresses —
  O! leave them apart!
They are light on the tresses,
  But lead on the heart.

  Ligeia! Ligeia!
    My beautiful one!
  Whose harshest idea
    Will to melody run,
  O! is it thy will
    On the breezes to toss?

Or, capriciously still,
  *Like the lone Albatross,
Incumbent on night
  (As she on the air)
To keep watch with delight
  On the harmony there?
Ligeia! wherever
  Thy image may be,
No magic shall sever
  Thy music from thee.
Thou hast bound many eyes
  In a dreamy sleep —
But the strains still arise
  Which *thy* vigilance keep —
The sound of the rain
  Which leaps down to the flower,
And dances again
  In the rhythm of the shower —
†The murmur that springs
  From the growing of grass
Are the music of things —
  But are modell'd, alas! —
Away, then my dearest,
  O! hie thee away
To springs that lie clearest
  Beneath the moon-ray —
To lone lake that smiles,
  In its dream of deep rest,

* The Albatross is said to sleep on the wing.
† I met with this idea in an old English tale, which I am now
unable to obtain and quote from memory: — "The verie essence
and, as it were, springeheade and origine of all musiche is the verie
pleasaunte sounde which the trees of the forest do make when they
growe."

At the many star-isles
   That enjewel its breast —
Where wild flowers, creeping,
   Have mingled their shade,
On its margin is sleeping
   Full many a maid —
Some have left the cool glade, and
   *Have slept with the bee —
Arouse them, my maiden,
   On moorland and lea —
Go! breathe on their slumber,
   All softly in ear,
The musical number
   They slumber'd to hear —
For what can awaken
   An angel so soon
Whose sleep hath been taken
   Beneath the cold moon,
As the spell which no slumber
   Of witchery may test,
The rhythmical number
   Which lull'd him to rest?"

Spirits in wing, and angels to the view,
A thousand seraphs burst th' Empyrean thro',

* The wild bee will not sleep in the shade if there be moonlight.
  The rhyme in this verse, as in one about sixty lines before, has
an appearance of affectation. It is, however, imitated from Sir
W. Scott, or rather from Claud Halcro — in whose mouth I admired its affect:

        O! were there an island,
          Tho' ever so wild
       Where woman might smile, and
          No man be beguil'd, &c.

Young dreams still hovering on their drowsy flight —
Seraphs in all but "Knowledge," the keen light
That fell, refracted, thro' thy bounds, afar
O Death! from eye of God upon that star:
Sweet was that error — sweeter still that death —
Sweet was that error — ev'n with *us* the breath
Of Science dims the mirror of our joy —
To them 't were the Simoom, and would destroy —
For what (to them) availeth it to know
That Truth is Falsehood — or that Bliss is Woe?
Sweet was their death — with them to die was rife
With the last ecstasy of satiate life —
Beyond that death no immortality —
But sleep that pondereth and is not "to be" —
And there — oh! may my weary spirit dwell —
*Apart from Heaven's Eternity — and yet how far
　　　from Hell!
What guilty spirit, in what shrubbery dim,
Heard not the stirring summons of that hymn?

* With the Arabians there is a medium between Heaven and Hell,
where men suffer no punishment, but yet do not attain that tran-
quil and even happiness which they suppose to be characteristic
of heavenly enjoyment.

　　　　　Un oo rompido sueoo —
　　　　　Un dia puro — allegre — libre
　　　　　Quiera —
　　　　　Libre de amor — de zelo —
　　　　　De odio — de esperanza — de rezelo. — *Luis Ponce de Leon.*

Sorrow is not excluded from "Al Aaraaf," but it is that sorrow
which the living love to cherish for the dead, and which, in some
minds, resembles the delirium of opium. The passionate excitement of Love and the buoyancy of spirit attendant upon intoxica-
tion are its less holy pleasures — the price of which, to those souls
who make choice of "Al Aaraaf" as their residence after life, is
final death and annihilation.

But two: they fell: for Heaven no grace imparts
To those who hear not for their beating hearts.
A maiden-angel and her seraph-lover —
O! where (and ye may seek the wide skies over)
Was Love, the blind, near sober Duty known?
*Unguided Love hath fallen — 'mid "tears of perfect
     moan."
He was a goodly spirit — he who fell:
A wanderer by moss-y-mantled well —
A gazer on the lights that shine above —
A dreamer in the moonbeam by his love:
What wonder? for each star is eye-like there,
And looks so sweetly down on Beauty's hair —
And they, and ev'ry mossy spring were holy
To his love-haunted heart and melancholy.
The night had found (to him a night of wo)
Upon a mountain crag, young Angelo —
Beetling it bends athwart the solemn sky,
And scowls on starry worlds that down beneath it lie.
Here sate he with his love — his dark eye bent
With eagle gaze along the firmament:
Now turn'd it upon her — but ever then
It trembled to the orb of EARTH again.

"Ianthe, dearest, see! how dim that ray!
How lovely 't is to look so far away!
She seem'd not thus upon that autumn eve
I left her gorgeous halls — nor mourn'd to leave.
That eve — that eve — I should remember well —
The sun-ray dropp'd, in Lemnos, with a spell
On th' Arabesque carving of a gilded hall
Wherein I sate, and on the draperied wall —

    *There be tears of perfect moan
    Wept for thee in Helicon. — *Milton.*

And on my eye-lids — O the heavy light!
How drowsily it weigh'd them into night!
On flowers, before, and mist, and love they ran
With Persian Saadi in his Gulistan:
But O that light! — I slumber'd — Death, the while,
Stole o'er my senses in that lovely isle
So softly that no single silken hair
Awoke that slept — or knew that he was there.
The last spot of Earth's orb I trod upon
* Was a proud temple call'd the Parthenon —
More beauty clung around her column'd wall
† Than ev'n thy glowing bosom beats withal,
And when old Time my wing did disenthral
Thence sprang I — as the eagle from his tower,
And years I left behind me in an hour.
What time upon her airy bounds I hung
One half the garden of her globe was flung
Unrolling as a chart unto my view —
Tenantless cities of the desert too!
Ianthe, beauty crowded on me then,
And half I wish'd to be again of men."
"My Angelo! and why of them to be?
A brighter dwelling-place is there for thee —
And greener fields than in yon world above,
And woman's loveliness — and passionate love."

"But, list, Ianthe! when the air so soft
‡ Fail'd, as my pennon'd spirit leapt aloft,
Perhaps my brain grew dizzy — but the world
I left so late was into chaos hurl'd —

* It was entire in 1687 — the most elevated spot in Athens.
    † Shadowing more beauty in their airy brows
        Than have the white breasts of the Queen of Love. — *Marlowe.*
‡ Pennon — for pinion. — *Milton.*

Sprang from her station, on the winds apart,
And roll'd, a flame, the fiery Heaven athwart.
Methought, my sweet one, then I ceased to soar
And fell — not swiftly as I rose before,
But with a downward, tremulous motion thro'
Light, brazen rays, this golden star unto!
Nor long the measure of my falling hours,
For nearest of all stars was thine to ours —
Dread star! that came, amid a night of mirth,
A red Dædalion on the timid Earth.

"We came — and to thy Earth — but not to us
Be given our lady's bidding to discuss:
We came, my love; around, above, below,
Gay fire-fly of the night we come and go,
Nor ask a reason save the angel-nod
She grants to us, as granted by her God —
But, Angelo, than thine grey Time unfurl'd
Never his fairy wing o'er fairier world!
Dim was its little disk, and angel eyes
Alone could see the phantom in the skies,
When first Al Aaraaf knew her course to be
Headlong thitherward o'er the starry sea —
But when its glory swell'd upon the sky,
As glowing Beauty's bust beneath man's eye,
We paus'd before the heritage of men,
And thy star trembled — as doth Beauty then!"

Thus, in discourse, the lovers whiled away
The night that waned and waned and brought no
day.
They fell: for Heaven to them no hope imparts
Who hear not for the beating of their hearts.

↓ ROMANCE

ROMANCE, who loves to nod and sing,
With drowsy head and folded wing,
Among the green leaves as they shake
Far down within some shadowy lake,
To me a painted paroquet
Hath been — a most familiar bird —
Taught me my alphabet to say —
To lisp my very earliest word
While in the wild wood I did lie,
A child — with a most knowing eye.

Of late, eternal Condor years
So shake the very Heaven on high
With tumult as they thunder by,
I have no time for idle cares
Through gazing on the unquiet sky.
And when an hour with calmer wings
Its down upon my spirit flings —
That little time with lyre and rhyme
To while away — forbidden things!
My heart would feel to be a crime
Unless it trembled with the strings.

SONG

I saw thee on thy bridal day —
  When a burning blush came o'er thee,
Though happiness around thee lay,
  The world all love before thee:

And in thine eye a kindling light
  (Whatever it might be)
Was all on Earth my aching sight
  Of Loveliness could see.

That blush, perhaps, was maiden shame —
  As such it well may pass —
Though its glow hath raised a fiercer flame
  In the breast of him, alas!

Who saw thee on that bridal day,
  When that deep blush *would* come o'er thee,
Though happiness around thee lay,
  The world all love before thee.

DREAMS

Oh! that my young life were a lasting dream!
My spirit not awakening, till the beam
Of an Eternity should bring the morrow.
Yes! tho' that long dream were of hopeless sorrow,
'T were better than the cold reality
Of waking life, to him whose heart must be,
And hath been still, upon the lovely earth,
A chaos of deep passion, from his birth.
But should it be — that dream eternally
Continuing — as dreams have been to me
In my young boyhood — should it thus be given,
'T were folly still to hope for higher Heaven.
For I have revell'd when the sun was bright
I' the summer sky, in dreams of living light,
And loveliness, — have left my very heart
Inclines of my imagining, apart
From mine own home, with beings that have been
Of mine own thought — what more could I have seen?
'T was once — and only once — and the wild hour
From my remembrance shall not pass — some power
Or spell had bound me — 't was the chilly wind
Came o'er me in the night, and left behind
Its image on my spirit — or the moon
Shone on my slumbers in her lofty noon
Too coldly — or the stars — howe'er it was
That dream was as that night-wind — let it pass.

I *have been* happy, tho' in a dream.
I have been happy — and I love the theme:

Dreams! in their vivid colouring of life
As in that fleeting, shadowy, misty strife
Of semblance with reality which brings
To the delirious eye, more lovely things
Of Paradise and Love — and all our own!
 Than young Hope in his sunniest hour hath known.

SPIRITS OF THE DEAD

I

THY soul shall find itself alone
'Mid dark thoughts of the gray tomb-stone —
Not one, of all the crowd, to pry
Into thine hour of secrecy:

II

Be silent in that solitude,
   Which is not loneliness — for then
The spirits of the dead who stood
   In life before thee are again
In death around thee — and their will
Shall overshadow thee: be still.

III

The night — tho' clear — shall frown —
And the stars shall look not down,
From their high thrones in the heaven,
With light like Hope to mortals given —
But their red orbs, without beam,
To thy weariness shall seem
As a burning and a fever
Which would cling to thee for ever.

IV

Now are thoughts thou shalt not banish —
Now are visions ne'er to vanish —
From thy spirit shall they pass
No more — like dew-drop from the grass.

V

The breeze — the breath of God — is still —
And the mist upon the hill
Shadowy — shadowy — yet unbroken,
Is a symbol and a token —
How it hangs upon the trees,
A mystery of mysteries! —

EVENING STAR

'T WAS noontide of summer,
  And mid-time of night;
And stars, in their orbits,
  Shone pale, thro' the light
Of the brighter, cold moon,
  'Mid planets her slaves,
Herself in the Heavens,
  Her beam on the waves.
    I gazed awhile
    On her cold smile;
Too cold — too cold for me —
    There pass'd, as a shroud,
    A fleecy cloud,
And I turn'd away to thee,
    Proud Evening Star,
    In thy glory afar,
And dearer thy beam shall be;
    For joy to my heart
    Is the proud part
Thou bearest in Heaven at night,
    And more I admire
    Thy distant fire,
Than that colder, lowly light.

TO ———[1]

TAKE this kiss upon thy brow!
And, in parting from you now,
Thus much let me avow —
You are not wrong, to deem
That my days have been a dream;
Yet if Hope has flown away
In a night, or in a day,
In a vision, or in none,
Is it therefore the less *gone?*
All that we see or seem
Is but a dream within a dream.

I stand amid the roar
Of a surf-tormented shore,
And I hold within my hand
Grains of the golden sand —
How few! yet how they creep
Through my fingers to the deep,
While I weep — while I weep!
O, God! can I not grasp
Them with a tighter clasp?
O, God! can I not save
One from the pitiless wave?
Is *all* that we see or seem
But a dream within a dream?

[1] Poe's title in the *Flag of Our Union* was "A Dream within a Dream."

"IN YOUTH HAVE I KNOWN ONE WITH WHOM THE EARTH"[1]

How often we forget all time, when lone
Admiring Nature's universal throne;
Her woods — her wilds — her mountains — the intense
Reply of HERS to our intelligence![2]

I

IN youth have I known one with whom the Earth
In secret communing held — as he with it,
In daylight, and in beauty from his birth:
Whose fervid, flickering torch of life was lit
From the sun and stars, whence he had drawn forth
A passionate light — such for his spirit was fit —
And yet that spirit knew not, in the hour
Of its own fervour, what had o'er it power.

2

Perhaps it may be that my mind is wrought
To a ferver by the moonbeam that hangs o'er,
But I will half believe that wild light fraught
With more of sovereignty than ancient lore
Hath ever told — or is it of a thought
The unembodied essence, and no more,
That with a quickening spell doth o'er us pass
As dew of the night-time o'er the summer grass?

[1] The late E. C. Stedman gave this the title of "Stanzas" in the Stedman-Woodberry edition of Poe's poems, which all succeeding editions have followed.
[2] Byron, "The Island."

3

Doth o'er us pass, when, as th' expanding eye
To the loved object — so the tear to the lid .
Will start, which lately slept in apathy?
And yet it need not be — (that object) hid
From us in life — but common — which doth lie
Each hour before us — but *then* only, bid
With a strange sound, as of a harp-string broken,
To awake us — 'T is a symbol and a token

4

Of what in other worlds shall be — and given
In beauty by our God, to those alone
Who otherwise would fall from life and Heaven
Drawn by their heart's passion, and that tone,
That high tone of the spirit which hath striven,
Tho' not with Faith — with godliness — whose throne
With desperate energy 't hath beaten down;
Wearing its own deep feeling as a crown.

A DREAM

In visions of the dark night
   I have dreamed of joy departed —
But a waking dream of life and light
   Hath left me broken-hearted.

Ah! what is not a dream by day
   To him whose eyes are cast
On things around him with a ray
   Turned back upon the past?

That holy dream — that holy dream,
   While all the world were chiding,
Hath cheered me as a lovely beam
   A lonely spirit guiding.

What though that light, thro' storm and night,
   So trembled from afar —
What could there be more purely bright
   In Truth's day-star?

"THE HAPPIEST DAY, THE HAPPIEST HOUR"

THE happiest day — the happiest hour
  My sear'd and blighted heart hath known,
The highest hope of pride and power,
  I feel hath flown.

Of power! said I? yes! such I ween;
  But they have vanish'd long, alas!
The visions of my youth have been —
  But let them pass.

And, pride, what have I now with thee?
  Another brow may even inherit
The venom thou hast pour'd on me —
  Be still, my spirit!

The happiest day — the happiest hour
  Mine eyes shall see — have ever seen,
The brightest glance of pride and power,
  I feel — have been:

But were that hope of pride and power
  Now offer'd, with the pain
Even *then* I felt — that brightest hour
  I would not live again:

For on its wing was dark alloy,
  And, as it flutter'd — fell
An essence — powerful to destroy
  A soul that knew it well.

THE LAKE

To ——

IN youth's spring it was my lot
To haunt of the wide world a spot
The which I could not love the less,
So lovely was the loneliness
Of a wild lake with black rock bound,
And the tall pines that tower'd around —

But when the night had thrown her pall
Upon that spot, as upon all,
And the ghastly wind went by
In a dirge-like melody,
Then — ah then I would awake
To the terror of that lone lake.

Yet that terror was not fright,
But a tremulous delight —
A feeling not the jewell'd mine
Could teach or bribe me to define,
Nor love — although the love were thine.

Death was in that poison'd wave,
And in its depth a fitting grave
For him who thence could solace bring
To his lone imagining —
Whose solitary soul could make
An Eden of that dim lake.

TO ——

THE bowers whereat, in dreams, I see
  The wantonest singing birds,
Are lips — and all thy melody
  Of lip-begotten words —

Thine eyes, in Heaven of heart enshrined
  Then desolately fall,
O God! on my funereal mind
  Like starlight on a pall —

Thy heart — *thy* heart! — I wake and sigh,
  And sleep to dream till day
Of the truth that gold can never buy —
  Of the baubles that it may.

TO THE RIVER ——

FAIR river! in thy bright, clear flow
    Of crystal, wandering water,
Thou art an emblem of the glow
        Of beauty — the unhidden heart —
        The playful maziness of art
    In old Alberto's daughter;

But when within thy wave she looks —
    Which glistens then, and trembles —
Why, then, the prettiest of brooks
    Her worshipper resembles;
For in his heart, as in thy stream,
    Her image deeply lies —
His heart which trembles at the beam
    Of her soul-searching eyes.

TO ——

I HEED not that my earthly lot
    Hath — little of Earth in it —
That years of love have been forgot
    In the hatred of a minute: —
I mourn not that the desolate
    Are happier, sweet, than I,
But that *you* sorrow for *my* fate
    Who am a passer by.

FAIRY-LAND

Dim vales — and shadowy floods —
And cloudy-looking woods,
Whose forms we can't discover
For the tears that drip all over.
Huge moons there wax and wane —
Again — again — again —
Every moment of the night —
Forever changing places —
And they put out the star-light
With the breath from their pale faces.
About twelve by the moon-dial
One more filmy than the rest
(A kind which, upon trial,
They have found to be the best)
Comes down — still down — and down
With its centre on the crown
Of a mountain's eminence,
While its wide circumference
In easy drapery falls
Over hamlets, over halls,
Wherever they may be —
O'er the strange woods — o'er the sea —
Over spirits on the wing —
Over every drowsy thing —
And buries them up quite
In a labyrinth of light —
And then, how deep! — O, deep!
Is the passion of their sleep.

In the morning they arise,
And their moony covering
Is soaring in the skies,
With the tempests as they toss,
Like —— almost any thing —
Or a yellow Albatross.
They use that moon no more
For the same end as before —
Videlicet a tent —
Which I think extravagant:
Its atomies, however,
Into a shower dissever,
Of which those butterflies,
Of Earth, who seek the skies,
And so come down again
(Never-contented things!)
Have brought a specimen
Upon their quivering wings.

TO HELEN

HELEN, thy beauty is to me
    Like those Nicéan barks of yore,
That gently, o'er a perfumed sea,
    The weary, way-worn wanderer bore
    To his own native shore.

On desperate seas long wont to roam,
    Thy hyacinth hair, thy classic face,
Thy Naiad airs have brought me home
    To the glory that was Greece,
And the grandeur that was Rome.

Lo! in yon brilliant window-niche
    How statue-like I see thee stand,
    The agate lamp within thy hand!
Ah, Psyche, from the regions which
    Are Holy-Land!

✓ FROM AN ALBUM (ALONE)

FROM childhood's hour I have not been
As others were — I have not seen
As others saw — I could not bring
My passions from a common spring —
From the same source I have not taken
My sorrow — I could not awaken
My heart to joy at the same tone —
And all I lov'd — *I* lov'd alone —
Then — in my childhood — in the dawn
Of a most stormy life — was drawn
From ev'ry depth of good and ill
The mystery which binds me still —
From the torrent, or the fountain —
From the red cliff of the mountain —
From the sun that 'round me roll'd
In its autumn tint of gold —
From the lightning in the sky
As it pass'd me flying by —
From the thunder, and the storm —
And the cloud that took the form
(When the rest of Heaven was blue)
Of a demon in my view —

POEMS NOW FIRST COL-
LECTED

Spiritual Song

Hark, echo! — Hark; echo!
   'Tis the sound
Of archangels, in happiness wrapt

POEMS NOW FIRST COL-LECTED

SPIRITUAL SONG

HARK, echo! — Hark; echo!
'T is the sound
Of archangels, in happiness wrapt

ELIZABETH

ELIZABETH — it surely is most fit
[Logic and common usage so commanding]
In thy own book that *first* thy name be writ,
Zeno[1] and other sages notwithstanding;
And *I* have other reasons for so doing
Besides my innate love of contradiction;
Each poet — *if* a poet — in persuing
The muses thro' their bowers of Truth or Fiction,
Has studied very little of his part,
Read nothing, written less — in short 's a fool
Endued with neither soul, nor sense, nor art,
Being ignorant of one important rule,
Employed in even the theses of the school —
Called — I forget the heathenish Greek name —
[Called anything, its meaning is the same]
"Always write *first* things uppermost in the heart."

[1] It was a saying of this philosopher " that one's own name should never appear in one's own book."

FROM AN ALBUM

ELIZABETH it is in vain you say
"Love not" — thou sayest it in so sweet a way:
In vain those words from thee or L. E. L.
Zantippe's talents had enforced so well:
Ah! if that language from thy heart arise,
Breathe it less gently forth — and veil thine eyes.
Endymion, recollect, when Luna tried
To cure his love — was cured of all beside —
His folly — pride — and passion — for he died.

TO SARAH

WHEN melancholy and alone,
I sit on some moss-covered stone
Beside a murm'ring stream;   ·
I think I hear thy voice's sound
In every tuneful thing around,
Oh! what a pleasant dream.

The silvery streamlet gurgling on,
The mock-bird chirping on the thorn,
Remind me, love, of thee.
They seem to whisper thoughts of love,
As thou didst when the stars above
Witnessed thy vows to me; —

The gentle zephyr floating by,
In chorus to my pensive sigh,
Recalls the hour of bliss,
When from thy balmy lips I drew
Fragrance as sweet as Hermia's dew,
And left the first fond kiss.

In such an hour, when are forgot,
The world, its cares, and my own lot,
Thou seemest then to be,
A gentle guardian spirit given
To guide my wandering thoughts to heaven,
If they should stray from thee.

THE GREAT MAN

THE great man lives forever shrined in the hearts of men,
Albeit form and feature may fade from human ken;
Recorded are his actions on history's living page —
They shine with purer lustre with each successive age.
Immortal aye immortal, undying as a God
The sands of time are printed wherever his feet have
     trod.
Above his dust no monument may proudly rear its
     head
To mark the spot where resteth, the mighty and the
     dead.
He needeth no mausoleum, nor shaft need pierce the sky
To point to coming ages, where his sacred ashes lie.
No! that may be forgotten, but around his glorious
     name
Will shine the dazzling halo of a never dying fame.
His requiem will be chanted in the wild bird's sweetest
     song,
The summer breeze and wintry gale the sad notes will
     prolong,
The flowers of spring time and the leaves of autumn
     be his pall,
Long as the one shall blossom, long as the other fall.
Here is a noble lesson. Oh! let it graven be
In characters unfading on the page of memory.
Like the needle to the mariner amidst the tempest wrath
Let it fire your hopes and guide you as you tread life's
     thorny path.

GRATITUDE

To ⸺

As turns the eye to bless the hand that led its infant
      years,
As list'ning still for that sweet voice which every tone
      endears,
So I to thee, through mental power, would each remem-
      brance trace,
And bless the hand that led me on to fonts of lasting
      grace.
As sailor on the billowy deep hath seen some light afar,
And shunned the rock that lies between his pathway
      and the star,
So hast thou been o'er stormy wave to me, 'mid sorrow's
      night,
A beacon true whose glory spreads afar its rays of light.
As flow sweet sounds of melody from strings drawn out
      by skill,
As roll its wavelets o'er the soul and all its chambers
      fill,
So came the words of holy truth endued with wisdom's
      zeal,
So fell their impress on my heart and stamped it with
      their seal.

As runs the rivulet its course and swifter as it flows,
Still murmuring of the hidden depths where first its
      waters rose,

So evermore as life glides on expanding far and wide,
Will turn the heart to where at first was ope'd its holiest
tide.
As pours the captive bird its song to him who sets it
free,
So flows my breath in song of praise in gratitude to thee.
As o'er the earth the sun reflects its rays of living light,
So thou by thy pure rays of thought art power to men-
tal sight.

AN ENIGMA

FIRST, find out a word that doth silence proclaim,
And that backwards and forwards is always the same,
Then next you must find out a feminine name
That backwards and forwards is always the same;
An act, or a writing on parchment whose name
Both backwards and forwards is always the same;
A fruit that is rare, whose botanical name
Read backwards and forwards is always the same;
A note, used in music, which time doth proclaim,
And backwards and forwards is always the same;
Their initials connected, a title will frame,
That is justly the due of the fair married dame,
Which backwards and forwards is always the same.

IMPROMPTU

To Kate Carol

WHEN from your gems of thought I turn
To those pure orbs, your heart to learn,
I scarce know which to prize most high —
The bright *i-dea*, or bright *dear-eye*.

STANZAS

LADY! I would that verse of mine
Could fling, all lavishly and free,
Prophetic tones from every line,
Of health, joy, peace, in store for thee.

Thine should be length of happy days,
Enduring joys and fleeting cares,
Virtue that challenge envy's praise,
By rivals loved, and mourned by heirs.

Thy life's free course should ever roam,
Beyond this bounded earthly clime,
No billow breaking into foam
Upon the rock-girt shore of Time.

The gladness of a gentle heart,
Pure as the wishes breathed in prayer,
Which has in others' joys a part,
While in its own all others share.

The fullness of a cultured mind,
Stored with the wealth of bard and sage,
Which Error's glitter cannot blind,
Lustrous in youth, undimmed in age;

The grandeur of a guileless soul,
With wisdom, virtues, feeling fraught,
Gliding serenely to its goal,
Beneath the eternal sky of Thought: —

These should be thine, to guard and shield,
And this the life thy spirit live,
Blest with all bliss that earth can yield,
Bright with all hopes that Heaven can give.

THE DIVINE RIGHT OF KINGS

THE only king by right divine
Is Ellen King, and were she mine
I'd strive for liberty no more,
But hug the glorious chains I wore.

Her bosom is an ivory throne,
Where tyrant virtue reigns alone;
No subject vice dare interfere,
To check the power that governs here.

Oh! would she deign to rule my fate
I'd worship Kings with kingly state,
And hold this maxim all life long,
The King — *my* King — can do no wrong.

THE VITAL STREAM

FLOW softly — gently — vital stream;
Ye crimson life-drops, stay;
Indulge me with this pleasing dream
Thro' an eternal day.

See — see — my soul, her agony!
See how her eye-balls glare!
Those shrieks, delightful harmony,
Proclaim her deep despair.

Rise — rise — infernal spirits, rise,
Swift dart across her brain
Thou Horror, with blood-chilling cries,
Lead on thy hidious train.

O, feast my soul, revenge is sweet,
Louisa, take my scorn; —
Curs'd was the hour that saw us meet,
The hour when we were born.

" *Poeta* *Curse* " *Byron*

COUPLET

DEEP in earth my love is lying
And I must weep alone.

LINES TO JOE LOCKE

As for Locke, he is all in my eye,
May the d—l right soon for his soul call,
He never was known to lie —
In bed at a reveillé " roll call."

John Locke was a notable name;
Joe Locke is a greater; in short,
The former was well known to fame,
But the latter 's well known " to report."

ADDITIONAL POEMS WITH POETRY ATTRIBUTED TO POE

ADDITIONAL POEMS WITH POETRY ATTRIBUTED TO POE

SONG OF TRIUMPH

(From tale Four Beasts In One)
Southern Literary Messenger

WHO is king but Epiphanes?
  Say — do you know?
Who is king but Epiphanes?
  Bravo — bravo!
There is none but Epiphanes,
  No — there is none:
So tear down the temples,
  And put out the sun!
Who is king but Epiphanes?
  Say — do you know?
Who is king but Epiphanes?
  Bravo — bravo!

LATIN HYMN

(From tale Four Beasts In One)
Southern Literary Messenger

A THOUSAND, a thousand, a thousand,
A thousand, a thousand, a thousand,
We, with one warrior, have slain!
A thousand, a thousand, a thousand, a thousand,
    Sing a thousand over again!
    Soho! — let us sing
Long life to our king,
Who knocked over a thousand so fine!
    Soho! — let us roar,
  He has given us more
    Red gallons of gore
Than all Syria can furnish of wine !

THE SKELETON–HAND

(Attributed to Poe)

[*From The Yankee, August, 1829.*]

Lo! one is on the mountain side,
  While the clouds are passing by —
With their black wings flapping heavily,
  Like eagles in the sky;
Or lying up in the forest trees,
  And waiting there for the mountain-breeze.

And now he passes through the clouds —
  And up to the mountain-top,
Nor yet to look for the joyous sun
  Does the hasty traveller stop.

But he leapeth down in the broken path
  With a step as light and free —
As ever in his days of mirth,
  In the dance and revelry.

Why endeth he his hasty speed?
  Why stoppeth on his way?
In truth it is a fearful thing,
  For human tongue to say.

He fears that toward him pointeth there,
  A fleshless human hand;
Where the mountain rains have swept away,
  Its covering of sand;

That hand his very soul doth stir,
  For it proveth him a murderer.

Ay long ago on the mountain side,
  The fearful deed was done;
And the murderer thought him safe, that none
  Could see, save the broad bright sun,
As he rolled in the heavens the dead above,
  And flooded the earth with his rays of love.

Now lifted he his clouded eye,
  To the mountain crests behind;
And o'er them came the broad black clouds,
  Upheaving with the wind;
And on them their thick darkness spread —
  A crown upon the mountain's head.

And then shone out the flaming sun,
  From the waters of the sea;
And God's own bow came in the clouds,
  And looked out gloriously;
But its colours were of wo and wrath,
  That threw their light o'er the murderer's path.

And now God's chariots — the clouds,
  Came rolling down with might;
Their wheels like many horsemen were,
  In battle or in flight.
And yet no power to move hath *he*,
  His soul is in an agony.

Over the murderer and dead
  They rolled their mighty host;

Old ocean's waves come not so thick,
  By northern tempests tost.

Forth from their mighty bosom came,
  A flash of heaven's wrath,
And away the heavy clouds — and dun,
  Rolled from the murder-path.
And the sun shone out where the murderer lay,
Before the dead in the narrow way —
With his hand all seared, and his breast torn bare —
God's vengeance had been working there.

P.

THE MAGICIAN [1]

(*Attributed to Poe*)

[*From The Yankee, December, 1829.*]

MAGICIAN

THOU dark, sea-stirring storm,
Whence comest thou in thy might —
Nay — wait, thou dim and dreamy form —
Storm spirit, I call thee — 't is mine of right —
Arrest thee in thy troubled flight.

STORM SPIRIT

Thou askest me whence I came —
I came o'er the sleeping sea,
It roused at my torrent of storm and flame,
And it howled aloud in its agony,
And swelled to the sky — that sleeping sea.

Thou askest me what I met —
A ship from the Indian shore,
A tall proud ship with her sails all set —
Far down in the sea that ship I bore,
My storms wild rushing wings before.

And her men will forever lie,
Below the unquiet sea;
And tears will dim full many an eye,

[1] The punctuation throughout is the author's — *by desire.*

Of those who shall widows and orphans be,
And their days be years — for their misery.

A boat with a starving crew —
For hunger they howled and swore;
While the blood from a fellow's veins they drew
I came upon them with rush and roar —
Far under the waves that boat I bore.

Two ships in a fearful fight —
When a hundred guns did flash
I came upon them — no time for flight —
But under the sea their timbers crash
And over their guns the wild waters dash

A wretch on a single plank —
And I tossed him on the shore —
A night and a day of the sea he drank,
But the wearied wretch to the land I bore —
And now he walketh the earth once more.

MAGICIAN

Storm spirit — go on thy path —

The spirit has spread his wings —
And comes on the sea with a rush of wrath,
As a war horse when he springs —
And over the earth his winds he flings —
And over the earth — nor stop nor stay —
The winds of the storm king go out on their way.

P——

QUEEN OF MAY ODE

FAIRIES guard the Queen of May,
Let her reign in Peace and Honor —
Every blessing be upon her;
May her future pathway lie,
All beneath a smiling sky.

NOTE

Mrs. Harriet Virginia Thomson, née Scott, of Austin, Texas, who is over ninety years of age, knew Poe in Richmond, Va. She lived there with her parents when a girl, residing on the Main street near the *Southern Literary Messenger* office. She saw Poe pass her house several times daily, and in those early days looked upon him as a great poet.

Her school was to have a May Queen celebration, and she was required to recite verses to the May Queen. In company with a cousin, an attorney, of Richmond, and a warm friend of Mr. Poe's, she called at the *Messenger* office, and asked Mr. Poe to write her a May Queen Ode.

He readily complied, and sent her the lines the following day. The manuscript was preserved for some time, but finally went astray.

Mrs. Thomson remembers that there were four or five stanzas, as she committed them to memory, and recited them on the occasion. One of the stanzas, she says, she never forgot, and gives it as above from memory.

The school celebration was published in some pamphlet or periodical at the time and the lines printed, but she does not think they were credited to Mr. Poe.

FANNY

THE dying swan by northern lakes
Sings its wild death song, sweet and clear,
And as the solemn music breaks
O'er hill and glen dissolves in air;
Thus musical thy soft voice came,
Thus trembled on thy tongue my name.

Like sunburst through the ebon cloud,
Which veils the solemn midnight sky,
Piercing cold evening's sable shroud
Thus came the first glance of that eye;
But like the adamantine rock,
My spirit met and braved the shock.

Let memory the boy recall
Who laid his heart upon thy shrine,
When far away his footsteps fall,
Think that he deem'd thy charms divine;
A victim on love's altar slain,
By witching eyes which looked disdain.

NOTE

The above was printed in the *Baltimore Saturday Visiter* of May 18, 1833. Like the poem "To ——" on the following page, which also appeared in the same newspaper May 11, 1833, the verses were signed "Tamerlane."

TO ——

SLEEP on, sleep on, another hour —
I would not break so calm a sleep,
To wake to sunshine and to show'r,
To smile and weep.

Sleep on, sleep on, like sculptured thing,
Majestic, beautiful art thou;
Sure seraph shields thee with his wing
And fans thy brow —

We would not deem thee child of earth,
For, O, angelic is thy form!
But that in heav'n thou had'st thy birth,
Where comes no storm

To mar the bright, the perfect flow'r,
But all is beautiful and still —
And golden sands proclaim the hour
Which brings no ill.

Sleep on, sleep on, some fairy dream
Perchance is woven in thy sleep —
But, O, thy spirit, calm, serene,
Must wake to weep.

OH, TEMPORA! OH, MORES!

The Baltimore *No Name Magazine* of October, 1889, printed the following as an unpublished poem by Poe: —

"The following verses which have never before appeared in print were written by Edgar Allan Poe at the age of seventeen, and were for more than half a century in the possession of the late John H. MacKenzie [1] of Henrico County, Virginia, whose mother adopted Rosalie Poe, Edgar's sister, at the same time that Edgar was adopted by Mrs. Allan of Richmond. The satire is interesting as perhaps the earliest of Poe's writings known to exist. The luckless Pitts, lampooned by Poe, was a clerk in the leading fashionable dry-goods store of Richmond at the time, and was paying court to a youthful belle of the period who afterwards married a prominent Virginia politician and member of Congress, and who sometimes smiled *dans sa premiere jeunesse* on the wayward young Edgar with the bright eyes and hyacinthine curls. Doubtless that lady's escritoire contained many a woful ballad and lovesick sonnet of the precocious madcap. The frequent use of parliamentary phrases, and the mention of member's claws and member's logic shows that '*Oh, Tempora! Oh, Mores!*' was written chiefly for the ridicule of Pitts in the eyes of certain members of the Virginia legislature who were then boarding in the same house with him.

"All the parties in any manner connected with this lampoon — the fair lady, the distinguished M. C., the author and his victim — have long since passed away, and its publication now can wound the sensibility of no human being,

[1] He was a youthful companion of Poe.

while the numberless admirers of the author of 'The Raven' will read with interest an authentic poem written by him when a boy, — an interest similar in kind — if not as great in degree — to that which would be inspired by a juvenile production of Tennyson or Sir Walter Scott."

OH, TEMPORA! OH, MORES!

Oh Times! Oh Manners! It is my opinion
That you are changing sadly your dominion —
I mean the reign of manners hath long ceased,
For men have none at all, or bad at least;
And as for times, although 't is said by many
The "good old times" were far the worst of any,
Of which sound doctrine I believe each tittle,
Yet still I think these worse than them a little.

I 've been a thinking, is n't that the phrase?
— I like your Yankee words and Yankee ways —
I 've been a thinking, whether it were best
To take things seriously or all in jest;
Whether with Heraclitus of yore
To weep, as he did, till his eyes were sore,
Or rather laugh with him, that queer Philosopher,
Democritus of Thrace, who used to toss over
The page of life and grin at the dog-ears,
As though he 'd say, "Why who the devil cares?"

This is a question which, Oh Heaven, withdraw
The luckless query from a Member's claw!
Instead of two sides, Job has nearly eight,
Each fit to furnish forth four hours debate.
What shall be done? I 'll lay it on the table,
And take the matter up when I 'm more able,

And in the meantime, to prevent all bother,
I 'll neither laugh with one or cry with t'other,
Nor deal in flattery or aspersions foul,
But, taking one by each hand, merely growl.

Ah growl, say you, my friend, and pray at what?
Why really, sir, I almost had forgot —
But damn it, sir, I deem it a disgrace
That things should stare us boldly in the face,
And daily strut the street with bows and scrapes,
Who would be men by imitating apes.
I beg your pardon, reader, for the oath,
The monkey made me swear, though something
    loath;
I 'm apt to be discursive in my style,
But pray be patient: yet a little while
Will change me, and as politicians do
I 'll mend my manners and my measures too.

Of all the cities, and I 've seen no few, —
For I have travelled, friend, as well as you, —
I don't remember one, upon my soul,
But take it generally upon the whole,
(As Members say they like their logic taken
Because divided it may chance be shaken)
So pat, agreeable, and vastly proper
As this for a neat, frisky counter-hopper;
Here he may revel to his heart's content,
Flounce like a fish in his own element,
Toss back his fine curls from their forehead fair
And hop o'er counters with a Vestris air,
Complete at night what he began A. M.,
And having cheated ladies, dance with them;

For at a ball what fair one can escape
The pretty little hand that sold her tape,
Or who so cold, so callous to refuse
The youth who cut the ribbon for her shoes!

One of these fish, par excellence the beau,
God help me, it has been my lot to know,
At least by sight, for I 'm a timid man
And always keep from laughing when I can;
But speak to him, he 'll make you such grimace.
Lord! to be grave exceeds the power of face.
The hearts of all the ladies are with him,
Their bright eyes on his Tom and Jerry brim
And dove-tailed coat, obtained at cost; while then
Those won't turn on anything like men.

His very voice is musical delight,
His form once seen becomes a part of sight,
In short his shirt-collar, his look, his tone is
The "beau ideal" fancied for Adonis.
Philosophers have often held dispute
As to the seat of thought in man and brute,
For that the power of thought attend the latter
My friend, the beau, hath made a settled matter,
And spite all dogmas current in all ages,
One settled fact is better than ten sages.

For he does think, although I 'm oft in doubt
If I can tell exactly what about.
Ah yes! his little foot and ancle trim,
'T is there the seat of reason lies in him;
A wise philosopher would shake his head,
He then, of course, must shake his foot instead.

At me in vengeance shall that foot be shaken —
Another proof of thought, I 'm not mistaken —
Because to his cat's eyes I hold a glass
And let him see himself a proper ass?
I think he 'll take this likeness to himself,
But if he won't *he shall*, the stupid elf,
And, lest the guessing throw the fool in fits,
I close the portrait with the name of PITTS.

NOTE

The Editor of the Magazine, Mr. Eugene L. Didier, wrote me that the poem was sent him by John R. Thompson of the *Southern Literary Messenger*, and that the introduction was written by Thompson.

The original manuscript of this poem in Poe's autograph was once in the possession of John H. MacKenzie. It was destroyed with other Poe papers by fire during the Civil War. A copy reading like the above verses is still preserved by a step-daughter of Mr. MacKenzie, with an account of how it came to be written by Poe in the year 1826.

APPENDIX

APPENDIX

I

THE BALTIMORE SATURDAY VISITER, ETC.

A VOLUME of *The Baltimore Saturday Visiter* for the year 1833 is preserved at Catonsville, Md. In all probability Poe contributed to that newspaper the two poems "Fanny" and "To ———" appearing on pages 165 and 166 of the present volume. *The Visiter* of April 20, 1833, also published the following verses: —

SERENADE — BY E. A. POE

So sweet the hour — so calm the time,
I feel it more than half a crime
When Nature sleeps and stars are mute,
To mar the silence ev'n with lute.
At rest on ocean's brilliant dies
An image of Elysium lies:
Seven Pleiades entranced in Heaven,
Form in the deep another seven:
Endymion nodding from above
Sees in the sea a second love:
Within the valleys dim and brown,
And on the spectral mountain's crown
The wearied light is dying down:
And earth, and stars, and sea, and sky
Are redolent of sleep, as I
Am redolent of thee and thine
Enthralling love, my Adeline.
But list, O list! — so soft and low
Thy lover's voice to-night shall flow
That, scarce awake, thy soul shall deem
My words the music of a dream.
Thus, while no single sound too rude,

Upon thy slumber shall intrude,
Our thoughts, our souls — O God above!
In every deed shall mingle, love.

A prize of fifty dollars was awarded Poe, October 12, 1833, for his tale "MS. Found in a Bottle," which was published in the *Visiter* of October 19. The text mainly follows the version of the *Southern Literary Messenger*. The poem "Coliseum" appeared in the *Visiter* of October 26, 1833. The version closely follows that of the *Southern Literary Messenger* with the exception of a new line at the beginning: "Lone amphitheatre! Grey Coliseum!"

A file of the Philadelphia *United States Military Magazine* has been located by the present editor. It contains selections believed to be Poe's, but nothing is signed with his name. A Poe couplet has been discovered in the last issue of the *Broadway Journal* for January 3, 1846, by Mr. Thomas Ollive Mabbott. It reads: —

I thought Kit North a bore — in 1824 —
I find the thought alive — in 1845.

A translation of Frederick Spielhagen from *Westermanns Monats-Hefte* on the Poe-Longfellow war by Mr. Carl A. Weyerhauser points out for the first time that Longfellow in his tale called *Kavanagh*, Chapter XX, has a character (Mr. Hathaway) representing Poe, while that of Mr. Churchill represents Longfellow.

II

The following are from *The Yankee and Boston Literary Gazette*, New Series, July–December, 1829, John Neal, Editor: —

"To Correspondents.[1] If E. A. P. of Baltimore — whose lines about *Heaven*, though he professes to regard

[1] September, 1829.

them as altogether superior to anything in the whole range
of American poetry, save two or three trifles referred to, are,
though nonsense, rather exquisite nonsense — would but do
himself justice, he might make a beautiful and perhaps a
magnificent poem. There is a good deal here to justify such a
hope:

> Dim vales and shadowy floods,
> And cloudy-looking woods,
> Whose forms we can't discover
> For the tears that — drip all over.
>   The moonlight
> ————————————————————falls
> Over hamlets, over halls.
> Wherever they may be,
> O'er the strange woods, o'er the sea —
> O'er spirits on the wing,
> O'er every drowsy thing —
> And buries them up quite
> In a labyrinth of light,
> And then how deep! — *Oh deep!*
> *Is the passion of their sleep!*

"He should have signed it, Bah! . . . We have no room for
others."

" To Correspondents [1] Many papers intended for this
number have been put aside for the next, . . . Among others
are Night — The Magician — Unpublished Poetry (being
specimens of a book about to appear at Baltimore)."

" Unpublished Poetry [2] The following passages are
from the manuscript-works of a young author, about to be
published in Baltimore. He is entirely a stranger to us, but
with all their faults, if the remainder of Al Aaraaf and Tamerlane are as good as the body of the extracts here given — to
say nothing of the more extraordinary parts, he will deserve

[1] November, 1829.   [2] December, 1829.

to stand high — very high — in the estimation of the shining brotherhood. Whether he *will* do so however, must depend, not so much upon his worth now in mere poetry, as upon his worth hereafter in something yet loftier and more generous — we allude to the stronger properties of the mind, to the magnanimous determination that enables a youth to endure the present, whatever the present may be, in the hope, or rather in the belief, the fixed, unwavering belief, that in the future he will find his reward. 'I am young,' he says in a letter to one who has laid it on our table for a good purpose, 'I am young — not yet twenty — *am* a poet — if deep worship of all beauty can make me one — and wish to be so in the more common meaning of the word. I would give the world to embody one half the ideas afloat in my imagination. (By the way, do you remember — or did you ever read the exclamation of Shelley about Shakspeare? — "What a number of ideas must have been afloat before such an author could arise!") I appeal to you as a man that loves the same beauty which I adore — the beauty of the natural blue sky and the sunshiny earth — there can be no tie more strong than that of brother for brother — it is not so much that they love one another, as that they both love the same parent — their affections are always running in the same direction — the same channel — and cannot help mingling.

I am and have been, from my childhood, an idler. It cannot therefore be said that

> "I left a calling for this idle trade,
> A duty broke — a father disobeyed" —

for I have no father — nor mother.

I am about to publish a volume of "Poems," the greater part written before I was fifteen. Speaking about "Heaven," [1]

[1] A poem by the author of "Al Aaraaf," mentioned in No. III: 168.

MRS. FRANCES KEELING ALLAN
POE'S FOSTER-MOTHER

the editor of the Yankee says, "He might write a beautiful, if not a magnificent poem" — (the very first words of
encouragement I ever remember to have heard). I am very
certain that as yet I have not written *either* — but that I *can*,
I will take oath — if they will give me time.

The poems to be published are "Al Aaraaf" — "Tamerlane" — one about four, and the other about three hundred
lines, with smaller pieces. "Al Aaraaf" has some good poetry, and much extravagance, which I have not had time
to throw away.[1]

"Al Aaraaf" is a tale of another world — the star discovered by Tycho Brahe, which appeared and disappeared so
suddenly — or rather, it is no tale at all. I will insert an extract, about the palace of its presiding Deity, in which you
will see that I have supposed many of the lost sculptures of
our world to have flown (in spirit) to the star "Al Aaraaf"
— a delicate place, more suited to their divinity.

> Uprear'd upon such height arose a pile
> Of gorgeous columns on th' unburthened air —
> * Flashing, from Parian marble, that twin-smile
> Far down upon the wave that sparkled there,
> And nursled the young mountain in its lair:
> Of molten stars their pavement — such as fall
> Thro' the ebon air — besilvering the pall
> Of their own dissolution while they die —
> Adorning, then, the dwellings of the sky;
> A dome by linked light [2] from Heaven let down,
> Sat gently on these columns as a crown;
> A window of one circular diamond there

---

[1] This will remind the reader of the following anecdote. Your sermon was too
long sir — why did n't you make it shorter? *I had n't time.* — [Editor's Note.]

* Alluding to a prior part.

[1] The idea of linked light is beautiful ; but, the moment you *read* it aloud, the
beauty is gone. To say link-ed light would be queer enough, notwithstanding
Moore's "wreath-ed shell "; but to say link'd-light would spoil the rhythm.
[Editor's Note.]

Looked out above into the purple air,
And rays from God shot down that meteor chain
And hallow'd all the beauty twice again,
Save when, between th' Empyrean, and that ring,
Some eager spirit flapp'd a dusky wing:
But, on the *pillars*, seraph eyes have seen
The dimness of this world: that grayish green
That nature loves the best for Beauty's grave,
Lurked in each cornice — round each architrave —
And every sculptur'd cherub thereabout
That from his marble dwelling ventured [1] out,
Seemed earthly in the shadow of his niche —
Archaian statues in a world so rich?
Friezes from Tadmor and Persepolis —
From Balbec and the stilly, clear abyss —
Of beautiful Gomorrah! — oh! the wave
Is now upon thee — but too late to save!
Far down within the crystal of the lake
Thy swollen pillars tremble — and so quake
The hearts of many wanderers who look in
Thy luridness of beauty — and of sin.

Another —

— Silence is the voice of God —
Ours is a world of words: quiet we call
"Silence" — which is the merest word of all.
Here Nature speaks — and ev'n ideal things
Flap shadowy sounds from visionary wings;
But ah! not so, when in the realms on high,
The eternal voice of God is moving by,
And the red winds are withering in the sky!

From Tamerlane —

The fever'd diadem on my brow
I claimed and won usurpingly:
Hath not the same fierce heirdom given
Rome to the Cæsar — this to me?

[1] The word in the original was *peered :* we have changed it for the reason stated above. — [Editor's Note.]

The heritage of a kingly mind
And a proud spirit, which hath striven
Triumphantly with human-kind.

* * * *

On mountain soil I first drew life,
    The mists of the Taglay have shed
    Nightly their dews upon my head;
And, I believe, the winged strife
And tumult of the headlong air
Hath nestled in my very hair.

* * * *

So late from Heaven, that dew, it fell.
    Mid dreams of one unholy night,
Upon me with the touch of Hell —
    While the red flashing of the light
From clouds that hung, like banners, o'er,
Seem'd then to my half-closing eye
The pageantry of monarchy;
And the deep trumpet-thunder's roar
Came hurriedly upon me telling
Of human battle (near me swelling).

* * * *

The rain came down upon my head
Unshelter'd, and the heavy wind
Was giantlike — so thou, my mind!
It was but man, I thought, who shed
Laurels upon me — and the rush —
The torrent of the chilly air
Gurgled within my ear the crush
Of empires — with the captive's prayer;
The hum of suitors, and the tone
Of flattery round a sovereign-throne.

* * * *

Young Love's first lesson is the heart:
    For mid that sunshine and those smiles,
When, from our little cares apart,
    And laughing at her girlish wiles,
I 'd throw me on her throbbing breast,
    And pour my spirit out in tears,

There was no need to speak the rest —
  No need to quiet any fears
Of her — who ask'd no reason why,
But turned on me her quiet eye.

Tamerlane dying —

Father! I firmly do believe —
  I know — for Death, who comes for me
From regions of the blest afar,
(Where there is nothing to deceive)
  Hath left his iron gate ajar;
And rays of truth you cannot see
Are flashing through Eternity —
I do believe that Eblis hath
A snare in every human path;
Else how when in the holy grove
I wandered of the idol, Love,
Who daily scents his snowy wings
With incense of burnt offerings
From the most undefiled things —
Whose pleasant bowers are yet so riven
Above with trelliced rays from Heaven
No mote may shun — no tiniest fly
The lightning of his eagle eye.
How was it that Ambition crept
  Unseen, amid the revels there,
Till, growing bold, he laugh'd and leapt
  In the tangles of Love's brilliant hair?

Passage from the minor poems.

If my peace hath flown away
In a night — or in a day —
In a vision — or in none —
Is it therefore the less gone?
I am standing mid the roar
Of a weatherbeaten shore,
And I hold within my hand
Some particles of sand —

How few! and how they creep
Through my fingers to the deep!
My early hopes? — No — they
Went gloriously away,
Like lightning from the sky
At once — and so will I."

Having allowed our youthful writer to be heard in his own behalf, — what more can we do for the lovers of genuine poetry? Nothing. They who are judges will not need more; and they who are not — why waste words upon them? We shall not.

III

MYTHICAL POE POEMS

Quite a number of mythical Poe poems have been published. The three widest circulated of such poems are "The Fire Legend," "Leonainie," and "Kelah."

The following named pamphlet written in heroic couplets and comprising nine hundred and fifty lines and signed Lavante has also been reprinted with an effort to show that Poe was the author: "The Poets and Poetry of America. A *Satire*. Philadelphia William S. Young — No. 173 Race Street 1847."

IV

LETTERS RELATING TO POE

A collection of eight autograph letters of Thomas W. White, proprietor of the *Southern Literary Messenger*, written to Lucian Minor (at one time associated with him on the *Messenger*), during Poe's first year with the magazine, have never been published. They serve to throw new light on Poe's connections with the *Messenger* during his early career in Richmond, Virginia.

(1) *A. L. S.*, 1 p., 4to.

RICHMOND, *August* 18, 1835.

I have, my dear sir, been compelled to part with Mr. Sparhawk as regular editor. . . . He will, however, continue to assist me. Mr. Poe is here also. He tarries one month and will aid me all that lies in his power.

(2) *A. L. S.*, 2 pp., 4to.

RICHMOND, *September* 8, 1835.

Poe is now in my employ — not as editor. He is unfortunately rather dissipated — and therefore I can place very little reliance upon him. His disposition is quite amiable. He will be some assistance to me in proof-reading — at least I hope so.

(3) *A. L. S.*, 2 pp., 4to.

RICHMOND, *September* 21, 1835.

Poe has flew the track already. His habits were not good. He is in addition a victim of melancholy. I should not be at all astonished to hear that he had been guilty of suicide.

(4) *A. L. S.*, 3 pp., 4to.

RICHMOND, *October* 1, 1835.

I have just seen Mr. Heath. He thinks he can manage the autography for me. He proposes striking out Cooper's and Irving's names. I will not put the article in till I hear from you. Give me your candid opinion of it. Poe is its author.

(5) *A. L. S.*, 1 p., 4to.

RICHMOND, *October* 20, 1835.

Mr. Poe, who is with me again, read (your address) over by copy with great care. He is very much pleased with it —

in fact he passes great encomiums upon it to me, and intends noticing it under the head of Reviews.

(6) *A. L. S.*, 1 p., small folio.

RICHMOND, *October* 24, 1835.

Suppose you send me a modest paragraph, mentioning . . . the paper is now under my own editorial management, assisted by several gentlemen of distinguished literary attainments. You may introduce Mr. Poe's name as amongst those engaged to contribute for its columns — taking care not to say as editor.

(7) *A. L. S.*, 3 pp., 4to.

RICHMOND, *November* 23, 1835.

You are altogether right about the Leslie critique. Poe has evidently shown himself no lawyer — whatever else he may be.

(8) *A. L. S.*, 2 pp. 4to.

RICHMOND, *December* 25, 1835.

All the critical notices are from the pen of Poe — who, I rejoice to tell you, still keeps from the Bottle.

There is also among the collection a letter addressed to Lucian Minor altogether in Poe's autograph, but signed by Thomas W. White.

V

THE ELLIS–ALLAN PAPERS [1]

New light is thrown upon the life of Edgar Allan Poe by letters and documents; also original manuscripts in the handwriting of the poet, to be found among the Ellis-Allan papers, deposited in the Library of Congress at Washington. The collection consists of some four hundred and forty-two portfolios, and volumes of office books and letters of an old Richmond, Virginia, firm. John Allan, Poe's foster-father, was a member of the firm until near the time of his death in 1834. His executor, James Galt, has left the statement through his son, Major John Allan Galt, that John Allan, previous to taking into his home a second wife, packed all his first wife's personal letters and papers, as well as his own, into a trunk and stowed it away in the establishment of Ellis & Allan. James Galt afterwards removed this trunk and contents to his home in Fluvanna County, Virginia, where the younger Galt had gone over them. From his recollections there were more unpublished letters of Poe's than are now deposited with the Valentine Museum at Richmond, Virginia. The second Mrs. Allan had later access to these papers and took away mainly all the Poe letters, upon the margins of which her husband had written caustic comments, in answer to Poe's own arguments, as well as other Allan family letters, in some of which there were references to Poe's early trip to Scotland. The Poe letters taken away were recalled, as touching largely about financial assistance given to, and sought after by Poe. The letters in the Valen-

[1] Acknowledgments are due Miss Mary E. Phillips, Mr. Gaillard Hunt and Mr. J. C. Fitzpatrick for research assistance among the Ellis-Allan papers in the Library of Congress. Extracts from these papers by the writer were published in the New York *Nation*, July 18, 1912, and January 27, 1916.

tinc Museum are thought to number about thirty, if they have all that were taken by Mrs. Allan, while nearly a dozen more were left in the trunk. A few of those left were addressed to the first Mrs. Allan, and couched in the most passionate terms of an affectionate son. The Ellis-Allan papers were long in the possession of Colonel Thomas H. Ellis, a son of a member of the old firm. He furnished abstracts from them to Professor G. E. Woodberry, who made the first reference to them in his revised Life of Poe. After the death of Colonel Ellis the papers were offered for sale. I purchased books, newspapers and other effects belonging to the old firm, but the bulk of the material went to the Library of Congress as economic papers. There still remain in private hands, however, important personal papers of a similar nature to some of those already discovered about Poe in the Ellis-Allan papers at Washington, and having reference to the poet's earlier career. I have talked with one most familiar with these letters and papers, and know their present whereabouts, but the owner does not feel that the time has yet arrived to allow an examination of them. A letter written by Poe to the Mills Nursery of Philadelphia, mentioned in the memoir to this volume, and returned to John Allan, as well as letters from Poe to Allan, bitterly denouncing his foster-father for bad treatment, are all missing from the collection of the papers in Washington. While Colonel Ellis has stated that he destroyed some of the papers — probably from a kind feeling for the Allan family — yet there is a possibility that some part of them still exist, and may come to light later, with other Poe matters.

Poe in his youth spent much of his time about the Ellis & Allan place of business, which is shown in an illustration elsewhere in this volume. The building, as well as that of the *Southern Literary Messenger* adjoining, were condemned in the fall of the year 1916, and have both been taken down. The material, however, has been saved and arrangements are in process to have a reconstructed building of the old Messenger architectural type erected, as a National Poe Museum.

Poe was employed at the Ellis & Allan concern just after his return from college early in the year 1827. James Galt in his recollections of Poe now gives the first and only contemporaneous account of Poe for this period as follows: "Poe was employed in the Ellis & Allan establishment as a clerk in charge of dry goods. He never had much heart in his work, and John Allan frequently had occasion to find fault, and censure him for inattention to business. During the early years of the firm they handled popular London periodicals, as well as sheet music. In 1827 while that branch of the business was being gradually curtailed, because other competing houses had begun to make more of a specialty in that line, still the firm carried a considerable assortment of leading periodicals and songs. Poe's fondness for the upper floor of the building where these literary matters were kept was remarked upon long before he left Richmond for college, and it was there that he spent most of his time when he returned, whenever the vigilant eyes of John Allan were not upon him. Poe was fond of music, having both a musical and cultivated voice, and in the earlier years sang frequently; but after his return from college showed less vivacity, and sang fewer of his favorite songs. It was generally known among his associates that Poe had poetry he expected to have published in a book, and that some pieces had already appeared in newspapers. He was shy about reciting, or discussing his own poetry, but was familiar with the verse of the popular poets, and occasionally would recite some favorite poem to those about the Ellis & Allan store."

James Galt recalled Poe as a lad of uncommon good appearance, who attracted general attention wherever he went; that his manners were always cheerful and gay, and although at times reserved, nothing of a morose character was observed in him, until after his return from college. He was known to drink-wine and toddies at home, but no excessive appetite for liquor was noticed. Like John Allan, James Galt did not censure Poe's faults at college so much for drinking, as he did gambling, and what he further regarded as a lack of proper respect and obedience on Poe's part for his patron John Allan. It was his impression that Poe was of an impatient disposition from his infancy, being always fond of a change of scene and excitement. He believed that Poe was fully imbued in his early youth with an idea that he would one day become a great writer, and was impatient to have his writings published, for a try to become famous. It was James Galt's opinion that in order to seek his fortune, and reach London or some great literary centre, Poe had run away from his home in the year 1827.

The name of Poe has not been found on any pay roll of the Ellis & Allan firm, which is taken as a further proof of the parsimony shown by Allan towards Poe, who doubtless received his sole pay in board and lodgings. An early reference to Poe in the Ellis-Allan papers is a letter from his aunt Eliza Poe, dated Baltimore (Md.), February 8, 1813, about two years after Poe had been taken into the Allan family. It is addressed to Mrs. Allan, and asks about the welfare of little Edgar. A previous letter from her had met with no response and it would seem that up to that date there had been no intercourse between the two families. Eliza Poe, the writer of this letter, afterwards married Henry Herring. It was her daughter, and Poe's cousin Elizabeth Herring, to whom Poe made love and wrote verses in her album about the year 1832.

A letter from John Allan to Charles Ellis of May 14, 1813, contains the information that "Edgar has caught the whooping caugh." There are small tailor bills during the year 1813–14, for cutting suits for Edgar. A charge of $2, on May 3, 1815, is for making a suit of clothes for Edgar. There is a letter from a Richmond schoolmaster named William Ewing, to John Allan, from which it might be surmised that Poe was a pupil with him during the years 1814–15. In Poe's tale of "The Narrative of A. Gordon Pym " he says: "He sent me at six years of age to the school of old Mr. Ricketts, a gentleman with only one arm, and of eccentric manners. . . . I staid at his school until I was sixteen when I left for Mr. E. Ronald's academy on the hill." This in a measure tallies with the location of Poe's schools in Richmond and the matter of locality is further clinched by the reference to "on the hill " — a typical Richmond expression in Poe's day for one part of the city. I find that there was a one-armed Richmond school-teacher in Poe's day named "Ricketts," and the poet may possibly have gone to his school, or substituted the name for "Ewing."

A copy of a letter written by John Allan to William Henry Poe, brother of the poet, is dated November 1, 1824. At that date Poe was fifteen years old, a member of the Junior Morgan Riflemen, and very likely knew something of the town, as well as the confessed fault of his foster-father John Allan, whom he stated in after years "treated him with as much kindness as his gross nature admitted." This letter of Allan's to Poe's brother reads: "I have just seen your letter of the 25th ult. to Edgar and am much afflicted, that he has not written you. He has had little else to do; for me he does nothing & seems quite miserable, sulky & ill tempered to all the Family — How we have acted to produce this is beyond my conception; why I have put up so long with his conduct is less wonderful. The boy possesses not a Spark of affection for us, not a particle of gratitude for all my care and kindness towards him. I have given him a much superior Education than ever I received myself. If Rosalie has to relie on any affection from him God in his mercy preserve her — I fear his associates have led him to adopt a line of thinking & acting very contrary to what he possessed in England. I feel proudly the difference between your principles & his, & hence my desire to Stand as I aught to do in your Estimation. Had I done my duty as faithfully to my God as I have to Edgar — then had Death come when he will, had no terrors for me, but I must end this with a devout wish that God may yet bless him & you & that success may crown all your endeavors & between you your poor sister Rosalie may not suffer. At least she is half your Sister & God forbid dear Henry that we should visit upon the living the Errors and frailties of the dead. Believe me Dear Henry we take an affectionate interest in your destinies and our United Prayers will be that the God of Heaven will bless & protect you, rely on him my Brave & excellent Boy, who is willing & ready to save to the uttermost. May he keep you in Danger, preserve you always, is the prayer of your Friend & Servant.''

This letter shows that the strife between John Allan and Poe, which was to end in the latter leaving home a few years later, had now surely started. When Poe's mother died in Richmond John Allan took charge of the few effects she left, including a packet of old letters. Some of these letters are said to have let out a skeleton in the Poe family closet. Poe was known to have had these letters, and at his death they passed to Mrs. Clemm, his aunt and mother-in-law. She hinted of dark family troubles that had worried "Eddie," as she called Poe, but believed that in destroying the letters before she died, all knowledge of the matters had been blotted out.

It is to be noted that Allan was careful to keep a copy of his letter, possibly to show Poe, fearing that he was telling tales in Baltimore, like at home. With Poe's knowledge of Allan's fault it is an impression that Allan held over him his own family secret in order to keep him quiet. This charge of Allan's, if true, might have been the cause for the alleged desertion of Poe's father from the family. The matter alluded to in Allan's letter seems to have been known and talked about by others intimate in the Allan household, and William MacKenzie, a patron of Rosalie Poe, wrongfully accused.

A number of entries and notes among the papers have reference to John Allan's departure on the ship "Lothair" for Europe June 22, 1815, accompanied by his wife, her sister Miss Ann M. Valentine and Edgar. Among the entries is shown the purchase of one "Olive Branch," one "Murray's Reader," and two "Murray's Spellers," all likely intended for Edgar's use on the voyage.

A letter brought back by the pilot boat to Norfolk showed that the water trip had already proved a severe trial to the women folks, but it added, "Ned cares but little about it, poor fellow." Another Allan letter is dated Liverpool, July 29, 1815, giving an account of the trip across the Atlantic, and states that "Edgar was a little sick, but had recovered." A letter of Allan's dated Greenock, September 21, 1815, has in it, "Edgar says, Pa: Say something for me; say I was not afraid coming across the sea." Allan in another letter dated Blake's Hotel, London, October 10, 1815, announces the arrival of the family there on the 7th, by way of Glasgow, Newcastle and Sheffield, also mentioning the attractions of the Scotland trip as "high in all respects."

In a letter written by Allan, dated October 15, 1815, from his residence in Southampton Row, London, the family are represented as "seated before a snug fire in a nice little sitting parlour with Edgar reading a little story book." A pathetic reminder of Poe's earliest childish romance is a message in a letter from his first little sweetheart, Catherine Poitiaux, the god-child of the first Mrs. Allan, mentioned in the memoir to this volume. She said: "Give my love to Edgar and tell him I want to see him very much. I expect Edgar does not know what to make of such a large city as London. Tell him Josephine [Miss Poitiaux's younger sister] and all the children want to see him." In the *Philadelphia Saturday Museum* sketch of Poe's life he had it stated that only a portion of his five years' stay in London was spent at the school of the Rev. Dr. John Bransby. There remain documents to substantiate this. He also attended the boarding school of the Misses Dubourg at 146 Sloan Street, Chelsea, London. In his tale of "The Murders in the Rue Morgue," Poe has a character named Pauline Dubourg. The documents show that he was a pupil there from about April, 1816, until probably early in December, 1817. He was at Bransby's school from the autumn of 1817 until the summer of 1820 when he returned to America, as is also shown by documents. This leaves a hiatus of some months in his school history. The references of Poe to Rev. Dr. John Bransby have been questioned, as no degree of doctor has yet been found. It is presumed that if there was no academical degree for the title, it was erroneously used during Poe's day, and that it was Poe's belief that Bransby was entitled to be called doctor. There are a number of references to "Edgar" and his schooling abroad in Allan's letters, and one dated June 22, 1818, says: "Edgar is both able and willing to receive instructions," which might infer that

Poe's earlier dispositions in these respects were not so amiable. The papers show that Poe with the family arrived at New York on July 21, 1820, after a passage of thirty-six days, and reached Richmond, Virginia, on the 2d of August following.

There are bills for Edgar's schooling at Richmond to both Masters Joseph H. Clarke and William Burke during the years 1821–24. The few charges for money given to Poe in his youth warrant the belief that Allan's allowances were always restricted. There are entries for less than a dozen small amounts for postage charged against both Poe and his sister Rosalie. In January, 1825, $8.50 is charged for "Edgar's clothes."

There remain letters and bills to substantiate the charge made that Allan's allowances to Poe at college were inadequate for his needs. There are also other bills besides "debts of honor" Allan refused to pay, among them a bill from S. Leitch, Jr., for haberdashery amounting to $68.46. Two letters from G. W. Spotswood dated in April and May, 1827, are addressed to Allan, urging settlement of a bill for servant attendance to Poe's room at the University of Virginia; another letter from E. G. Crump of March 25, 1827, relates to money matters not a debt of honor. It is addressed to Poe and was evidently received by Allan after Poe had left Richmond on his ocean trip towards Europe. The letter is endorsed on the back, presumably by Allan, "To E. A. Poe, alias Henri Le Rennét." This is thought to have been the name Poe used on his first trip from Richmond in the year 1827. It should seem that Allan about the time of the receipt of this letter had in some manner learned of Poe's whereabouts, or had seen one of his first letters written to Mrs. Allan. In a copy of a letter from Allan to his sister in Scotland dated March 27th, he wrote: "I am thinking Edgar has gone to sea to seek his fortune." There is a signed order in the handwriting of John Allan dated March 4, 1828, as follows: "Mr. Ellis. Please to furnish Edgar A. Poe with a suit of clothes, 3 pair socks, or thread Hose. McCrery will make them, also a pair of suspenders, and Hat & knife, pair of gloves." An entry in the Ellis Journal under date of March 3, 1829, is against John Allan. Pr. order to "E.A.P." for just about what the preceding order called for, or the palpable error in the date of Allan's order might make it appear as if Poe had been in Richmond during the year 1828. In the Journal entry it is also further shown that the clothes were eventually made by McCrery. Allan was no doubt disturbed by the death of his wife and wrote the year date of 1828 by mistake. It has been stated that Poe arrived in Richmond after the funeral of his foster-mother, Mrs. Allan, who died February 28, 1829. It is mentioned in an official army letter that Poe was granted a leave of absence about this period, but the record has not been found. The testimony of James Galt, however, now clears up this matter, and what he tells is borne out by the burial records of Mrs. Allan. James Galt stated that "Poe was at the funeral, and that the final burial was delayed until his arrival in Richmond. It was the dying wish of Mrs. Allan that she take Poe once again in her arms before she died, and that in the event she passed away before his arrival, that she would not be buried until he saw her." The scene of Poe's arrival at the house is depicted as most harrowing, as well as great sorrow shown afterwards by Poe at his foster-mother's grave in Shockoe Cemetery.

Among other books at one time with the Ellis-Allan effects, now in my possession, is a large day-book containing the transactions of Pumfrey & Fitzwhylsown, old-time stationers and bookbinders of Richmond, Virginia, dating from April, 1804, to August, 1805. This contains interesting early items, among them one, dated April 12, 1804: "John W. Green (Comedian) To half binding a book of playbills, 4/6"; another of June 27, same year, is "Mr. Hopkins, (Comedian), To Black lead pencil, /1." These entries as well as the fact of the volume being among the Ellis-Allan effects, led me to believe that the book must have been the property of Poe. It looked like an effort on the part of Poe, mentioned by him later to Judge R. W. Hughes, to trace his own early history. That like his brother, William Henry Poe, he knew little concerning the career or final end of his father, David Poe, Jr., seems evident, for while he had possession of his mother's letters and papers, he had not so much as an autograph of his father's. This is shown by an unpublished manuscript letter written by Poe to Joseph H. Hedges, dated Philadelphia, November 16, 1843, as follows: "I presume the request you make, in your note of the 14th, has reference to my grandfather Gen. David Poe, and not to my father David Poe, Jr. I regret to say, however, that, owing to peculiar circumstances, I have in my possession no autograph of either." The entries about the "Green Players" in the old day-book seemed to be an index to the early career of Poe's father, and further investigation verified this conclusion. It has hitherto been the impression of all Poe's biographers that David Poe, Jr., played upon the Charleston (S.C.) stage about December, 1803, and that he began his theatrical engagement with the "Green Players," including Mrs. Hopkins, his future wife, at Petersburg, Virginia, in November, 1804. The old day-book showed, at least, that the "Green Players" were in Richmond during the year 1804, and from that data I was able to lighten up the dark period in the life of David Poe, Jr., from the spring of 1804 until the following November. It should appear that Poe's father left Charleston at the end of the spring season there, if not earlier, and at once joined the company of the "Green Players." The *Virginia Gazette* of June 30, 1804, has David Poe, Jr., with this company in the cast of "Speed the Plow," as "Hewey," and the same paper of July 25 following gives him in the play of the "Heir at Law" in the character of "Henry Moreland." So it is conclusive that not only the "Green Players," including Mrs. Hopkins, Poe's mother, but his father David Poe, Jr., performed upon the Richmond stage during the year 1804. This is the earliest found record of Poe's father in Richmond. The theatrical company left Richmond and are on record at Petersburg, November 3–20, 1804. The company were at Norfolk, March 19–June 12 following, and the *Virginia Gazette* of August 28, 1805, states that "Mrs. Hopkins and other members of the Charleston theatre made a one night stop over at Richmond, on the way to the Federal city." There is a recent hint of David Poe, Jr., in Scotland, where it is said that he ran away to America with a pretty blonde married woman named Wilson. The story shows Edgar Allan Poe as, later on, meeting in school at Irvine, Scotland, with a son of this Mrs. Wilson; one of those "wise children who know their own father," and named after the injured husband, William Wilson. This boy is presumed to have been the hero of Poe's later well-known tale called "William Wilson." Mr. R. M. Hogg, of Irvine, Scotland, vouches for the facts, as told to him by the descendants of the Wilson family. I heard previous hints of a runaway escapade of Poe's father, but the woman's name was mentioned as Thomas. A reference to this matter will be found in G. E. Woodberry's revised Life of Poe, vol. i, p. 368. An entry in the Ellis-Allan papers under date of January 8, and another of May 12, 1830, show that Allan rendered assistance to Poe. The later entry was for blankets, probably for Poe's use at the West Point Academy.

Most important among the Ellis-Allan papers are a number of manuscripts in Poe's own hand. As he wrote F. W. Thomas later in life, that nothing could seduce him from the noble profession of literature, these also indicate that his mind at the time was strongly bent towards a career in the world of letters. The documents are browned by age and written upon paper similar to that used by the firm of Ellis & Allan about the year 1827.

A manuscript entirely in Poe's autograph called "Hope," is copied from Goldsmith's "Song from the Oratorio of the Captivity." This should show the trend of Poe's thought at the time it was written, and its influence upon his later writings. Another manuscript is a copy of an early song called "Ally Croaker." In this song Poe may have gained some of his later conceptions of the repetend in his poetry. The idea in these lines of a pawned coat losing a lady love, with some gambling and drinking episodes, show a parody on Poe's own self about the time they were copied. In them he also shows an early fondness for reconstructing verse to suit his own taste, having made alterations from the original construction of the song. The original song Poe copied from was probably found by him among the early collection, then in the possession of the firm of Ellis & Allan.

On a strip of paper, much in his usual later manner, and in a handwriting closely approximating his well-known later day autograph, Poe copied verses on "The Burial of Sir John Moore" and "Extract from Byron's Dream." As if he had intended to send the copy of "The Burial of Sir John Moore" to some periodical, Poe headed his paper, "The Soldier's Burial," and wrote the following lines which remain as Poe's first known criticism: "These verses have been often and justly admired as the only original essay on so hackney'd a subject as a Burial which has appeared for a long time —

They are on the burial of Sir John Moore — Much dispute has arisen concerning the writer of this really elegant & original production, Moore, Campbell, Scott & Byron have all been mentioned as the supposed writers. It has since been pretty well ascertained to he Byron — As for the piece itself it is inimitable. The poet — the Patriot, and the man of feeling breathes thro' the whole, and a strain of originality gives zest to this little piece, which is seldom felt on the perusal of others of the same kind."

This criticism tends to show Poe at that period a close reader of the periodical literature of the day, and that he knew this poem had been ascribed to Moore, Campbell and Scott, and finally believed to be Byron's. That he was not aware at the moment that it was written by the Rev. Charles Wolfe is not to be wondered at, for Medwin in his delightful *Journal of the Conversations of Lord Byron* tells of Byron's praise of this gem, and how he himself had thought that it was Byron's own verse. It was only in a later edition of his book that Medwin told of his discovery of the name of the real author.

There has hitherto been much guessing at the sources for Poe's extraordinary learning, which was not only varied, but thorough. In his "Marginalia" notes may be noted the thoughtful man of letters, and in them is also to be detected signs of Poe's own education. It had been supposed that Poe discovered his critical capacity for the first time while engaged on the *Southern Literary Messenger*. The criticism on "The Burial of Sir John Moore," however, shows a knowledge and indications of earlier handling of some necessary critical apparatus in literature. Poe's studies among the periodicals and songs at the Ellis & Allan establishment go far towards establishing conclusive proof, not only of the beginning of his scholastic habit, but his unconscious education in the critical line, from the mere love of it.

There is to be found in the Ellis & Allan firm record among the periodicals kept by them, and such as Poe likely consulted, the London *Critical Review or Annals of Literature*, for the years 1791 to 1803, bound in thirty-nine volumes, and the *Ladies Magazine*, London, for that period, bound in thirty volumes.

On the same strip of paper with the criticism of "The Burial of Sir John Moore," Poe continued the Byron lines. He wrote the caption, "Lord Byron's Last Poem," which he afterwards ran his pen through, and substituted, "Extract from Byron's Dream." He commenced his lines from "Byron's Dream" at the beginning of Canto VI. and followed the text along closely into Canto VII. where it reads,

> A change came over the spirit of his dream.
> The lady of his love — oh, she was changed
> As by the sickness of

Poe stopped right there. It was eighteen years afterwards when Poe in a magazine article on "Byron and Mary Chaworth," wrote the following: "'The Dream,' in which the incident of his parting with her when about to travel, and said to be delineated or at least paralleled, has never been excelled (certainly never excelled by him) in the blended fervor, delicacy, truthfulness and ethereality which sublime and adorn it."

It is the supposition that in writing the early copy of the "Dream" verses Poe likened his own sad love affairs at that time to Byron's, and on a sudden impulse stopped, as appears above, and improvised and wrote on another sheet of paper the original verses, "The Vital Stream," which have now been first collected into his poems in this volume. It is to be lamented that the original manuscript of this poem has disappeared from among the Ellis-Allan papers at the Library of Congress. It is thought that the wind carried it into a waste-paper basket at the library, and that it was destroyed. There is, however, slight hope that it may yet come to light in the collection.

That Poe's poem "An Enigma" appeared anonymously in the Philadelphia *Casket* for May, 1827, bears out the statement of James Galt that Poe's poetry found publication at that period. It should also seem Poe's habit from that year to send out his writings anonymously. As is mentioned in the memoir to this volume, Poe was writing for the Philadelphia newspapers about the year 1832.

There appears without name in the *Philadelphia Saturday Courier* for the year 1832, the following well-known tales by Poe: "Metzengerstein," January 14; "Duc de l'Omelette," March 3; "A Tale of Jerusalem," June 9; "Loss of Breath," entitled "A Decided Loss," November 10, and "Bon-Bon," called "The Bargain Lost," December 1. There also appears in this same paper for October 14, 1843, "Raising the Wind, or Diddling considered as one of the Exact Sciences."

VI

POE IN SCOTLAND [1]

The visits of Poe to Scotland must have left vivid marks of remembrance upon his memory of that classic region of which so many scenes and incidents are sketched with truth and beauty. Poe arrived at Liverpool with the Allan

[1] Acknowledgment is due R. M. Hogg, Esq., of Irvine, Scotland, for valuable assistance in obtaining many facts connected with Poe's trip into Scotland. Some portions of this account of Poe's visits into Scotland by the writer were published in the September, 1916, New York *Bookman*.

family in the latter part of the year 1815, and proceeded at once to Scotland, to visit the Allan relatives. While the visit was partly one of pleasure, Allan was about to establish a branch of his business in London with tobacco as a main staple. He had important trade connections to make in Scotland, besides the pleasure of meeting again with his kinsfolk and wandering about the scenes of his youth.

The first journey was to Irvine, Ayrshire, the birthplace of John Allan, where Poe and the Allan family stopped with a spinster sister of Allan's named Mary Allan. There lived at Irvine at that time other near relatives of Allan's named "Galt." Among them was James Galt, then under fifteen years of age, who afterwards came to America with the Allan family when they returned home in 1820. Young Galt was a relative of William Galt of Richmond, an uncle to John Allan, who assisted the Ellis & Allan firm financially, and from whom Allan later obtained a large legacy. The uncle, as is shown by his letters among the Ellis-Allan papers, was not in accord with Allan's conduct in London, and it looks as if James Galt was about the London business establishment to keep him fully informed of Allan's doings. After James Galt's arrival in Richmond, this uncle took good care for his future. He finally settled on the James River above Richmond, in Virginia, and was the progenitor of the well-known family of Goldsboroughs of Maryland.

He lived to a ripe old age, and a son named after Allan, Major John Allan Galt, left interesting reminiscences of his father, which throw important new lights upon Poe's early career.

Irvine is a seaport twenty-three miles from Glasgow, and at the time of Poe's visit differed somewhat from the present day. There is an illustration showing the town about 1780, and in it is to be seen the dwelling where John Allan was born, while opposite is a house where Henry Eckford, the constructor of the American Navy of 1812, also first saw the light.

At the head of the old Kirkgate was the ancient grammar school where Allan was educated, it is said, with his relative John Galt the novelist, and Henry Eckford. The school was a continuation of the Pre-Reformation school in connection with the church. The old school building was taken down in 1816, and a new academy erected. There is a possibility that Poe had the old Irvine school building in his mind while writing his description of the ancient school in his tale of "William Wilson," or at least made a composite picture of it with his recollections of the school at Stoke Newington, England, better known as "Bransby's."

It was John Allan's early intention to have Poe remain at this school while abroad for his education, but his wife demurred and Poe was also opposed to being left so far away from his foster-mother.

In the same square with the Allan house in Irvine, was "Templeton's" book-shop, where Burns the poet delighted to browse among old sheets of song. It was in the year 1781 that Burns went to Irvine to learn flax dressing, and the old shop stands within a stone's throw of where John Allan was born. The well-known incidents in John Galt's "Annals of the Parish" are taken from the old town of Irvine. The Irvine burial-ground is situated on a rise of a bank of the river Irvine, and alongside the parish church. There all the Allan ancestors are buried. The Allan section adjoins that of "Dainty Davie," the friend of Burns. Here Poe could have acquired much of his early impressions of a grave-yard, since the death of his own mother. The first grave-yard he probably ever entered was the historic St. John's at Richmond, Virginia, where Patrick Henry delivered his patriotic address, and where it is now definitely ascertained Poe's mother is buried. The Irvine church-yard was the second, and the third, "Shockoe Cemetery," at Richmond, Virginia, where pleasant legends relate that he kept vigils with the spirit of his first departed "Helen." It is certain that Poe was fond of visiting this latter grave-yard, and that he was not only about the grave of Mrs. Stanard, his "Helen," but also that of Mrs. Allan, his foster-mother, who in reality may have been the original of Poe's "Helen."

"Of all melancholy topics," Poe once asked himself, "what according to the universal understanding of mankind, is the most melancholy?" "Death!" was the obvious reply.

There was much about the old Scotch kirk-yard at Irvine to inspire Poe with awe, and with his love for the odd, the rhyming tombstones, and the "dregy," or lengthy funeral services must have left lasting impressions on his mind. The epitaphs on the tombstones there are most original and in the olden time the grammar school scholars are said to have been required to write some of them out for their examinations. In Irvine near the printing office of the erratic Maxwell Dick, was a house where Dr. Robinson, the poet preacher, lodged. Here one day the well-known writer De Quincey came from Glasgow to visit him, but unfortunately the genial doctor was out. The canny Scot's landlady took De Quincey, with a suspicious looking volume under his arm, to be a book-canvasser, and would not permit him to come in and await the doctor's return. De Quincey in high dudgeon returned to the station, and went back to Glasgow. On his way to and from the station De Quincey had to pass the house where Poe stopped.

In this connection it might be recalled that Poe later on proved an admirer of De Quincey, whose declamatory interpolations may be detected in his writings, especially in the

THE FOWLDS HOUSE, KILMARNOCK, SCOTLAND,
WHERE POE STAYED

WHERE POE WENT TO SCHOOL, AT IRVINE, SCOTLAND

tale of "William Wilson." While at Irvine Poe lived at the Bridgegate house. It was a two-story tenement dwelling owned by the Allan family, and taken down about thirty years ago to make room for a street improvement. After leaving Irvine, Poe with the Allans went to Kilmarnock, about seven miles distant from Irvine. He remained there about two weeks and stopped with another of Allan's sisters named Agnes, but called Nancy, who married a nurseryman named Allan Fowlds. The site of the old nursery is now Fowlds, Clark and Prince Streets. The house in which Poe lodged was a small affair and stood on the present site of the building occupied by the *Kilmarnock Standard*. A house opposite was occupied by a family named Gregory, who perfectly remembered the visit of John Allan and his family, with little Edgar Poe. In the rear of the Fowlds house ran the grounds of "Kilmarnock House," the residence of Lord Kilmarnock, executed for his share in the '45 Rebellion. There stood nearby a large grove of trees and a beautiful walkway where the lord's widow passed much of her time after his death. Here is also what was once called the "Ghost walk," and there the lord's widow might be seen after sundown in her pensive perambulations, alone, and sometimes in company with her murdered husband. No doubt Poe had heard of this incident, and perchance looked himself for what they called the "allagrugous bawsy-broon," or the ghastly, grim hobgoblin.

Nelson Street extended by a crooked lane to the cross of Kilmarnock, in the croon of which was the shop where Burns' first edition of his poems was issued. The town exhibits relics of Burns, and was formerly noted for its manufacture of "Kilmarnock cowles."

One end of Nelson Street led to the old Irvine road, and a number of visits to and from Irvine were made by Allan during his stay, on which occasions Poe invariably accompanied him. The old red riding carts then abounded about Irvine and Kilmarnock, with their creaking wheels, and are said to have had a special attraction for Poe. He was most contented in one of them, sitting alongside the driver, usually attired in coarse woolen cloth "green duffle apron," and thick nap "red kilmarnock cap." Close to the Fowlds house in Kilmarnock lived William Anderson, an intimate neighbor of the family. His son James Anderson died December 26, 1887, aged 84 years. In early life he was an accountant in the Union Bank and for a long period auditor for the corporation of Kilmarnock, as well as chairman of the Bellfield Trust. He had vivid recollections of Poe's visit to Kilmarnock, and spoke with pride of having played in the streets of the town with Poe. He recalled Poe as "much petted by the Allans, and a 'carmudgeon,' or forward, quick-witted boy, but very self-willed."

Poe went from Kilmarnock with the Allans to Greenock, situated on the Clyde. From there he went to Glasgow, thence to Edinburgh, and also stopped at Newcastle and Sheffield, landing with the Allans at London October 7, 1815.

There are many persons now living in Irvine who have had the statement handed down to them from their ancestors that Edgar Allan Poe attended the old Irvine grammar school. This is now confirmed by the reminiscences of James Galt, although the stay of Poe there must have been brief. It was Allan's intention to leave Poe at the school when he visited the town, but the women members of the family as well as Poe objected and a compromise was effected by allowing Poe to finish out the Scotland pleasure trip, with an understanding that he was later to accompany James Galt back from London, to the Irvine school.

The exact time of this second trip is not mentioned, but

there are several gaps in Poe's school record. It is presumed that the visit must have been towards the close of the year 1815. James Galt said that there were pleadings from the women folks as well as Poe, of "not to go," when the time came to depart for Scotland. It was the opinion, however, that Poe would be better satisfied after settling down there and out of the sight of the home folks. The start on the part of Poe was unwilling, and Galt said he kept up "an unceasing fuss all the way over." His aunt Mary, as he called Miss Allan, sent him to the school, but there he sulked, and no manner of coaxing or threats could induce him to attempt any studies.

At Miss Allan's home he talked boldly about returning back to England alone. She feared that he might try to carry out this threat and had young Galt remain at her home on guard over Poe. He slept in the same room with Poe in the Bridgegate house at Irvine; was impressed with Poe's old-fashioned talk for one so young, and like Miss Allan he believed that if Poe had not been restrained he would have attempted the trip back to England alone. Galt said Poe's self-reliance and total absence of fear impressed him then, and up to the time he left John Allan's home.

Poe showed no inclinations to become satisfied with his surroundings at Irvine, and in many ways made it unpleasant for aunt Mary Allan; so much so that she finally packed up his "duds," as Galt said, and sent him back to London.

This Scotland and other school episodes in Poe's life possibly account for his own statements of unhappy schoolboy days.

When Poe published his tale, the "M. Valdemar Case," a druggist at Stonehaven, Scotland, named A. Ramsay, to make sure the story was true wrote a letter to Poe. This letter of Ramsay's to Poe has been published, but no reply of Poe's has appeared in book form, until now, although a mention and its date was made in the first edition of this volume. A nephew of Ramsay's still occupies the old Stonehaven warehouse. He had many of his relative's letters, but none from Poe. The search, however, was continued among other relatives, and Poe's letter finally brought to light. It is interesting in connection with the story of Poe's visits to Scotland. The letter reads: —

NEW YORK, December 30, '46.

DEAR SIR:

Hoax *is* precisely the word suited to M. Valdemar Case. The story appeared originally in the "American Review," a monthly magazine published in this city. The London papers, commencing with the "Morning Post" and the "Popular Record of Science," took up the theme. The article was generally copied in England and is now circulating in France. Some few persons believe it — but *I* don't — and don't you.

Very Resp'y, yr. Ob St.

EDGAR A. POE

P.S. I have some relatives, I think, in Stonehaven, of the name of Allan, who again are connected with the Allan's and Galt's of Kilmarnock. My name is Edgar *Allan* Poe. Do you know any of them? If so, and it would not put you to too much trouble, I would like it as a favor if you could give me some account of the family.

The postscript to this letter written at so late a date reads a bit odd. It is said, however, that Poe felt bitterly to the end that Allan should have brought him up and educated him as an only child, until he had reached the advanced age of fifteen years, and then turn suddenly against him and make him feel as a menial instead of a member of the family. The

STREET IN IRVINE, SHOWING BRIDGEGATE HOUSE, WHERE POE STAYED,
AT EXTREME RIGHT

relatives of Allan in Scotland have stated that Allan, while on his visit to them, made the statement that after providing for his wife and Edgar it was his intention to leave the remainder of his estate to relatives in Scotland. Poe in the *Philadelphia Saturday Museum* sketch of the year 1843 had it stated that Allan made it a practice in the early days to tell every one that he intended to make him his heir. In a letter to Poe's brother Allan mentioned doing "his duty towards Edgar," but near his death he is said to have had doubts in the matter.

VII

POE'S REVISION OF OTHERS' POETRY

The F. W. Thomas *Recollections of E. A. Poe* states that the poetry written in part, and revised by Poe for others in his lifetime, if known and collected, would make a respectable volume. Mrs. Shew is the only contemporary of Poe's, who has given any hint of collaboration with Poe in the making of any poetry. But Mrs. Shew had no poetical ambitions, or, perhaps, like Chivers and the others, she might have claimed "The Bells" as her own production.

The letters of Poe to Mrs. Whitman, at least, show that she sought his criticisms and corrections of her poetry. It remains a question, however, as to how many of her poems besides "To Arcturus" Poe revised. There is also little way to find out now what literary aid Poe rendered Mrs. Ellet, Mrs. Osgood, and the balance of the literary coterie who surrounded and flattered him in order to obtain his favors.

The most persistent of the female poets who followed Poe about and endeavored by her arts to gain his assistance to help her mount the pinnacles of Parnassus was Mrs. Lewis. Her baptismal name was "Sarah Anna," but she adopted that of "Estelle" as more æsthetic. Poe wrote an enigma to her as "Sarah Anna," but afterwards, to please her, called her "Stella."

' There remains a note of Poe's, and his corrections of some poetry of "Stella's," which forms a striking illustration of literary labors performed by Poe, into which the general reader has had little insight. In returning Mrs. Lewis a manuscript copy of her lines entitled "The Prisoner of Perotè," Poe wrote her as follows: —

"DEAR MRS. LEWIS,

Upon the whole I think this the most spirited poem you have written. If I were you, I would retain *all* the prose prefix. You will observe that I have taken the liberty of making some *suggestions* in the body of the poem — the force of which, I think, would be *much* increased by the introduction of an occasional *short* line, for example: —

> Hurtled by the blast.
> Sadly fell his eye.
> Heard her shrieks of wo.
> As now they flock to Rome.
> And to Palestine.
> Woke him from his dream.
> And God will guide thy bark.
> And the sun will shine.
> Is a throne to me.
> Pours a Paradise.
> Sheds its holy light.
> Will I cling to thee.

These short lines should be indented — as for instance: —

> So, to cheer thy desolation,
>   Will I cling to thee."

The alterations shown in the following poem are Poe's and although evidently made hastily they make an improvement in the verses.

THE PRISONER OF PEROTÈ

In the Prison of Perotè
Silently the Warrior sate,
With ∧ His eye bent sadly downward,
∧Like one stricken sore by Fate;
Broken visions of his Glory
~~Before his Spirit passed,~~ *Quick before his spirit passed*
Like clouds ~~across the Heaven~~ *Athwart the summer*
Hurtled ∧ ∧~~Driven onward~~ by the Blast. *Heaven.*
sullen ∧ The booming of the Cannon,
And the clash of blade and spear —
"Death — death, unto the Tyrant!"
Still were ringing in his ear.
Much he sorrowed for the people,
For whose weal he fain would die —
On the Tablets of the Future,
Sadly ~~bent his mental eye.~~ *fell his eye*
There he saw his weeping country
Close beleaguered by the foe;
He saw her ~~chained and bleeding,~~ *faint and bleeding*
~~He~~ heard her shrieks of Wo;
ward ∧ From the East and ~~from~~ the Westward
He ∧ ~~There~~ beheld the Pilgrims come
~~To ponder o'er her Ruins,~~ *To muse upon her ivied ruins*
As now they flock to Rome;

. . . .

Well he weighed the fate of Nations,
Well ⟩ ∧Their glory and their shame,
Well ∧ ∧The fleetness of all Power,
Well ∧ ∧The emptiness of Fame;
Well ∧ ∧The wasting wrecks of Empires
∧~~That choke Time's rapid stream,~~ *Choking Time's*
Till Beauty with ~~Till Beauty's gentle whispers~~ *impatient stream*
her gentle Woke him from his dream. —
whispers

NOTES
AND
VARIORUM TEXT
OF THE POEMS

NOTES AND VARIORUM TEXT

OF THE POEMS

THE sources of the text for E. A. Poe's poems are the editions published by him in 1827, 1829, 1831, and 1845; the manuscripts of poems in
Poe's own hand; copy of 1829 Poems with corrections made in Poe's
hand; the magazines and newspapers to which he contributed poems,
viz. : —

*The Yankee and Boston Literary Gazette ; The Philadelphia Casket ; The
Baltimore Saturday Morning Visiter ; Richmond Southern Literary Mes-
senger ; Godey's Lady's Book ; Baltimore American Museum ; Burton's
Gentleman's Magazine ; Graham's Magazine ; Philadelphia Saturday Mu-
seum ; Philadelphia Saturday Evening Post ; The New York Evening Mirror ;
New York Broadway Journal ; New York Literary Emporium ; New York
American Whig Review ; The London Critic ; New York Missionary Memorial ; New York Literary World ; New York Home Journal ; Sartain's
Union Magazine ; New York Union Magazine ; Boston Flag of Our Union ;
New York Tribune ; Philadelphia Leaflets of Memory ; Richmond Examiner ; Richmond Whig ;* Griswold's 1850 poems and "Poets and Poetry
of America," 1842 and 1855. The manuscript sources superior to the
texts are the J. Lorimer Graham copy of the 1845 poems, with corrections in Poe's hand, and the F. W. Thomas manuscript *Recollections
of E. A. Poe,* with poems contributed to the *Richmond Examiner,* corrected in proof in Poe's hand shortly before his death.

The editions of Poems issued by Poe were: —

1827

TAMERLANE / AND / OTHER POEMS / BY A BOSTONIAN
Young heads are giddy, and young hearts are warm,
And make mistakes for manhood to reform. — COWPER.

Boston./ CALVIN F. S. THOMAS . . . PRINTER / 1827

Collation : Title, p. 1; verso blank, p. 2; Preface, pp. 3–4; TAMER-
LANE, pp. 5–21; verso blank, p. 22; half title, Fugitive Pieces, p. 23;
verso blank, p. 24; Fugitive Pieces, pp. 25–34; half title, Notes, p. 35;

verso blank, p. 36; Notes, pp. 37–40. Contents: Tamerlane ; Fugitive Pieces: To ——; Dreams; Visit of the Dead; Evening Star; Imitation; Communion with Nature; A wilder'd being from my birth; The happiest day — the happiest hour; The Lake; Author's Notes (To Tamerlane).

The volume measures 6.37 by 4.13 inches, and was issued as a pamphlet in yellow covers. Only three copies are known. One is in the British Museum, and the other two are in the library of a New York collector. Mr. R. H. Shepherd made a reprint of the British Museum copy in 1884, with corrections of misprints in a separate list.

The preface reads as follows: "The greater part of the poems which compose this little volume were written in the year 1821–2, when the author had not completed his fourteenth year. They were of course not intended for publication; why they are now published concerns no one but himself. Of the smaller pieces very little need be said: They perhaps savor too much of egotism; but they were written by one too young to have any knowledge of the world but from his own breast.

"In 'Tamerlane' he has endeavored to expose the folly of even *risking* the best feelings of the heart at the shrine of Ambition. He is conscious that in this there are many faults (besides that of the general character of the poems), which he flatters himself he could, with little trouble, have corrected, but unlike many of his predecessors, has been too fond of his early productions to amend them in his *old age.*

"He will not say that he is indifferent as to the success of these Poems — it might stimulate him to other attempts — but he can safely assert that failure will not at all influence him in a resolution already adopted. This is challenging criticism — let it be so. *Nos haec novimus esse nihil.*"

1829

AL AARAAF, / TAMERLANE, / AND / MINOR POEMS / (Rule) BY EDGAR A. POE. / (Rule) BALTIMORE: / HATCH & DUNNING / (Rule) 1829.

Collation: Title, p. 1; verso (copyright secured), p. 2 (in lower right hand corner: Matchett & Woods Printers); p. 3, quotation:

> Entiendes, Fabio, lo que voi deciendo?
> Toma, si, lo entendio: — Mientes, Fabio.

p. 4, blank; p. 5, half title: AL AARAAF; verso, p. 6:

> What has night to do with sleep? — Comus.

p. 7, Dedication:

> Who drinks the deepest? — here 's to him. — CLEAVELAND.

p. 8, blank; p. 9, "A star was discovered by Tycho Brahe which burst forth in a / moment, with a splendor surpassing that of Jupiter — then gradually / faded away and became invisible to the naked eye." p. 10, blank; p. 11, poem, Science; p. 12, blank; pp. 13–21, AL AARAAF, part I.; p. 22, blank; p. 23, half title, AL AARAAF; verso blank, p. 24; pp. 25–38, AL AARAAF, part II.; p. 39, half title, TAMERLANE; p. 40:

ADVERTISEMENT

This poem was printed for publication in Boston, in the year / 1827, but suppressed through circumstances of a private nature.

p. 41, Dedication: TO / JOHN NEAL / THIS POEM / IS RE-SPECTFULLY DEDICATED. / p. 42, blank; pp. 43–54, TAMER-LANE; / p. 55, half title, MISCELLANEOUS POEMS ; p. 56:

> My nothingness — my wants —
> My sins — And my contrition — SOUTHEY E. PERSIS.[1]

> And some flowers — but no bays. — MILTON.

p. 57, poem, Romance; p 58, blank; pp. 59–71, POEMS, numbered 1 to 9. Issued in boards, with tinted paper covering, muslin backs. Size of leaf untrimmed 8.75 by 5.25 inches. One copy in the library of a New York collector has the date 1820, which some think a printer's error, while others are of the opinion that Poe had that date put in on purpose. This was a presentation copy to his cousin Elizabeth (Herring). It also has his corrections in his own hand made for the 1845 edition of his poems. Some copies have the poem "Science" on the unpaged leaf. Some ten or more copies of the volume are known. One is in the New York Public Library, another in the Peabody Institute, Baltimore, and the others mainly in private libraries — five in New York City, one in Chicago, one in Washington, and one in Pittsburg.

1831

POEMS / By / Edgar A. Poe. / (Rule) Tout le Monde a Raison. — Rochefoucault. / (Rule) Second Edition / (Rule) New York: / Published by Elam Bliss. / (Rule) 1831.

Collation: p. 1, half title, Poems; verso blank, p. 2; p. 3, title; p. 4, imprint; p. 5, Dedication, To The U. S. / Corps Of Cadets / This vol-

---

[1] Error for SOUTHEY'S PERSIS.

ume / is Respectfully Dedicated; verso blank, p. 6; p. 7, Contents; verso blank, p. 8; half title, "Letter," p. 9; verso blank, p. 10; p. 11, Quotation; verso blank, p. 12; pp. 13–29, text of letter to Mr. —— ; verso blank, p. 30; p. 31, half title, "Introduction"; verso blank, p. 32; pp. 33–124, POEMS : Helen, Israfel, The Doomed City, Fairy-land, Irene, A Pæan, The Valley Nis, Science, Al Aaraaf, Tamerlane. Size of leaf untrimmed 6.75 by 3.75 inches. Issued in cloth binding. Some copies have the word "The End" on the last leaf. Six copies are known, but there are likely others.

The original form of the 1831 letter,[1] with the *Southern Literary Messenger* variations, follows : —

It has been said that a good critique on a poem may be written by one who is no poet himself. This, according to *your* idea and *mine* of poetry, I feel to be false — the less poetical the critic, the less just the critique, and the converse. On this account, and because there are but few B——'s in the world, I would be as much ashamed of the world's good opinion as proud of your own. Another than yourself might here observe, "Shakespeare is in possession of the world's good opinion, and yet Shakespeare is the greatest of poets. It appears then that the world judge correctly, why should you be ashamed of their favorable judgment?" The difficulty lies in the interpretation of the word "judgment" or "opinion." The opinion is the world's, truly, but it may be called theirs as a man would call a book his, having bought it; he did not write the book, but it is his; they did not originate the opinion, but it is theirs. A fool, for example, thinks Shakespeare a great poet — yet the fool has never read Shakespeare. But the fool's neighbor, who is a step higher on the Andes of the mind, whose head (that is to say, his more exalted thought) is too far above the fool to be seen or understood, but whose feet (by which I mean his every-day actions) are sufficiently near to be discerned, and by means of which that superiority is ascertained, which *but* for them would never have been discovered — this neighbor asserts that Shakespeare is a great poet — the fool believes him, and it is henceforward his *opinion*. This neighbor's own opinion has, in like manner, been adopted from one

[1] Printed, with the following note in the *Southern Literary Messenger* of July, 1836: "Letter To B—— These detached passages form part of the preface to a small volume printed some years ago for private circulation. They have vigor and much originality — but of course we shall not be called upon to endorse all the writer's opinions. — Ed."

above *him*, and so, ascendingly, to a few gifted individuals who kneel around the summit, beholding, face to face, the master spirit who stands upon the pinnacle. * * *

You are aware of the great barrier in the path of an American writer. He is read, if at all, in preference to the combined and established wit of the world. I say established; for it is with literature as with law or empire — an established name is an estate in tenure, or a throne in possession. Besides, one might suppose that books, like their authors, improve by travel — their having crossed the sea is, with us, so great a distinction. Our antiquaries abandon time for distance; our very fops glance from the binding to the bottom of the title-page, where the mystic characters which spell London, Paris, or Genoa, are preciscly so many letters of recommendation. * * *

I mentioned just now a vulgar error as regards criticism. I think the notion that no poet can form a correct estimate of his own writings is another. I remarked before, that in proportion to the poetical talent, would be the justice of a critique upon poetry. Therefore, a bad poet would, I grant, make a false critique, and his self-love would infallibly bias his little judgment in his favor; but a poet, who is indeed a poet, could not, I think, fail of making a just critique. Whatever should be deducted on the score of self-love, might be replaced on account of his intimate acquaintance with the subject; in short, we have more instances of false criticism than of just, where one's own writings are the test, simply because we have more bad poets than good. There are of course many objections to what I say: Milton is a great example of the contrary; but his opinion with respect to the Paradise Regained is by no means fairly ascertained. By what trivial circumstances men are often led to assert what they do not really believe! Perhaps an inadvertent word has descended to posterity. But, in fact, the Paradise Regained is little, if at all, inferior to the Paradise Lost, and is only supposed so to be, because men do not like epics, whatever they may say to the contrary, and reading those of Milton in their natural order, are too much wearied with the first to derive any pleasure from the second.

I dare say Milton preferred Comus to either — if so — justly. * * *

As I am speaking of poetry, it will not be amiss to touch slightly upon the most singular heresy in its modern history — the heresy of what is called very foolishly, the Lake School. Some years ago I might have been induced, by an occasion like the present, to attempt a formal refutation of their doctrine; at present it would be a work of supererogation. The wise must bow to the wisdom of such men as Coleridge and Southey, but being wise, have laughed at poetical theories so prosaically exemplified.

Aristotle, with singular assurance, has declared poetry the most philosophical of all writings;* but it required a Wordsworth to pronounce it the most metaphysical. He seems to think that the end of poetry is, or should be, instruction — yet it is a truism that the end of our existence is happiness; if so, the end of every separate part of our existence — every thing connected with our existence should be still happiness. Therefore the end of instruction should be happiness; and happiness is another name for pleasure; — therefore the end of instruction should be pleasure: yet we see the above mentioned opinion implies precisely the reverse.

To proceed: *ceteris paribus*, he who pleases, is of more importance to his fellow men than he who instructs, since utility is happiness, and pleasure is the end already obtained which instruction is merely the means of obtaining.

I see no reason, then, why our metaphysical poets should plume themselves so much on the utility of their works, unless indeed they refer to instruction with eternity in view; in which case, sincere respect for their piety would not allow me to express my contempt for their judgment; contempt which it would be difficult to conceal, since their writings are professedly to he understood by the few, and it is the many who stand in need of salvation. In such case I should no doubt be tempted to think of the devil in "Melmoth," who labors indefatigably through three octavo volumes to accomplish the destruction of one or two souls, while any common devil would have demolished one or two thousand. * * *

Against the subtleties which would make poetry a study — not a passion — it becomes the metaphysician to reason — but the poet to protest. Yet Wordsworth and Coleridge are men in years; the one imbued in contemplation from his childhood, the other a giant in intellect and learning. The diffidence, then, with which I venture to dispute their authority, would he overwhelming, did I not feel, from the bottom of my heart, that learning has little to do with the imagination — intellect with the passions — or age with poetry. * * *

"Trifles, like straws, upon the surface flow,
He who would search for pearls must dive below,"

are lines which have done much mischief. As regards the greater truths, men oftener err by seeking them at the bottom than at the top; the depth

* Spoudaiotaton kai philosophikotaton genos.   S. L. M. text.

lies in the huge abysses where wisdom is sought — not in the palpable places where she is found. The ancients were not always right in hiding the goddess in a well: witness the light which Bacon has thrown upon philosophy; witness the principles of our divine faith — that moral mechanism by which the simplicity of a child may overbalance the wisdom of a man. (*Poetry above all things is a beautiful painting whose tints to minute inspection are confusion worse confounded, but start boldly out to the cursory glance of the connoisseur.)

We see an instance of Coleridge's liability to err, in his "Biographia Literaria" — professedly his literary life and opinions, but, in fact, a treatise *de omni scibili et quibusdam aliis*. He goes wrong by reason of his very profundity, and of his error we have a natural type in the contemplation of a star. He who regards it directly and intensely sees, it is true, the star, but it is the star without a ray — while he who surveys it less inquisitively is conscious of all for which the star is useful to us below — its brilliancy and its beauty. * * *

As to Wordsworth, I have no faith in him. That he had, in youth, the feelings of a poet I believe — for there are glimpses of extreme delicacy in his writings — (and delicacy is the poet's own kingdom — his *El Dorado*) — but they have the appearance of a better day recollected; and glimpses, at best, are little evidence of present poetic fire — we know that a few straggling flowers spring up daily in the crevices of the (†avalanche).

He was to blame in wearing away his youth in contemplation with the end of poetizing in his manhood. With the increase of his judgment the light which should make it apparent has faded away. His judgment consequently is too correct. This may not be understood, — but the old Goths of Germany would have understood it, who used to debate matters of importance to their State twice, once when drunk, and once when sober — sober that they might not be deficient in formality — drunk lest they should be destitute of vigor.

The long wordy discussions by which he tries to reason us into admiration of his poetry, speak very little in his favor: they are full of such assertions as this — (I have opened one of his volumes at random) "Of genius the only proof is the act of doing well what is worthy to be done, and what was never done before" — indeed! then it follows that in doing what is *un*worthy to be done, or what *has* been done before, n●

* Lines in parenthesis erased from S. L. M. text.
† Glacier in S. L. M. text.

genius can be evinced; yet the picking of pockets is an unworthy act, pockets have been picked time immemorial, and Barrington, the pick-pocket, in point of genius, would have thought hard of a comparison with William Wordsworth, the poet.

Again—in estimating the merit of certain poems, whether they be Ossian's or M'Pherson's, can surely be of little consequence, yet, in order to prove their worthlessness, Mr. W. has expended many pages in the controversy. *Tantæne animis?* Can great minds descend to such absurdity? But worse still: that he may bear down every argument in favor of these poems, he triumphantly drags forward a passage, in his abomination of which he expects the reader to sympathize. It is the beginning of the epic poem * "*Temora*." "The blue waves of Ullin roll in light; the green hills are covered with day; trees shake their dusky heads in the breeze." And this — this gorgeous, yet simple imagery, where all is alive and panting with immortality — this, William Wordsworth, the author of "Peter Bell," has *selected* for his contempt. We shall see what better be. in his own person, has to offer.   Imprimis:

> " And now she 's at the pony's head,
> And now she 's at the pony's tail,
> On that side now, and now on this,
> And almost stifled her with bliss —
> A few sad tears does Betty shed,
> She pats the pony where or when
> She knows not: happy Betty Foy!
> O, Johnny! never mind the Doctor!"

Secondly:

> "The dew was falling fast, the — stars began to blink,
> I heard a voice; it said ——— drink, pretty creature, drink;
> And, looking o'er the hedge, be — fore me I espied
> A snow-white mountain lamb, with a — maiden at its side.
> No other sheep were near, the lamb was all alone,
> And by a slender cord was — tether'd to a stone."

Now, we have no doubt this is all true; we *will* believe it, indeed, we will, Mr. W. Is it sympathy for the sheep you wish to excite? I love a sheep from the bottom of my heart.

But there *are* occasions, dear B———, there are occasions when even Wordsworth is reasonable. Even Stamboul, it is said, shall have an end

* No italics in S. L. M. text.

and the most unlucky blunders must come to a conclusion. Here is an extract from his preface —

"Those who have been accustomed to the phraseology of modern writers, if they persist in reading this book to a conclusion (*impossible!*) will, no doubt, have to struggle with feelings of awkwardness; (ha! ha! ha!) they will look round for poetry (ha! ha! ha! ha!) and will be induced to inquire by what species of courtesy these attempts have been permitted to assume that title." Ha! ha! ha! ha! ha!

Yet let not Mr. W. despair; he has given immortality to a wagon, and the bee Sophocles has transmitted to eternity a sore toe, and dignified a tragedy with a chorus of turkeys. * * *

Of Coleridge I cannot speak but with reverence. His towering intellect! his gigantic power![1] (He is one more evidence of the fact) (To use an author quoted by himself, "J'ai trouvé souvent)[2] que la plupart des sectes ont raison dans une bonne partie de ce qu'elles avancent, mais non pas en ce qu'elles nient," (and to employ his own language,)[3] he has imprisoned his own conceptions by the barrier he has erected against those of others. It is lamentable to think that such a mind should be buried in metaphysics, and, like the Nyctanthes, waste its perfume upon the night alone. In reading [that man's[4]] poetry, I tremble, like one who stands upon a volcano, conscious, from the very darkness bursting from the crater, of the fire and the light that are weltering below.

. . . .

What is Poetry? — Poetry! that Proteus-like idea, with as many appellations as the nine-titled Corcyra! Give me, I demanded of a scholar some time ago, give me a definition of poetry. "Très-volontiers," and he proceeded to his library, brought me a Dr. Johnson, and overwhelmed me with a definition. Shade of the immortal Shakespeare! I imagine to myself the scowl of your spiritual eye upon the profanity of that scurrilous Ursa Major. Think of poetry, dear B——, think of poetry, and then think of — Dr. Samuel Johnson! Think of all that is airy and fairy-like, and then of all that is hideous and unwieldy; think of his huge bulk, the Elephant! and then — and then think of the Tempest — the Midsummer Night's Dream — Prospero — Oberon — and Titania! * * *

A poem, in my opinion, is opposed to a work of science by having, for its *immediate* object, pleasure, not truth; to romance, by having for its

[1] S. L. M. text.　　　　　　[2] Erased from S. L. M. text.
[3] Erased from S. L. M. text.　　[4] "his" in S. L. M. text.

object an *indefinite* instead of a *definite* pleasure, being a poem only so far as this object is attained; romance presenting perceptible images with definite, poetry with *in*definite sensations, to which end music is an *essential*, since the comprehension of sweet sound is our most indefinite conception. Music, when combined with a pleasurable idea, is poetry; music without the idea is simply music; the idea without the music is prose from its very definitiveness.

What was meant by the invective against him who had no music in his soul? * * *

To sum up this long rigmarole, I have, dear B——, what you no doubt perceive, for the metaphysical poets, *as* poets, the most sovereign contempt. That they have followers proves nothing —

> No Indian prince has to his palace
> More followers than a thief to the gallows.

1845

The Raven / And / Other Poems. / By / Edgar A. Poe. / New York: / Wiley & Putnam, 161 Broadway. / 1845.

Collation: half-title. Wiley And Putnam's / Library Of / AMERI-CAN BOOKS. / The Raven and Other Poems. Title, p. I ; with copyright and imprint on verso, p. II; dedication, p. III; verso blank, p. IV; Preface, p. V; verso, Contents, p. VI. The Raven and Other Poems, pp. 1–51; blank verso, p. 52 ; half-title, Poems Written In Youth, p. 53; verso blank, p. 54; Poems Written In Youth, pp 55–91. Issued in paper covers. Size 7.50 by 5.25 inches. The same edition was issued by the same firm in London with the imprint 1846.

THE RAVEN

The *American Whig Review*, February, 1845; the *Evening Mirror*, January 29, 1845; *Southern Literary Messenger*, March, 1845; *London Critic*, June, 1845; 1845; J. Lorimer Graham copy of 1845 poems; *Literary Emporium*, 1845; *Richmond Examiner*, September 25, 1849.

Text, *Richmond Examiner.*

Variations from the text : —

II. 3. *sought :* tried. all others except 1845.

6. *here :* no italics except J. Lorimer Graham, 1845.

III. 6. *This :* That. L. E.; S. L. M.

V. 3. *stillness:* darkness, all others except J. Lorimer Graham, 1845.

VI. 1. *Back:* Then, all others except 1845 and J. Lorimer Graham, 1845.

2. *again I heard:* I heard again, all others except J. Lorimer Graham, 1845.

VII. 3. *minute:* instant, all others except J. Lorimer Graham, 1845.

IX. 3. *living human:* sublunary. A. W. R.

X. 6. *Then the bird said:* Quoth the raven. A. W. R.; E. M.; S. L. M.

XI. 1. *Startled:* wondering. A. W. R.; S. L. M.

4. *songs:* song. C.

4–6. *till . . . nevermore:* so when Hope he would adjure Stern Despair returned, instead of the sweet Hope he dared adjure.

That sad answer, "Nevermore." A. W. R.; E. M.; S. L. M.

5. *That:* the, all others except 1845, and J. Lorimer Graham, 1845.

6. *Of "Never — Nevermore":* of "Nevermore" all others except 1845 and J. Lorimer Graham, 1845.

XII. 1. *My sad fancy:* all my sad soul, all others; my fancy; J. Lorimer Graham, 1845.

XIII. 1. *This:* Thus. C.

XIV. 2. *seraphim whose:* angels whose faint, all others except J. Lorimer Graham, 1845.

5. *Quaff, oh:* Let me. A. W. R.; S. L. M.

XVIII. 1. *still:* No italics except J. Lorimer Graham, 1845.

3. *demon's:* demon, all others except 1845.

Notes: In the *Broadway Journal*, May 24, 1845, a variant reading of the poem is given as follows: —

> "While I pondered nearly napping
> Suddenly there came a rapping,
> As of some one gently tapping,
> Tapping at my chamber door."

The Shea manuscript recorded elsewhere also gives variant readings, and in the quotations from the poem in Poe's " Philosophy of Composition," two verbal variations are found — VII. 3. *minute* for *moment* and X. 1. *that* for *the.*

The above readings of " The Raven " show the poem in eight states. First as sent to the *American Whig Review,* February, 1845; second as revised in the *Evening Mirror,* January 29, 1845; third as revised in the *Southern Literary Messenger,* March, 1845; fourth as revised in the *Lon-*

don Critic, June, 1845; fifth as revised in the edition of the 1845 poems; sixth as revised in the J. Lorimer Graham copy of the 1845 poems in Poe's own hand; seventh as revised in the *Literary Emporium,* 1845; eighth and finally in the *Richmond Examiner,* September 25, 1849.

Many theories as to the composition of "The Raven" have been published. Dr. William Elliot Griffis, in the *Home Journal,* November 5, 1884, stated that Poe mentioned "The Raven" and showed a draft of the poem to a contributor to the *New York Mirror,* in the summer of 1842, at the Barhyte trout Ponds, Saratoga Springs, New York.

Mr. Rosenback in the *American,* February 26, 1887, claimed that he read "The Raven" long before it was published, and was in George R. Graham's office, when the poem was offered there. Poe said that his wife and Mrs. Clemm were starving, and that he was in pressing need of funds. Fifteen dollars was contributed to Poe as charity, but the poem was not accepted. This date was about the winter of 1843–44.

F. G. Fairfield has an account in *Scribner's Magazine,* October, 1875, that the poem was written at the Fordham cottage, 1844–45; also that it was a sort of joint stock affair, the stanzas being produced at intervals by Colonel Du Solle, and others.

Poe did not move to Fordham until the spring of 1846.

Colonel J. A. Joyce attributed the poem to "The Parrot," published in the *Milan Art Journal,* for 1809, by Leo Penzoni, but failed to give further authenticated data.

The generally accepted theory is that given by Judge George Shea, formerly of the Marine Court of New York. Poe wrote Shea's father the following letter without date: —

"DEAR SHEA, — Lest I should have made some mistake in the hurry I transcribe the whole alteration. Instead of the whole stanza commencing 'Wondering at the stillness broken &c.' substitute this:

'Startled at the stillness broken by reply so aptly spoken,
"Doubtless," said I, " what it utters is its only stock and store
Caught from some unhappy master whom unmerciful Disaster
Followed fast and followed faster till his songs one burden bore —
Till the dirges of his Hope the melancholy burden bore,
          Nevermore — Ah Nevermore."'

" At the close of the stanza preceding this, instead of Quoth the raven Nevermore, substitute 'Then the bird said "Nevermore." ' — Truly yours, POE."

This is written on a glazed paper without lines, and on the back "J. Augustus Shea Esq. — to be delivered as soon as he comes in." The manuscript is now in the library of J. Pierpont Morgan, Esq., of New York City. Judge Shea stated that his father and Poe were cadets together at West Point and close associates; that in later life they were often together, and that Poe consulted his father about the publication of his poems. In this way he committed to Shea the publication anonymously of "The Raven" which appeared in the *Whig Review*.

The circumstantial evidences, however, do not fully accord with this theory. Poe was well acquainted with the editor of the *Whig Review* who alluded to the poem as from a correspondent. No good reason appears for Poe sending the poem by Shea. It is in evidence that Poe was a correspondent of the journal, but not Shea. The lines sent to Shea did not appear in the *Whig Review*. Some of the alterations sent Shea do not appear to have ever been published by Poe. Shea was known to have London literary correspondents, and the text sent him may have had some reference to "The Raven" sent by Poe to the *London Critic* in June, 1845. In the *Broadway Journal* of August 23, 1845, Poe made the following notice of Shea's death: "We note with regret the death of James Augustus Shea, Esq., a native of Ireland, for many years a citizen of the United States, and a resident of this city. He died on Friday morning, the 17th inst. at the early age of 42. As a poet his reputation was high — but by no means as high as his deserts. His 'Ocean' is really one of the most spirited lyrics ever published. Its rhythm strikingly resembles 'The Bridge of Sighs.'"

F. W. Thomas's *Recollections of E. A. Poe* states that Poe informed him that "The Raven" was written in one day; that in having it appear anonymously he had merely followed a whim like Coleridge, who published his "Raven" in the same way. Thomas further stated that Poe was constantly urged by himself and others to revise the lines in the poem referring to the "shadow on the floor" and "seraphin whose foot-falls tinkled on the tufted floor." To criticisms of the former he claimed a conception of the bracket candelabrum affixed high up against the wall, while he argued for the latter that his idea was good and came from Isaiah iii. 16 : "The daughters of Zion making a tinkling with their feet."

For Poe's commentary on "The Raven," see his "Philosophy of Composition." The text of "The Raven" given in editions of Poe's poems since Griswold's time as revised by Poe for the *Broadway Journal*, February 8, 1845, is an error. Poe at that time was employed on the *Mirror*, and in a letter to Thomas dated May 4, 1845, said: "I send you an early number of the *Broadway Journal*, containing my 'Raven.' It was copied by Briggs, my associate, before I joined the paper. 'The Raven' had a great 'run,' Thomas — but I wrote it for the express purpose of running — just as I did the 'Gold Bug,' you know. The bird beat the bug though, all hollow." The supposition also advanced that the *Mirror* text of the poem followed that of the *Whig Review* is also an error. The *Mirror* text, as will be seen here, was considerably revised by Poe.

The Thomas *Recollections* state that Poe made up the *Literary Emporium* volume, which was further confirmed by printers who worked on the book. Poe himself said about this period that he would devote his time, "getting out books." The poem in that volume is in all probabilities the text of "The Raven," seen in proof with Poe while on the *Broadway Journal* by the office boy Alexander T. Crane, whose recollections have been published. Thomas also states that Poe made repeated efforts to have his poems appear in London during the year 1845. He did succeed in having some notices of his journal and "The Raven" appear in the *London Critic*.

THE RAVEN. BY — QUARLES

American Whig Review, February, 1845: The following lines from a correspondent — besides the deep quaint strain of the sentiment, and the curious introduction of some ludicrous touches amidst the serious and impressive, as was doubtless intended by the author — appear to us one of the most felicitous specimens of unique rhyming which has for some time met our eye. The resources of English rhythm for varieties of melody, measure, and sound, producing corresponding diversities of effect, have been thoroughly studied, much more perceived, by very few poets in the language. While the classic tongues, especially the Greek, possess, by power of accent, several advantages for versification over our own, chiefly through greater abundance of spondaic feet, we have other and very great advantages of sound by the modern usage of rhyme. Alliteration is nearly the only effect of that kind which the ancients had in common with us. It will be seen that much of the melody of "The Raven" arises from alliteration, and the studious use of similar sounds in unusual places. In regard to its measure, it may be noted that, if all the verses were like the second, they might properly be placed merely in short lines, producing a not uncommon form; but the presence in all the others of one line —

mostly the second in the verse — which flows continuously, with only an aspirate pause in the middle, like that before the short line in the Sapphic Adonic, while the fifth has at the middle pause no similarity of sound with any part beside, gives the versification an entirely different effect. We could wish the capacities of our noble language, in prosody, were better understood. — ED. AM. REV.

Evening Mirror, January 29, 1845: We are permitted to copy (in advance of publication) from the second number of *The American Review*, the following remarkable poem by Edgar Poe. In our opinion, it is the most effective single example of " fugitive poetry " ever published in this country; and unsurpassed in English poetry for subtile conception, masterly ingenuity of versification, and consistent sustaining of imaginative lift and "pokerishness." It is one of those "dainties bred in a book," which we *feed* on. It will stick to the memory of everybody who reads it.

Southern Literary Messenger, March, 1845: Mr. Brooks, editor of the *New York Express,* says: "There is a poem in this book (*The American Whig Review*) which far surpasses anything that has been done even by the best poets of the age: — indeed there are none of them who could pretend to enter into competition with it, except, perhaps, Alfred Tennyson; and he only to be excelled out of measure. Nothing can be conceived more effective than the settled melancholy of the poet bordering upon sullen despair in the Raven settling over the poet's door, to depart thence 'Nevermore.' In power and originality of versification the whole is no less remarkable than it is, psychologically, *a wonder*."

Richmond Examiner, September 25, 1849: Mr. Edgar A. Poe lectured again last night on the "Poetic Principle" and concluded his lecture as before with his now celebrated poem of "The Raven." As the attention of many in this city is now directed to this singular performance, and as Mr. Poe's poems from which only it is to be obtained in the bookstores, have been long out of print, we furnish our readers, to-day, with the only correct copy ever published—which we are enabled to do by the courtesy of Mr. Poe himself. "The Raven " has taken rank over the whole world of literature, as the very first poem as yet produced on the American continent. There is indeed but one other, the "Humble Bee" of Ralph Waldo Emerson, which can be ranked near it. The latter is superior to it as a work of construction and design while the former is superior to the latter as a work of *pure art*. They hold the same relation, the one to the other, that a masterpiece of painting holds to a splendid piece of Mosaic. But while this poem maintains a rank so high among all persons of catholic and general cultivated taste, we can conceive the wrath of many who will read it for the first time in the columns of this newspaper. Those who have formed their taste in the Pope and Dryden school, whose earliest poetical acquaintance is Milton, and whose latest Hamlet and Cowper — with a small sprinkling of Moore and Byron — will not be apt to relish on first sight a poem tinged so deeply with the dyes of the Nineteenth Century. The poem will make an impression on them which they will not be able to explain, — but that will irritate them, — criticism and explanation are useless with such. Criticism cannot reason people into an attachment. In spite of our plans, such will talk of the gaudiness of Keats and craziness of Shelley, until they see deep enough into their claims to forget or be ashamed to talk so. Such will angrily pronounce "The Raven" flat nonsense. Another class will be disgusted therewith because they can see no purpose, no allegory, no meaning as they express it in the poem. These people — and they constitute the majority of our practical race — are possessed with a false theory. They hold that every poem and poet should have some moral notion or other, which it is his "mission" to expound. That theory is all false. To build theories, principles, religions, etc., is the business of the argumentative, not of the poetic faculty. The business of poetry is to minister to the sense of the beautiful in human minds. — That sense is a simple element in our nature — simple, not compound; and therefore the art which ministers to it may safely be said to have an ultimate end in so ministering. This "The Raven" does in an eminent degree. It has no allegory in it, no purpose — or a very slight one — but it is a "thing of beauty" and will be a "joy forever" for that and no further reason. In the last stanza is an image of settled despair and despondency, which throws a gleam of meaning and allegory over the entire poem — making it all a personification of that passion — but that stanza is evidently an afterthought, and unconnected with the original poem. "The Raven" itself is a mere narrative of simple events. A bird which has been taught to speak by some former master is lost in a stormy night, is attracted by the light of a student's window, flies to it and flutters against it. Then against the door. The student fancies it a visitor, opens the door and the chance word uttered by the bird suggests to him memories and fancies connected with his own situation and his dead sweetheart or wife. Such is the poem. The last stanza is an afterthought. The worth of "The Raven" is not in any "moral," nor is its charm in the construction of its story. Its great and wonderful merits consist in the strange, beautiful, and fantastic imagery and color with which the simple subject is clothed, the grave and supernatural tone with which it rolls on the ear, the extraordinary vividness of the word-painting, and the powerful but altogether indefinable appeal which is made throughout to the organs of ideality and marvellousness. Added to these is a versification indescribably sweet and wonderfully difficult — winding and convoluted about like the mazes of some complicated overtures of Beethoven. To all who have a strong perception of tune there is a music in it which haunts the ear long after reading. These are great merits, and "The Raven" is a gem of art. It is stamped with the image of true genius — and genius in its happiest hour. It is one of those things an author never does but once. Y

NOTE. — It is known that Poe discussed the merits of " The Raven " with John M. Daniel, the author of the above, and some portions may have been inspired by him. This notice of the poem was found among Poe's clippings after his death, and is now among the " Griswold Papers."

THE VALLEY OF UNREST

American Whig Review, April, 1845; 1845; *Broadway Journal*, II. 9 ; "The Valley Nis," 1831; *Southern Literary Messenger*, February, 1836.
Text, 1845.

Variations from the text : —
  18. *rustle :* rustles.   A. W. R.
  19. *Uneasily :* Unceasingly.   A. W. R.; B. J.
After 27 insert: —

> They wave; they weep; and the tears as they well
> From the depth of each pallid lily-bell,
> Give a trickle and a tinkle and a knell.   A. W. R.

The earliest (1831) version runs as follows: The *Southern Literary Messenger* reading is noted below: —

THE VALLEY NIS

> Far away — far away —
> Far away — as far at least
> Lies that valley as the day
> Down within the golden east —
> All things lovely — are not they
> Far away — far away?

It is called the valley Nis.
And a Syriac tale there is
Thereabout which Time hath said
Shall not be interpreted.
Something about Satan's dart —
Something about angel wings —
Much about a broken heart —
All about unhappy things:
But "the valley Nis" at best
Means "the valley of unrest."
Once it smil'd a silent dell
Where the people did not dwell,
Having gone unto the wars —
And the sly, mysterious stars,
With a visage full of meaning,
O'er the unguarded flowers were leaning:
Or the sun ray dripp'd all red
Thro' the tulips overhead,
Then grew paler as it fell
On the quiet Asphodel.

Now the *unhappy* shall confess
Nothing there is motionless:
Helen, like thy human eye
There th' uneasy violets lie —
There the reedy grass doth wave
Over the old forgotten grave —
One by one from the tree top
There the eternal dews do drop —
There the vague and dreamy trees
Do roll like seas in northern breeze
Around the stormy Hebrides —
There the gorgeous clouds do fly,
Rustling everlastingly,
Through the terror-stricken sky,
Rolling like a waterfall
O'er the horizon's fiery wall —
There the moon doth shine by night
With a most unsteady light —

There the sun doth reel by day
" Over the hills and far away."

6. *Far away :* One and all, too.
24. *the :* tall.
27-46. *Now* each visiter shall confess
    Nothing there is motionless:
    Nothing save the airs that brood
    O'er the enchanted solitude,
    Save the airs with pinions furled
    That slumber o'er the valley-world.
    No wind in Heaven, and lo! the trees
    Do roll like seas, in Northern breeze,
    Around the stormy Hebrides —
    No wind in Heaven, and clouds do fly,
    Rustling everlastingly,
    Through the terror-stricken sky,
    Rolling, like a waterfall
    O'er th' horizon's fiery wall —
    And Helen, like thy human eye,
    Low crouched on Earth, some violets lie,
    And, nearer Heaven, some lilies wave
    All banner-like, above a *grave.*
    And, one by one, from out their tops
    Eternal dews come down in drops,
    Ah, one by one, from off their stems
    Eternal dews come down in gems !

BRIDAL BALLAD

Southern Literary Messenger, January, 1837, (Ballad); Philadelphia, *Saturday Evening Post,* July 31, 1841; Philadelphia, *Saturday Museum,* March 4, 1843, (Song of The Newly Wedded); 1845; *Broadway Journal,* II. 4 ; *Richmond Examiner,* October, 1849.

        Text, *Richmond Examiner.*

Variations from the text : —
I. 3. Insert after: —
      And many a rood of land. S. L. M.

II. 1. He has loved me long and well. S. L. M.

  2. *But:* And : *first,* omit. S. L. M.

  4. *as :* like. B. J.; S. M.

    rang as a knell: were his who fell. S. L. M. *rang like a knell.* B. J.

  5. Omit. S. L. M.

III. 1. *But:* And. S. L. M.

  3. *While:* But. S. L. M.

  6. Omit. S. L. M. Parenthesis omitted all others, except J. Lorimer Graham, 1845.

  7. Insert after: —

> And thus they said I plighted
> An irrevocable vow —
> And my friends are all delighted
> That his love I have requited —
> And my mind is much benighted
> If I am not happy now!
>
> Lo! the ring is on my hand,
> And the wreath is on my brow —
> Satins and jewels grand,
> And many a rood of land,
> Are all at my command,
> And I must be happy now! S. L. M.

IV. 1–2. I have spoken, I have spoken,
> They have registered the vow. S. L. M.
> It was spoken — it was spoken —
> Quick they registered the vow. S. E. P.

  5–6. Here is a ring as token
> That I am happy now. Omit all others, except J. Lorimer Graham, 1845.

V. 5. *Lest:* And. S. L. M.

Note : The addition of the two new lines in the fourth stanza of this poem shows the interesting way in which Poe derived his very characteristic varied repetend by doubling up two previous variant readings. The following from the *Southern Literary Messenger,* August, 1835, might well be read in connection with this poem. Authorities are of the opinion that it may have been the first draft of the poem. This might also apply to " Lenore."

The subjoined copy of an old Scotch ballad contains so much of the beauty and genuine spirit of bygone poetry that I have determined to risk a frown from the fair lady by whom the copy was furnished in submitting it for publication. The ladies sometimes violate their promises — may I not for once assume the privilege, in presenting to the readers of the *Messenger* this "legend of the olden time," although *I promised not?* Relying on the kind heart of the lady for forgiveness for *this breach of promise,* I have anticipated the pardon in sending you the lines which I have never as yet seen in print: —

" BALLAD

" They have giv'n her to another —
They have sever'd ev'ry vow ;
They have giv'n her to another
And my heart is lonely now;
They remember'd not our parting —
They remember'd not our tears,
They have sever'd in one fatal hour
The tenderness of years.
Oh! was it weel to leave me?
Thou couldst not so deceive me;
Lang and sairly shall I grieve thee,
Lost, lost Rosabel!

" They have giv'n thee to another —
Thou art now his gentle bride;
Had I lov'd thee as a brother,
I might see thee by his side;
But *I know with gold they won thee*
And thy trusting heart beguil'd;
Thy *mother,* too, did shun me,
For she knew I lov'd her child.
Oh! was it weel, etc.

" They have giv'n her to another —
She will love him, so they say;
If her mem'ry do not chide her,
Or, perhaps, perhaps she may;
But I know that she hath spoken

What she never can forget ;
And tho' my poor heart he broken,
It will love her, love her yet.
Oh! was it weel, etc."

THE SLEEPER

"The Poets and Poetry of America," 1842; *Philadelphia Saturday Museum*, March 4, 1843; 1845; *Broadway Journal*, I. 18; 1831, Title Irene; Poe MS. Irene The Dead; *Southern Literary Messenger*, May, 1836, Irene; *Richmond Examiner*, October, 1849.

Text, Richmond Examiner.

Variations from the text : —

11. *fog:* mist. P. P. A.

16. Insert after : —

> Her casement open to the skies. S. M.; 1845; B. J.; *Her :* with P. P. A.

17. Irene *with:* And. P. P. A.

19. WINDOW: lattice. S. M.

20–21. Omit. S. M.; P. P. A.

35. Stranger thy glorious length of tress. P. P. A.

39–47. Soft may the worms about her creep!

> This hed, being changed for one more holy,
> This room for one more melancholy
> I pray to God that she may lie
> Forever with uncloséd eye!
> My love she sleeps, O, may her sleep
> As it is lasting so be deep!
> Heaven have her in its sacred keep! P. P. A.

44. *pale:* dim. S. M.; 1845; B. J.

49. *vault:* tomh. P. P. A.

50. *vault:* tomh. P. P. A.

57. *tomb:* vault. P. P. A.

59. *thrilling :* nor thrill. P. P. A.

The (1831) earliest version reads as follows : —

IRENE

'T is now (so sings the soaring moon)
Midnight in the sweet month of June,

When winged visions love to lie
Lazily upon beauty's eye,
Or worse — upon her brow to dance
In panoply of old romance,
Till thoughts and locks are left, alas!
A ne'er-to-be untangled mass.

An influence dewy, drowsy, dim,
Is dripping from that golden rim;
Grey towers are mouldering into rest,
Wrapping the fog around their breast:
Looking like Lethe, see! the lake
A conscious slumber seems to take,
And would not for the world awake:
The rosemary sleeps upon the grave —
The lily lolls upon the wave —
And million bright pines to and fro,
Are rocking lullabies as they go,
To the lone oak that reels with bliss,
Nodding above the dim abyss.
All beauty sleeps: and lo! where lies
With casement open to the skies,
Irene, with her destinies!
  Thus hums the moon within her ear,
"O lady sweet! how camest thou here?
"Strange are thine eyelids — strange thy dress!
"And strange thy glorious length of tress!
"Sure thou art come o'er far-off seas,
"A wonder to our desert trees!
"Some gentle wind hath thought it right
"To open thy window to the night,
"And wanton airs from the tree-top,
"Laughingly thro' the lattice drop,
"And wave this crimson canopy,
"Like a banner o'er thy dreaming eye!
"Lady, awake! lady awake!
"For the holy Jesus' sake!
"For strangely — fearfully in this hall
"My tinted shadows rise and fall!"

The lady sleeps: the *dead* all sleep —
At least as long as Love doth weep:
Entranc'd, the spirit loves to lie
As long as — tears on Memory's eye:
But when a week or two go by,
And the light laughter chokes the sigh,
Indignant from the tomb doth take
Its way to some remember'd lake,
Where oft — in life — with friends — it went
To bathe in the pure element,
And there, from the untrodden grass,
Wreathing for its transparent brow
Those flowers that say (ah hear them now!)
To the night-winds as they pass,
"Ai! ai! alas! — alas!"
Pores for a moment, ere it go,
On the clear waters there that flow,
Then sinks within (weigh'd down by wo)
Th' uncertain, shadowy heaven below.
.   .   .   .

The lady sleeps: oh! may her sleep
As it is lasting so be deep —
No icy worms about her creep:
I pray to God that she may lie
Forever with as calm an eye,
That chamber chang'd for one more holy —
That bed for one more melancholy.

Far in the forest, dim and old,
For her may some tall vault unfold,
Against whose sounding door she hath thrown,
In childhood, many an idle stone —
Some tomb, which oft hath flung its black
And vampyre-winged pannels back,
Flutt'ring triumphant o'er the palls
Of her old family funerals.

Variations from the above : —
  1–2. I stand beneath the soaring moon
        At midnight in the month of June.   S. L. M.; MS.

3–8. omit S. L. M.; 10. *that :* yon. S. L. M.; her MS.; 18. *bright pines :* cedars. S. L. M.; 20. *reels with bliss,* nodding hangs. S. L. M.; 21. Above yon cataract of Serangs. S. L. M.

23–24. With : her ; transpose, MS.; 25 substitute : —

> And hark the sounds so low yet clear,
> (Like music of another sphere)
> Which steal within the slumberer's ear,
> Or so appear — or so appear! S. L. M.

35. Insert : —
> "So fitfully, so fearfully. S. L. M.

36. *Like :* As. S. L. M.; 37 substitute : —

> "That o'er the floor, and down the wall,
> "Like ghosts the shadows rise and fall —
> "Then, for thine own all radiant sake,
> "Lady, awake! awake! awake! " S. L. M.; MS.

37. *That o'er the floor :* thro' the floors. MS.

39. *All radiant :* beloved. MS.

40. *Awake! Awake :* Lady awake. MS.

40–58. Omit. S. L. M.

48. *Some remember'd like :* Heaven and sorrows forsake. MS.

49–59. Omit MS.

72. *Winged :* Wing-like. S. L. M.; MS.

Note : In a letter to R. W. Griswold dated April 19, 1845, Poe states, " In 'The Sleeper' the line Forever with unclosèd eye, should read: 'Forever with unopen'd eye.'

" Is it possible to make the alteration ? " This was never corrected by Griswold.

Poe's manuscript of this poem written in the album of his poet friend, John C. McCabe, is now in the possession of Captain W. Gordon Mc-Cabe of Richmond, Virginia. It is headed "Irene the Dead" and signed E. A. Poe. The handwriting is approximately the same as that in the manuscript of the "Spiritual Song."

THE COLISEUM

The Baltimore Saturday Morning Visiter, 1833; *Southern Literary Messenger*, title (The Coliseum, A Prize Poem), August, 1835; *Philadelphia Saturday Evening Post*, June 12, 1841, with subtitle (A Prize Poem); " The Poets and Poetry of America," 1842, title (Coliseum);

Philadelphia Saturday Museum, March 4, 1843; 1845; *Broadway Journal,* II. 1.

Text, 1845.

Variations from the text: —

1. *The:* Omit. S. M. V.

8. *Thy:* the. *So drink:* the dank. S. M. V.
   Amid: Within. P. P. A.

11. Insert after: —

Gaunt vestibules! and phantom peopled aisles! S. L. M.

20. *Gilded:* yellow. S. L. M.

21. Insert after: —

Here, where on ivory couch the Cæsar sate,
On bed of moss lies gloating the foul adder. S. L. M.

22. *Monarch lolled:* Cæsar sate. P. P. A.

23–24. On bed of moss lies gloating the foul adder!
    Here where on ivory couch the Monarch loll'd. P. P. A.

26. *But stay — these:* These crumbling; ivy clad: tottering. S. L. M.;

But hold! — these dark, these perishing arcades." P. P. A.

28. *Crumbling:* broken. S. L. M.; P. P. A.

31. *Famed:* Great. S. L. M.; proud. P. P. A.

35. *Unto:* to. P. P. A.

36. *Melody:* in old days. S. L. M.

39. *Impotent:* desolate. S. L. M.

34. To end, except after glory, l. 46, omit quotation marks. S. L. M.

Note: This was the poem offered for the prize in the *Baltimore Saturday Morning Visiter.*

The first nine lines of the poem are printed in *The Bibliophile,* of London, England, for May, 1909, from a fragment of a Poe MS. The only variation is, "stand" for "kneel" in the seventh line. It is stated there that no proof exists that the poem was published earlier than August, 1835, when it was issued in the *Southern Literary Messenger.* A copy of an early text from the *Baltimore Saturday Morning Visiter* is now in our possession from Professor J. H. Hewitt, who was the editor, and received the prize for the competing poem. The variant readings of same are given here for the first time.

The MS. in *The Bibliophile* is evidently a portion of the MS. of "Politian" — which ended with some of the lines from this poem.

LENORE

The Pioneer, February, 1843; *Philadelphia Saturday Museum*, March 4, 1843; *Graham's Magazine*, February, 1845; *Broadway Journal*, II. 6. "A Pæan," 1831; *Southern Literary Messenger*, January, 1836; *Richmond Whig*, September 18, 1849; *Richmond Examiner*, October, 1849.

Text, *Richmond Whig*.

Variations from the text: —
I. 5. *Come :* Ah. G. M.
II. 1. *And ye :* ye out all others.
 3. *Shall :* no italics. G. M.
III. 1. *Yet : but ; but :* and all others.
 3. *Gone before :* quotation marks all others.
 5. *Debonair :* Italics all others.
IV. 1. *to friends, from fiends :* from fiends below. J. Lorimer Graham, 1845.
 2. *Utmost :* out all others
 3. *Moan :* Grief. J. Lorimer Graham, 1845.
 4. *no :* no italics. J. Lorimer Graham, 1845.
 6. *no :* No all others.

The earliest version, 1831, is as follows: the readings of the *Southern Literary Messenger* being noted below: —

A PÆAN

I

How shall the burial rite be read?
 The solemn song be sung?
The requiem for the loveliest dead,
 That ever died so young?

II

Her friends are gazing on her,
 And on her gaudy bier,
And weep! — oh! to dishonor
Dead beauty with a tear!

III

They loved her for her wealth —
   And they hated her for her pride —
But she grew in feeble health,
   And they *love* her — that she died.

IV

They tell me (while they speak
   Of her "costly broider'd pall")
That my voice is growing weak —
   That I should not sing at all —

V

Or that my tone should be
   Tun'd to such solemn song
So mournfully — so mournfully,
   That the dead may feel no wrong.

VI

But she is gone above,
   With young Hope at her side,
And I am drunk with love
   Of the dead, who is my bride. —

VII

Of the dead — dead who lies
   All perfum'd there,
With the death upon her eyes,
   And the life upon her hair.

VIII

Thus on the coffin loud and long
   I strike — the murmur sent
Through the gray chambers to my song,
   Shall be the accompaniment.

IX

Thou died'st in thy life's June —
   But thou didst not die too fair:

Thou didst not die too soon,
Nor with too calm an air.

X

From more than fiends on earth,
Thy life and love are riven,
To join the untainted mirth
Of more than thrones in heaven —

XI

Therefore, to thee this night
I will no requiem raise,
But waft thee on thy flight
With a Pæan of old days.

II. 4. *Dead :* Her.
VII. 1. *dead who :* dead — who.
  2. *perfum'd there :* motionless.
  4. *her hair :* each tress.
VIII. Omit.
IX. 1–2. *In June she died :* in June
            Of life — beloved and fair.
  3. *Thou didst :* But she did.
X. *Thy life and love are :* Helen, thy soul is.
  3. *untainted :* all-hallowed.

The *Pioneer* version, 1843, is as follows: the *Saturday Museum* text is
made up of two lines less and the readings are noted below: —

LENORE

Ah, broken is the golden bowl!
  The spirit flown forever!
Let the bell toll! — A saintly soul
  Glides down the Stygian river!
And let the burial rite be read —
  The funeral song be sung —
A dirge for the most lovely dead
  That ever died so young!
    And, Guy De Vere,

Hast *thou* no tear?
　　Weep now or nevermore!
　See, on yon drear
　And rigid bier,
　　Low lies thy love Lenore!

"Yon heir, whose cheeks of pallid hue,
　With tears are streaming wet,
　Sees only, through
　Their crocodile dew,
　　A vacant coronet —
　　False friends! ye loved her for her wealth
　　And hated her for pride,
　And, when she fell in feeble health,
　　Ye blessed her — that she died.
　　　How *shall* the ritual, then, be read?
　　　The requiem *how* be sung
　　　　For her most wrong'd of all the dead
　　　　That ever died so young?"

Peccavimus!
But rave not thus!
　And let the solemn song
Go up to God so mournfully that *she* may feel no wrong!
　　The sweet Lenore
　　Hath "gone before"
　　　With young hope at her side,
　　　And thou art wild
　　　For the dear child
　　That should have been thy bride —
　　　For her, the fair
　　　And debonair,
　　　　That now so lowly lies —
　　　The life still there
　　　Upon her hair,
　　　　The death upon her eyes.

"Avaunt! — to-night
My heart is light —

No dirge will I upraise,
But waft the angel on her flight
    With a Pæan of old days!
        Let *no* bell toll!
        Lest her sweet soul,
            Amid its hallow'd mirth,
                Should catch the note
                As it doth float
            Up from the damnéd earth —
                To friends above, from fiends below,
                    Th' indignant ghost is riven —
                From grief and moan
                To a gold throne
            Beside the King of Heaven!"

I. 4. *Glides down :* Floats on.
II. 11. *how :* no italics.
Other readings are: —
IV.:
"Avaunt! to-night my heart is light. No dirge will I upraise.
"But waft the angel on her flight with a pæan of old days!
"Let *no* bell toll! — lest her sweet soul, amid its hallowed mirth,
"Should catch the note, as it doth float up from the damnéd Earth.
"To friends above, from fiends below, the indignant ghost is riven —
"From Hell unto a high estate far up within the Heaven —
"From grief and groan, to a golden throne, beside the King of Heaven."
—1845. G. M.; B. J.
    7. *Grief :* moan. B. J.; G. M.

Notes : The *Richmond Examiner* text follows the text with slight punctuation changes. In that newspaper was published October 12, 1849, a statement from Poe made to J. M. Daniel, that Mrs. Shelton to whom he was betrothed was "his ideal and the original of Lenore."

In a review of Amelia Welby's poem in the *Democratic Review*, of December, 1844, Poe said: "Her tone is not so much the tone of passion, as of a gentle and melancholy regret, interwoven with a pleasant sense of the natural loveliness surrounding the lost in the tomb, and a memory of her beauty while alive — Elegiac poems should either assume this character, or dwell purely on the beauty (moral or physical) of the departed, or better still, utter the note of triumph. I have endeavored to carry out this latter idea in some verses which I have called 'Lenore.' "

In his criticism on H. B. Hirst, in Griswold, 1850, Poe quotes the last three lines of the second stanza of " Lenore," and states that it was first published in 1830. The first known version was one year later. The manuscript in Poe's autograph of this criticism was among the papers of the late E. C. Stedman. Poe sent it to *Graham's Magazine*, but it was not published.

In his " Marginalia " in the *Southern Literary Messenger*, May, 1849, Poe quotes the first two lines of stanza four of "Lenore" and uses the "1845" text, which would indicate that his final revision of the poem was made late in that year.

In a letter to R. W. Griswold, no date (1849), Poe enclosed a copy of "Lenore" for a new edition of " The Poets and Poetry of America," and stated, "I would prefer the concluding stanza to run as here written." The J. Lorimer Graham edition of 1845 with corrections in Poe's hand was not in Griswold's possession prior to the issue of his first Poe volumes, Neilson Poe having failed to send it as promised. The text of stanza four of the poem is largely a reconstruction of the elements in the *Broadway Journal* version of that stanza.

HYMN

Poe MS. [Morella] about 1832–33; *Southern Literary Messenger*, April, 1835 [Morella]; *Burton's Gentleman's Magazine*, November, 1839 [Morella]; "Tales of the Grotesque and Arabesque," 1840 [Morella]; 1845; *Broadway Journal*, II. 6.

Text, 1845.

Variations from the text: —
Insert before: —

> Sancta Maria! turn thine eyes
> Upon the sinner's sacrifice
> Of fervent prayer, and humble love,
> From thy holy throne above. S. L. M.; MS.; B. G.

M.; except 2, *the:* a. B. G. M., 1840.

5. *the:* my; *brightly;* gently. S. L. M.; B. G. M.; MS. 6. *not a cloud obscured:* no storms were in. S. L. M.; B. G. M.; MS. 8. *grace:* love. S. L. M.; B. G. M.; MS. 9. *storms:* clouds. S. L. M.; B. G. M.; MS. 10. *Darkly:* All. S. L. M.; B. G. M.

Note: Poe struck out the word "Catholic" from the title of this poem in the J. Lorimer Graham copy of the 1845 poems.

ISRAFEL

1831; *Southern Literary Messenger*, August, 1836; *Graham's Magazine*, October, 1841; *Philadelphia Saturday Museum*, March 4, 1843; 1845; *Broadway Journal*, II. 3. *Richmond Examiner*, October, 1849.

Text, *Richmond Examiner*.

Variations from the text : —

II. 6. Transpose with 8. G. M.

III. 4. *Owing to :* due unto. G. M.

6. *The :* That. *Wire :* Lyre. G. M.

7. *Of :* With. G. M.

IV. 1. *Skies :* Heavens. G. M.

3. *Grown up :* Grown. *Loves :* Love is. G. M. *Where :* And. S. M.; B. J.

4. *Where :* And. S. M.; B. J.

6. Insert after : —

The more lovely, the more far! G. M.

V. 1. Thou art not, therefore. S. M.; B. J; G. M.

VIII. 1. *Could :* did. G. M.

4. *So wildly :* one half so. G. M.

5. One half so passionately. G. M.

Note : In the *Broadway Journal*, Poe's quotation in the footnote is attributed to *Sale's* Koran. In *Graham's Magazine*, it reads "And the angel Israfel, or Israfeli whose heart-strings are a lute, and who is the most musical of all God's creatures," Koran.

The 1831 version reads as follows : —

ISRAFEL [1]

I

In Heaven a spirit doth dwell
Whose heart-strings are a lute —
None sing so wild — so well
As the angel Israfel —
And the giddy stars are mute.

[1] And the angel Israfel, who has the sweetest voice of all God's creatures.

II

Tottering above
In her highest noon
The enamoured moon
Blushes with love —
While, to listen, the red levin
Pauses in Heaven.

III

And they say (the starry choir
And all the listening things)
That Israfeli's fire
Is owing to that lyre
With those unusual strings.

IV

But the Heavens that angel trod
Where deep thoughts are a duty —
Where Love is a grown god —
Where Houri glances are —
Stay! turn thine eyes afar! —
Imbued with all the beauty
Which we worship in yon star.

V

Thou art not, therefore, wrong
Israfeli, who despisest
An unimpassion'd song:
To thee the laurels belong
Best bard, — because the wisest.

VI

The extacies above
With thy burning measures suit
Thy grief — if any — thy love
With the fervor of thy lute —
Well may the stars be mute!

VII

Yes, Heaven is thine: but this
Is a world of sweets and sours:
Our flowers are merely — flowers,
And the shadow of thy bliss
Is the sunshine of ours.

VIII

If I did dwell where Israfel
Hath dwelt, and he where I,
He would not sing one half as well —
One half as passionately,
While a stormier note than this would swell
From my lyre within the sky.

Variations of Southern Literary Messenger from above : —

IV. 5. Omit.   7. *yon :* a ; VIII. 4. *So :* As ; 5. *While a stormier :* And a loftier.

DREAM–LAND

Graham's Magazine, June, 1844; 1845; *Broadway Journal,* I. 26; *Richmond Examiner,* October 29, 1849.

Text, *Richmond Examiner.*

Variations from the text : —

12. *dews :* tears.   J. Lorimer Graham, 1845.

20. Insert after 1–6. except 5, read my home for *these lands* and 6. this for *an.*   G. M.

25. Mountain.   G. M.; B. J.

38. *earth :* worms.   G. M.; B. J.

Insert after 1–6. except 5, read journeyed home for *reached these lands* and 6. this for *an.*   G. M.

42. *O ! it is :* 'T is — oh, 't is, all others.

47. *Its :* the.   G. M.; B. J.

50. *Beholds :* Beyond.   E.

Note : Poe used lines nine to twelve of this poem with slight variations in his early poem on "Fairy-Land."

SONNET — TO ZANTE

Southern Literary Messenger, January, 1837; Poe MS., 1840; *Philadelphia Saturday Museum*, March 4, 1843; 1845; *Broadway Journal*, II. 2.
Text, 1845.

Note: The germ of this poem like others may be found in Poe's early composition. See "Al Aaraaf," Part I.

> "From struggling with the waters of the Rhone: —
> And thy most lovely purple perfume, Zante!
> Isola d'oro! — Fior di Levante!"

The MS. of this poem has an interesting history. The original owner was one of Poe's editors who gave his own recollections of Poe, but for some reason failed to mention this incident.

R. H. Stoddard made a request of Poe for his autograph, and in a letter dated Philadelphia, November 6, 1840, Poe expressed himself as much gratified at the request, "and now hasten to comply by transcribing a sonnet of my own composition." The letter and manuscript of the poem were included in a sale of Mr. Stoddard's books by the late E. C. Stedman, his executor, who related the incident as above.

The text of the MS. poem only varies from others in the omission of italics and a few punctuation changes.

—— THE CITY IN THE SEA

American Whig Review (sub-title, "A Prophecy"), April, 1845; 1845; *Broadway Journal*, II. 8. "The Doomed City," 1831; "The City of Sin," *Southern Literary Messenger*, August, 1836.
Text, 1845.

Variations from the text: —

3. Far off in a region unblest. A. W. R.
4. *And:* where. S. L. M.
14–19. Omit. S. L. M.
20. No holy rays from heaven come down. S. L. M.
22. But light from out the lurid sea. S. L. M.
25. Around the mournful waters lie. A. W. R.
28–35. Omit   A. W. R.
36. *For no:* No murmuring. A. W. R.
39. *Some:* a. A. W. R.
41. *Seas less hideously:* oceans not so sad. A. W. R.

The 1831 version reads as follows: —

THE DOOMED CITY

Lo! Death hath rear'd himself a throne
In a strange city, all alone,
Far down within the dim west —
And the good, and the bad, and the worst, and the best,
Have gone to their eternal rest.

There shrines and palaces and towers
Are — not like anything of ours —
O! no — O! no — *ours* never loom
To heaven with that ungodly gloom!
Time-eaten towers that tremble not!
Around, by lifting winds forgot,
Resignedly beneath the sky
The melancholy waters lie.
A heaven that God doth not contemn
With stars is like a diadem —
We liken our ladies' eyes to them —
But there! That everlasting pall!
It would be mockery to call
Such dreariness a heaven at all.

Yet tho' no holy rays come down
On the long night-time of that town,
Light from the lurid, deep sea
Streams up the turrets silently —
Up thrones — up long-forgotten bowers
Of sculptur'd ivy and stone flowers —
Up domes — up spires — up kingly halls —
Up fanes — up Babylon-like walls —
Up many a melancholy shrine
Whose entablatures intertwine
The mask — the viol — and the vine.

There open temples — open graves
Are on a level with the waves —
But not the riches there that lie
In each idol's diamond eye,

Not the gayly-jewell'd dead
Tempt the waters from their bed:
For no ripples curl, alas!
Along that wilderness of glass —
No swellings hint that winds may be
Upon a far-off happier sea:
So blend the turrets and shadows there
That all seem pendulous in air,
While from the high towers of the town
Death looks gigantically down.
But lo! a stir is in the air!
The wave! there is a ripple there!
As if the towers had thrown aside,
In slightly sinking, the dull tide —
As if the turret-tops had given
A vacuum in the filmy heaven:
The waves have now a redder glow —
The very hours are breathing low —
And when, amid no earthly moans,
Down, down that town shall settle hence,
Hell rising from a thousand thrones
Shall do it reverence,
And Death to some more happy clime
Shall give his undivided time.

Note : The earliest form of this poem is found in the first thirty-nine lines of " Al Aaraaf," Part II, with note "O, the Wave."

TO ONE IN PARADISE

Southern Literary Messenger, "The Visionary," July, 1835; *Broadway Journal,* I. 19, I. 23, "The Assignation "; "To Ianthe in Heaven," *Burton's Gentleman's Magazine,* July, 1839; Tales, "The Visionary," 1840; *Philadelphia Saturday Museum,* March 4, 1843; 1845; *Godey's Lady's Book,* "The Visionary," January, 1834.

      Text, J. Lorimer Graham copy 1845.

Variations from the text : —

I. 1. *That all :* all that, all others.

     5. *With fairy fruits and :* round with wild. Go. around about with. S. L. M.; B. G. M.; 1840.

6. *All the flowers :* the flowers — they all. S. L. M.; B. G. M.; 1840.

II. 1. But the dream — it could not last. Go.; S. L. M.; B. G. M.; 1840.

2. Young Hope! thou didst arise. Go. And the star of Hope did rise. S. L. M.; B. G. M.; 1840. *Ah :* Oh. S. M.

5. *"On ! on" — but :* "Onward." Go.; S. L. M.; B. G. M.; 1840; B. J. *but :* while. Go.; S. L. M.; B. G. M.; 1840.

III. 2. Ambition — all — is o'er. Go.; S. L. M.; B. G. M.; 1840.

4. *Solemn :* breaking. Go.

IV. 1. *Days :* hours. Go.; S. L. M.; B. G. M.; 1840. *And :* now. B. J.

3. *Grey :* dark, all others.

5–6. In the maze of flashing dances
By the slow Italian streams. Go.

6. *Eternal :* Italian. Go.; S. L. M.; 1840; B. J. *What :* far. Go. Insert after : —

> Alas! for that accursed time
> They bore thee o'er the billow,
> From Love to titled age and crime
> And an unholy pillow —
> From me, and from our misty clime
> Where weeps the silver willow. S. L. M.; 1840; Go. except : —

3. *Love :* me.

5. *me :* Love.

The Literary World of February 5, 1853, reprinted from the London *Spectator*, January 1, 1853, a manuscript version of this poem. The correspondent had supposed the lines to be by Tennyson, and charged Poe with plagiarism. Tennyson wrote to the *Spectator*, January 20, 1853, correcting the statement. The text of the manuscript follows the *Southern Literary Messenger*, except : —

I. 1. *That :* Omit.

II. 2. And the star of life did rise.

3. *But :* only.

III. 1–5. Like the murmur of the solemn sea
To sands on the sea-shore
A voice is whispering unto me
"The day is past," and nevermore.

IV. 1. And all mine hours.

2. *Nightly :* nights are.

3. *Are:* of.

5–6. In the maze of flashing dances
By the slow Italian streams.

EULALIE — A SONG

American Whig Review (sub-title "A Song "), July, 1845; *Broadway Journal*, II. 5; 1845.

Text, 1845.

Variations from the text : —

II. 6. morn tints. A. W. R.

III. 4. *And:* while. A. W. R.; B. J.

7. *While:* And. A. W. R.; B. J.

8. *While:* And. A. W. R.; B. J.

TO F——s S. O——d

1845; "Lines Written in an Album," *Southern Literary Messenger*, September, 1835, "To —— " *Burton's Gentleman's Magazine*, August, 1839, "To F——," *Broadway Journal*, II. 10, lines 1–4.

Text, 1845.

Variations from the text : —

1. Eliza let thy generous heart. S. L..M.

Fair maiden let thy generous heart. B. G. M.

6. *Grace, thy more than :* unassuming. S. L. M.; B. G. M.

7. *Shall be an endless :* And truth shall be a. S. L. M. Thy truth — shall be a. B. G. M.

8. Forever — and love a duty. S. L. M.; B. G. M.

Note: The poem was addressed to Frances S. Osgood by Poe in 1845. The lines were also written in his wife's album. Her name was Virginia *Eliza* Clemm.

TO F——

1845; *Broadway Journal*, I. 17, "To Mary " ; *Southern Literary Messenger*, July, 1835, "To One Departed"; *Graham's Magazine*, March, 1842; *Philadelphia Saturday Museum*, March 4, 1843.

Text, 1845.

Variations from the text : —

I. 1. Mary amid the cares — the woes. S. L. M.

For 'mid the earnest cares and woes. G. M.; S. M.

2. *That crowd :* crowding. S. L. M.

3. *Drear :* sad. S. L. M.; G. M.; S. M.

7. *Bland :* sweet. S. L. M.

II. 1. *And thus :* Seraph. G. M.; S. M.

4. Some lake beset as lake can be. S. L. M.

   throbbing far and free : vexed as it may be. G. M.; S. M.

Reverse the order of stanzas. G. M.; S. M.

SONNET — SILENCE

Burton's Gentleman's Magazine, April, 1840; *Philadelphia Saturday Museum,* March 4, 1843; 1845; *Broadway Journal,* II. 3.

Text, 1845.

Variations of B. G. M. from the text : —

2. *Which thus is :* life aptly.

3. *A :* The.

9. *No more :* italics.

12. *Untimely lot :* no parenthesis.

13. *Shadow :* italics.

14. *That :* who; *lone :* dim.

Notes : There are several early references to "Silence" in "Al Aaraaf." In Part I appears: —

> "Ours is a world of words: Quiet we call
> "Silence," — which is the merest word of all.
> All Nature speaks, and even ideal things
> Flap shadowy sounds from visionary wings."

Poe's tale, "Silence. A Fable," which was originally published in 1839 as "Siope," contained the first two lines of the above quotation from "Al Aaraaf."

A poem on "Silence," signed "P," as Poe had previously printed some of his lines, appeared in *Burton's Gentleman's Magazine,* for September, 1839, while he was editor. This was regarded as Poe's poem, until a recent chance reference to William Sharp's "Sonnets of this Century" disclosed the fact that it was Thomas Hood's sonnet.

Sharp's note, p. 297, referring to Hood's "Silence" (Nos. ciii-iv) says it "should be compared with the following well-known sonnet by Edgar Poe." He gives the lines of Poe's own "Silence," as first printed in *Burton's Gentleman's Magazine,* for April, 1840, while Poe was still the editor.

Hood's lines on "Silence," most assuredly printed by Poe in the September, 1839, *Burton's Gentleman's Magazine*, follow Hood's text; except in the eighth line, which has characteristic Poe punctuation. It seems a question whether Poe was influenced by Hood's lines in writing his own sonnet, or printed them as a hoax. If the latter had been his intention, as was his custom he would have called attention to the matter afterwards. The fact, however, that he remained quiet seven months and then wrote his own lines would indicate that he hoped that his lines might be compared with Hood's and cause public comment; or, like the lines of Cone's "Proud Ladye," which he reviewed in *Burton's Gentleman's Magazine* for July, 1840, and which are presumed to have inspired him to write "The Conqueror Worm" six months afterwards, Hood's "Silence" may have influenced him to some extent to write his own verse.

THE CONQUEROR WORM

Graham's Magazine, January, 1843; *Philadelphia Saturday Museum*, March 4, 1843; 1845; *Broadway Journal*, I. 21; II. 12 "Ligeia"; Poe MS.; *Richmond Enquirer*, October, 1849.

Text, *Richmond Enquirer*.

Variations from the text: —

I. 3. *An angel :* A mystic. G. M.; S. M.; B. J.

II. 5. *formless :* shadowy. G. M.

IV. 7. *seraphs :* the angels, all others except J. L. G., 1845 edition.

V. 2. *quivering :* dying. G. M.; B. J.

5. *while :* And, all others, except J. L. G., 1845 edition. *Angels :* seraphs; *pallid :* haggard. G. M.

8. *And :* Omit. G. M.; S. M.; B. J.

Notes : In "Ligeia," in the *Broadway Journal*, Poe wrote "angels" in the fourth line of the first stanza of this poem instead of "Mystic," and in the fourth verse changed "angels" to "seraph," as he did in his later corrections.

A MS. copy of the poem, originally sent to Griswold by Poe and noted in Griswold's hand "Last poem sent by Poe," has been compared. It follows the early texts with slight punctuation changes.

In Poe's review of Spencer Wallace Cone's poems in *Burton's Gentleman's Magazine*, June, 1840, he says: "Here is a passage which breathes the true soul of poetry, and gives evidence of a purity of taste as well as a vigor of thought which *may* lead to high eminence in the end: —

"'Spread o'er his rigid form
The banner of his pride,
And let him meet the conqueror worm
With his good sword by his side.'"

THE HAUNTED PALACE

Baltimore Museum, April, 1839; *Burton's Gentleman's Magazine*, "The Fall of the House of Usher," September, 1839; Tales, "Fall of the House of Usher," 1840; *Philadelphia Saturday Museum*, March 4, 1843; *Graham's Magazine*, February, 1845; 1845; Tales, 1845, "The Fall of the House of Usher"; *Richmond Examiner*, October, 1849.

Text, *Richmond Examiner*.

Variations from the text: —
I. 4. *radiant:* snow white. B. M.; 1840; B. G. M.
III. 1. *all wanderers.* B. M.
    8. *ruler:* sovereign. B. M.; B. G. M.
IV. 5. *sweet:* sole. B. G. M.
VI. 2. *encrimson'd:* red *litten*, all others; 5. *ghastly rapid:* rapid ghastly. B. M.; B. G. M.; 1840; 1845.

Notes: In *Graham's Magazine* the fourth and sixth stanzas are entirely in italics. The MS. of this poem is now complete, the first half, originally in the possession of R. W. Griswold, having been found. It was evidently sent to Griswold late in 1849, as it closely follows the text, and the J. Lorimer Graham edition of 1845, with Poe's corrections. The Griswold collection now has only the last half, and the first part, supposed to have been lost, has been found and was used in comparing the texts.

In *Burton's Gentleman's Magazine*, at the end of "The Fall of the House of Usher," is the following note: "The ballad of 'The Haunted Palace' introduced in this tale was published separately some months ago in the *Baltimore Museum.*"

In a letter to Griswold, March 29, 1841, Poe stated: "By The Haunted Palace, I mean to imply a mind haunted by phantoms — a disordered brain."

In "Marginalia" in the *Southern Literary Messenger* for May, 1849, Poe quotes the first twelve lines of this poem, which follows the text, except "Radiant Palace" is in parenthesis instead of lines eleven and twelve.

SCENES FROM "POLITIAN"

AN UNPUBLISHED DRAMA

Southern Literary Messenger, December, 1835; January, 1836; 1845.
Text, 1845.

Variations of Southern Literary Messenger from the text: —

II. 1. Rome. 1845.

    114. *this sacred:* A vow — a.

III. 1. *Baldazzar:* Baldazzar his friend.

    7. *surely:* I live.

    69. *eloquent:* voice — that.

    70. *surely I:* I surely.

    76. *it:* that lattice.

    104. *Believe me:* Baldazzar! Oh!

IV. 5. *sob:* weep.

    6. *mourn:* weep.

    9. *turn here thine eyes:* and listen to me.

    30. *to me:* speak not.

V. 7. *Paradisal Hope:* hopes — give me to live.

After 50, insert: —

> If that we meet at all, it were as well
> That I should meet him in the Vatican —
> In the Vatican — within the holy walls
> Of the Vatican.

    66. *then at once:* have at thee then.

    72. *thy sacred:* hold off thy.

    73. *indeed I dare not:* I dare not, dare not.

After 73, insert: —

    Exceeding well! — thou darest not fight with me?

After 82, insert: —

    Thou darest not!

    84. *my lord:* alas!

    86. *the veriest:* I am — a.

    99. *thou liest:* By God; indeed — now this.

Notes: In the *Southern Literary Messenger* the title is "Scenes From An Unpublished Drama," and begins with Part II, of the text.

A portion of the drama is quoted in the "Longfellow War," *Broadway*

Journal, March 29, 1845. The lines about Jacinta and her mistress' jewels in the second scene are changed, and the line "This sacred vow" changed to "A pious vow."

The song in "Politian" which Poe says is English has been identified. It is among the poems of Sir Thomas Wyat, an early English poet. The full text follows: —

"THE LOVER'S APPEAL

"And wilt thou leave me thus?
 Say nay! say nay! for shame,
 To save thee from the blame
 Of all my grief and grame.
 And wilt thou leave me thus?
  Say nay! say nay!

"And wilt thou leave me thus,
 That hath loved thee so long,
 In wealth and woe among?
 And is thy heart so strong
 As for to leave me thus?
  Say nay! say nay!

"And wilt thou leave me thus,
 That hath given thee my heart
 Never for to depart
 Neither for pain nor smart;
 And wilt thou leave me thus?
  Say nay! say nay!

"And wilt thou leave me thus,
 And have no more pity
 Of him that loveth thee?
 Alas! thy cruelty!
 And wilt thou leave me thus?
  Say nay! say nay!"

The original manuscript of the drama of Politian is now in the library of J. Pierpont Morgan, Esq., of New York. It was once in the possession of Mrs. Lewis. The MS. consists of twenty folio pages, containing nearly six hundred and fifty lines, but is not complete; some pages have gone astray. At the top of the first page is the heading: —

> "Politian — a tragedy
> Scene — Rome in the — Century."

The drama ends with Politian, alone in the Coliseum at night, who utters a characteristic soliloquy — nothing less than a portion of the well-known lines from "The Coliseum." There are few alterations, but some interlineations and lines marked out. At the head of the first extract printed in the *Southern Literary Messenger*, Poe has written in pencil "Scenes from Politian. An unpublished Tragedy by Edgar A. Poe, Act II, Scene 3," which indicates that the MS. was evidently used for the *Messenger* text — the variations having been made in proof. The manuscript was probably written about 1831. A list of the *dramatis personæ* follows the heading and shows four additional characters. It also describes the characters "Lalage," an orphan and the ward of Di Broglio; Politian, "a young and noble Roman"; Baldazzar, "his friend." The two latter personages were subsequently transformed into the "Earl of Leicester" and the "Duke of Surrey."

The first act is a scene in the palazzo of the Duke Di Broglio in an apartment strewn with the débris of a protracted revel, with two of the Duke's servants, Benito and Ugo, the latter intoxicated, who are joined by Rupert a third servant. They discuss their master's son, Count Castiglione, who was —

> "Not long ago
> A very nobleman in heart and deed."

But of his treatment of the beautiful lady Lalage, Rupert says: —

> "His conduct there has damned him in my eyes."

> "O villain! villain! she his plighted wife
> And his own father's ward. I have noticed well
> That we may date his ruin — so I call it —
> His low debaucheries — his gaming habits —
> And all his numerous vices from the time
> Of that most base seduction and abandonment."

Benito: —

> "The sin sits heavily on his soul
> And goads him to these courses."

They speak further of Castiglione's approaching nuptials with his cousin Alessandra, who was "the bosom friend of the fair lady Lalage ere this mischance." Benito and Rupert retire to bed and leave Ugo, who while also about to depart meets Jacinta the maid servant of Lalage, with whom he is enamored. She displays some jewels, and intimates that they were given to her by Castiglione, but finally sets at rest the green-eyed monster, and ends the scene by confessing that they were given to her by Mistress Lalage "as a free gift and for a marriage present."

The second scene introduces Castiglione and his evil genius the Count San Ozzo, in the former's dressing room. The Count hints of the Duke's keeping Lalage in seclusion, and hums: —

> "Birds of so fine a feather,
>   And of so wanton eye,
> Should be caged — should be caged —
> Should be caged in all weather
>   Lest they fly."

To which Castiglione replies: —

> "San Ozzo! you do her wrong — unmanly wrong!
> Never in woman's breast enthronéd sat
> A purer heart! If ever woman fell
> With an excuse for falling, it was she!
> If ever plighted vows most sacredly —
> Solemnly-sworn, perfidiously broken,
> Will damn a man, that damned villain am I!
> Young, ardent, beautiful — and loving well —
> And pure as beautiful — how could she think —
>
> "How could she dream, being herself all truth,
> Of my black perfidy? Oh, that I were not
> Castiglione, but some peasant hind;
> The humble tiller of some humble field
> That I dare be honest!"

San Ozzo: —
> "Exceedingly fine!
> I never heard a better speech in all my life,
> Besides, you 're right. Oh, honesty 's the thing!

Honesty, poverty and true consent,
With the unutterable ecstasies,
Of bread, and milk and water!"

The third scene opens in a Hall in the Palace, and with minor alterations is what is now the first published. The next scene opens with Di
Broglio and his son in conversation about Politian. Castiglione "always
thought the Earl a gloomy man, but instead I have found him full of such
humor — such wit — such vim — such flashes of merriment."

They are disturbed by the entrance of Politian and Baldazzar. Castiglione attempts to introduce them to his father, but Politian suddenly re-
tires and is excused by Baldazzar, who claims for his friend sudden illness.
The scene which follows is the third published. The next third act of
the MS. is fourth of that published. The next, unpublished, shows
preparations for the wedding of Alessandra and Castiglione, and the bad
treatment of Ugo by Jacinta. This is followed by scene 5 as published. A
long hiatus occurs in the MS., where scene 5 now ends with Castiglione.
The whole of the first scene, 4th act, in which it is learned that Politian
again met Castiglione and

"In the public streets
Called him a coward!"

is missing, as also the first thirty-seven lines of the succeeding scene between San Ozzo and Ugo. The latter, apparently dejected by Jacinta's
treatment, attempts to commit suicide. San Ozzo remarks aside: —

"I 've heard before that such ideas as these
Have seized on human brains."

The third scene brings Politian alone in the moonlit Coliseum waiting
for Lalage, and with the soliloquy the MS. ends.

THE BELLS

Sartain's Union Magazine, November, 1849. *Richmond Examiner*,
October, 1849.

Text, *Richmond Examiner*.

Variations from Sartain's Union Magazine : —

I. 3. *What:* no italics.

II. 3. *What :* no italics.

12. *What:* no italics.

III. 3. *What:* no italics.

26. *Yes:* Yet.

IV. 3. *What:* no italics.

Notes: Sartain's Union Magazine, December, 1849.

"The singular poem of Mr. Poe's, called 'The Bells,' which we published in our last number, has been very extensively copied. There is a curious piece of literary history connected with this poem, which we may as well give now as at any other time. It illustrates the gradual development of an idea in the mind of a man of original genius. This poem came into our possession about a year since. It then consisted of *eighteen lines !* They were as follows: —

"THE BELLS. — A SONG

"The bells! — hear the bells!
The merry wedding bells!
The little silver bells!
How fairy-like a melody there swells
From the silver tinkling cells
Of the bells, bells, bells!
Of the bells!

"The bells! — ah, the bells!
The heavy iron bells!
Hear the tolling of the bells!
Hear the knells!
How horrible a monody there floats
From their throats —
From their deep-toned throats!
How I shudder at the notes
From the melancholy throats
Of the bells, bells, bells!
Of the bells!

"About six months after this we received the poem enlarged and altered nearly to its present size and form; and about three months since, the author sent another alteration and enlargement, in which condition the poem was left at the time of his death."

According to the above the last draft of "The Bells" was received by *Sartain's Union Magazine*, about September, 1849, at which period Poe was revising his writings at Richmond, Virginia. The second draft, much like the last, was sent to the same magazine in June, 1849, and the eighteen lines about December, 1848. In Gill's Life of Poe, page 205, it is stated that Poe composed and finished his greatest descriptive poem "The Bells" in the spring of 1849, a study of which he had previously made and sent to *Sartain's Union Magazine*. Ingram claims that it was the Summer of 1848 and not the Autumn that Poe wrote the first draft of "The Bells," at Mrs. Shew's residence. Professor Woodberry's revised Life of Poe, page 295, volume ii, says, that according to Annie he finished "The Bells," presumably the second draft, February 6, 1849, and on page 388, that he visited Lowell the last week in May, and there wrote the last draft of "The Bells."

Poe in a letter to Annie, February 8, 1849, says, "The day before I wrote a poem considerably longer than 'The Raven.' I call it 'The Bells.' How I wish 'Annie' could see it. I think 'The Bells' will appear in *The American Review*."

The second draft of "The Bells," claimed as sent to *Sartain's Union Magazine*, was shorter than "The Raven," so upon Poe's evidence the longer draft was made in February, 1849, and it was his intention to send it to the *American Whig Review*. F. W. Thomas states that he had a manuscript copy of "The Bells"; Griswold's, 1850, differs from *Sartain's Union Magazine* text, and it would seem that the claim that Poe left at least four manuscript copies of the poems is true. Only one copy, however, is known in America at the present time, now in the library of J. Pierpont Morgan, Esq., which lacks the last fourteen lines. A manuscript printed in a London magazine, in facsimile, is said to be a second copy, but does not differ materially from the American manuscript. In the original MS. the word "bells" is repeated five times in the twelfth line of the first stanza and twice in the line following. The same change is made in the corresponding lines of the next stanza. In the third stanza, sixth line, the word "much" is placed before "too." In the fifth line from the last of the stanza "clamor" was written and "anger" placed in the last line. The word "menace" in the sixth line of the fourth stanza was originally written "meaning." The eighth line of this stanza was first written "From out their ghostly throats," and the eleventh line changed twice, reading first "Who live up in the steeple," which was changed to "They that sleep," and finally "dwell" was printed instead of "sleep." After the eighteenth line, the following line was struck out: —

"But are pestilential carcasses disparted from their souls."

For this "They are ghouls" was substituted. The Stedman and Woodberry and Virginia Poe editions of the poems give *Sartain's Union Magazine* as their authorized text, but none of them agree.

F. W. Thomas, *Recollections of E. A. Poe*, states that the germ of this poem like most others was formed very early in Poe's career. In some manner Thomas had obtained possession of Poe's early "Marginalia Book" used by the poet while engaged on the *Southern Literary Messenger*. In a written statement made to me by John W. Fergusson, an apprentice, employed on the *Southern Literary Messenger*, and who carried proof sheets to Poe's home and helped celebrate his marriage in Richmond, it is claimed that the book was left at the *Messenger* office by Poe and was his property many years, but went astray.

Among the clippings in this book was one with a reference to "Bells" which Poe afterwards used again in *Burton's Gentleman's Magazine*. This clipping from Poulson's Philadelphia *American Daily Advertiser* about the Autumn of 1833 when Poe was engaged upon same is now in my possession. It is under the heading of VARIETIES, followed by the quotation: —

"Trahit quod cunque potest, atque addit acervo."

It reads: "Bells. — Bells were first brought into use by St. Paulinus, Bishop of Nola (409) in the Campania of Rome: hence a bell was called Nola or Campagna. At first they were called saints: hence coc-saint, or toc-sin, in process of time. But Pliny reports that, many ages before his time bells were in use, and called Tintin-nabula; and Suetonius says that Augustine had one put at the gate of the Temple of Jupiter, to call the meeting of the people." This was followed by a paragraph on the use of "Accents and Points."

Poe told Thomas that the "Chimes" by Dickens was his final inspiration to write his poem of "The Bells." That story left a deep impression on his mind after reading a copy sent him from abroad, and he reprinted it entire into the *Mirror*, probably its first publication in America.

He said : "Thomas, that ghostly story with beleaguered phantoms and goblins — up, up, up, up. — higher, high, high, higher up — haunted me day and night." A bell never sounded in his ear but he heard those chimes — "high, high, higher up," which afterwards took the form in his own poem of leaping — "high, higher, higher." " Many a time," continued Thomas, " after the din and clamor of some bells had died away he would say to his wife Virginia and Mrs. Clemm — 'I will have to do something to get those noisy creatures out of my way; they creep into my brain — confuse and disorder my ideas.'"

He gave this as an explanation for the lines in the *American Whig Review*, of April, 1845, in his poem of "The Valley of Unrest," which he afterwards suppressed: —

> "They wave; they weep; and the tears as they well
> From the depth of each pallid lily-bell,
> Give a trickle and a tinkle and a knell."

While the subject continually haunted his imagination Thomas states that it only assumed definite shape early in 1848. In two early numbers of the *Union Magazine*, Poe had observed several poems on "Bells," and at once wrote a draft of his own "Bells." When about to send to the *Union Magazine*, he noticed an editorial note in same, calling attention to a glut of manuscript on hand and suggesting a poem of twenty lines. Then he wrote a short poem on "The Bells" and sent it in, but it never appeared. He had rewritten the poem several times, had offered it to a number of magazines, but was never able to get his price or have it accepted. Still he always retained the greatest faith in the merits of the poem. Thomas did not think that *Sartain's Union Magazine* ever accepted or paid Poe for this poem.

John R. Thompson, in a notice in the *Southern Literary Messenger*, and also John M. Daniel in the *Richmond Examiner*, shortly after Poe's death, both state that it was the design of Poe, as he himself told them, to express in language the exact sounds of bells to the ear. They thought that he had succeeded far better than Southey, who attempted in a similar feat to tell how the waters "come down at Lodore."

Mrs. William Wiley, the daughter of Mrs. Shew, wrote me that she remembers how her mother told her that Poe wrote "The Bells" at her home. When a little girl going to school she was given some lessons on Poe, and her mother gave her the written lines of "The Bells" by Poe, to show her teacher. The manuscript was sold in New York at auction some years ago. The lines read as follows : —

"The bells! — ah, the bells!
The little silver bells!
How fairy-like a melody there floats
    From their throats —
From their merry little throats —
From the silver, tinkling throats
    Of the bells, bells, bells —
        Of the bells !

"The bells! — ah, the bells!
The heavy iron bells.
How horrible a monody there floats
    From their throats —
From their deep-toned throats —
From their melancholy throats!
How I shudder at the notes
    Of the bells, bells, bells —
        Of the bells!"

The manuscript of these lines was sent by Mrs. Shew to Mr. J. H. Ingram, of London, who, in his Life of Poe, states : "Poe wrote the first rough draft of 'The Bells' at Mrs. Shew's residence. 'One day he came in,' she records in her diary, and said, 'Marie Louise, I have to write a poem; I have no feeling, no sentiment, no inspiration!' His hostess persuaded him to have some tea. It was served in the conservatory, the windows of which were open, and admitted the sound of neighboring church bells. Mrs. Shew said playfully, 'Here is paper,' but the poet declining it declared, 'I so dislike the noise of bells to-night, I cannot write, I have no subject — I am exhausted!' The lady then took up the pen, and pretending to mimic his style, wrote, 'The Bells by E. A. Poe,' and then in pure sportiveness, 'The Bells, the little silver bells,' finishing off the stanza. She then suggested for the next verse 'The heavy iron bells !' and this Poe also expanded into a stanza. He next copied out the complete poem and headed it, 'By Mrs. M. L. Shew,' remarking that it was her poem, as she had composed so much of it. Mrs. Shew continues, 'My brother came in, and I sent him to Mrs. Clemm to tell her that "her boy would stay in town, and was well." My brother took Mr. Poe to his own room, where he slept twelve hours, and could hardly recall the evening's work.'"

TO M. L. S——

Poe's MS. To Mrs. M. L. S., February 14, 1847. *Home Journal,* March 13, 1847.

Text, Home Journal.

Variations in MS. from text: —

2. *Thine:* thy.

9. *Lying:* Laying them.

14. *Resembles:* approaches.

Notes: The poem was introduced in the *Home Journal* as follows: —

"The following seems said over a hand clasped in the speaker's two. It is by Edgar A. Poe, and is evidently the pouring out of a very deep feeling of gratitude." The poem was sent to Mrs. Marie Louise Shew. The manuscript copy dated February 14, 1847, is still in the possession of her daughter, Mrs. William Wiley, and was used in making comparisons of the text.

TO —— —— ——

Columbian Magazine, March, 1848.

Text, Columbian Magazine.

Notes: The tenth line of this poem is spoken by Lalage in "Politian," and some portions of "Israfel" are in lines fourteen and fifteen.

Poe sent a MS. copy of this poem to Mrs. Shew. The first seven lines follow the text.

TO MARIE LOUISE

Two gentle sounds made only to be murmured
By angels dreaming in the moon-lit " dew
That hangs like chains of pearl on Hermon hill"
Have stirred from out the abysses of my heart
Unthought-like thoughts — scarcely the shades of thought —
Bewildering fantasies — far richer visions
Than even the seraph harper, Israfel,
Who "had the sweetest voice of all God's creatures,"
Would hope to utter. Ah, Marie Louise!
In deep humility I own that now
All pride — all thought of power — all hopes of fame —

All wish for Heaven — is merged forevermore
Beneath the palpitating tide of passion
Heaped o'er my soul by thee. Its spells are broken —
The pen falls powerless from my shivering hand —
With that dear name as text I *cannot* write —
I cannot speak — I cannot even think —
Alas! I cannot feel; for 't is *not* feeling —
This standing motionless upon the golden
Threshold of the wide-open gates of Dreams,
Gazing, entranced, adown the gorgeous vista,
And thrilling as I see upon the right —
Upon the left — and all the way along,
Amid the clouds of glory: far away
To where the prospect terminates — *thee only.*

SONNET (AN ENIGMA)

Sonnet, *Union Magazine*, March, 1848; Griswold, 1850 (An Enigma).
Text, *Union Magazine.*
Variation of Griswold from the text: —
　　10. *Petrarchanities:* tuckermanities.
Note: The first letter of the first line, the second letter of the second
line, etc., form the name Sarah Anna Lewis.
This poem was sent to Mrs. Lewis (Stella) in November, 1847, and
Griswold's text follows that manuscript.

TO —— —— ——

"To Helen," Griswold, 1850. "The Poets and Poetry of America,"
1855. *Union Magazine*, November, 1848.
Text, *Union Magazine.*
Variations of Griswold from text: —
　　26. Insert after me : (Oh Heaven! oh, God! How my heart beats in
coupling those two words!)
Notes: It is claimed that the lines given by Griswold were omitted
from the *Union Magazine*, without Poe's authority. There appears no
direct evidence for this however. The authority for Griswold's text
is not found — likewise his title "To Helen." He discarded his early

text, and followed that of the *Union Magazine* in revising his later edition of "The Poets and Poetry of America."

Poe is presumed to have sent the lines for publication in the following letter to Bayard Taylor, June 15, 1848: "I would feel greatly indebted to you if you could spare the time to look over the lines enclosed and let me know whether they will be accepted for 'the Union,' — if so what you can afford to pay for them and when they can appear."

This poem was addressed to Mrs. Sarah Helen Whitman. In the *Union Magazine*, line eighteen, the word " see " is printed for " saw."

A VALENTINE TO —— —— ——

Flag of Our Union, March 3, 1849; *Sartain's Union Magazine*, March, 1849.

Text, *Flag of Our Union*.

Variations of Sartain's Union Magazine from the text: —

1. *These lines are :* this rhyme is.
4. *This :* the.
5. *This rhyme, which holds :* the lines! — they hold.
8. *Letters themselves :* Syllables!
12. *Understand :* comprehend.
13. *This page whereon :* the leaf where now.
14. Eyes scintillating soul, there lie *perdus*.
15. *A well-known name :* Three eloquent words.

Notes : The text is followed by the words "Valentine Eve, 1849."
A manuscript copy among the Griswold papers is as follows: —

TO ——

For her these lines are penned, whose luminous eyes,
     Bright and expressive as the stars of Leda,
Shall find her own sweet name, that, nestling, lies
     Upon this page, enwrapped from every reader.
Search narrowly these words, which hold a treasure
     Divine — a talisman — an amulet
That must be worn *at heart*. Search well the measure —
     The words — the letters themselves. Do not forget

The smallest point, or you may lose your labor.
And yet there is in this no Gordian knot
Which one might not undo without a sabre
If one could merely comprehend the plot.
Upon the open page on which are peering
Such sweet eyes now, there lies, I say, perdu
A musical name oft uttered in the hearing
Of poets, by poets — for the name is a poet's too.
In common sequence set, the letters lying,
Compose a sound delighting all to hear —
Ah, this you'd have no trouble in descrying
Were you not something of a dunce, my dear: —
And now I leave these riddles to their Seer.

Saturday, Feb. 14, 46.

The name Frances Sargent Osgood is spelled incorrectly in the above
lines. Another MS. copy in the Griswold collection dated Valentine's
Eve, 1848, shows the following variations from the above: —

A *Valentine*: By Edgar A. Poe. To : —— —— ——

1. *these lines*: this rhyme.
2. *Bright, stars, Leda*: Brightly, twins Lœda.
4. *this*: the.
5. *words, which*: lines, they.
8. *the letters themselves*: the syllables.
9. *smallest*: trivialest.
13. Enwritten upon the leaf where now are peering.
14. Eyes scintillating soul, their lie *perdus*.
15. *A musical name*: Three eloquent words.

After 16: —

Its letters, although naturally lying
(Like the knight Pinto — Mendez Ferdinando —)
Still form a synonym for Truth. — cease trying!
You will not read the riddle though you do the best you *can* do.

The following foreword appeared in the *Flag of Our Union*: —
"At a Valentine Soirée, in New York, the following enigmatical lines
were received, among others, and read aloud to the company. The verses
were enclosed in an envelope, addressed 'TO HER WHOSE NAME IS
WRITTEN WITHIN.' As no lady present could so read the riddle as

to find her name written in it the Valentine remained, and still remains, unclaimed. Can any of our readers of the *Flag* discover for whom it is intended?"

After the poem was the following note: "Should there be no solution furnished of the above, we will give the key next week."

It is evident that none of the readers sent in any answers, for in the issue of March 10 appears the following: —

"The Key to the Valentine.

"To transcribe the address of the Valentine which appeared in our last paper from the pen of Edgar A. Poe, read the first letter of the first line in connection with the second letter of the second line, the third letter of the third line, the fourth of the fourth, and so on to the end. The name of our contributor Frances Sargent Osgood will appear."

FOR ANNIE

Flag of Our Union, April 28, 1849; *Home Journal*, April 28, 1849; Poe MS. Griswold, 1850; "The Poets and Poetry of America," 1855. *Richmond Examiner*, October, 1849.

Text, *Richmond Examiner*.

Variations from the text: —

II. 1. Sadly I know I am. MS.; F. O. U.

Transpose stanzas IV and V, MS.; F. O. U.

IV. 3. Are quieted now with, MS.; Are quieted now; and the, F. O. U.

4. *That:* the. MS.; Horrible throbbing, F. O. U.

5. *Ah:* Oh. MS.; O, F. O. U.

VI. 1. *Oh:* Ah. MS.; F. O. U.

6. *Passion:* Glory. MS.; F. O. U.

VII. 3. *Spring:* Fountain. F. O. U.

VIII. 1. *But:* And. H. J.; Gr.; P. P. A.

And ah! let it never be. MS.; F. O. U.

2. *Be:* out. MS.; and F. O. U.

7. *Sleep:* italics out except Gr.; P. P. A.

IX. 1. My tantalized spirit here. MS.

X. 2. *It:* I. MS.

3. A holier odor about me. MS.

4. Of pansy. MS.

6. *Pansies:* pansy. MS.

XI. 1. *It:* I. MS.

    3. *Truth:* love. MS.; F. O. U.

XII. 5. Deeply to sleep from the. MS.; F. O. U.

    6. *From the:* out. MS.; F. O. U.

XIV. 3–7. Omit parenthesis. F. O. U.

XV. 3. *In:* of. All others except Gr. ; Stars of the Heaven — for it. MS.

    5. *Light:* though. MS.; fire. F. O. U.

A manuscript copy of "For Annie" was sold at the Pierce sale in Philadelphia, May 6, 1903. "Annie" was Mrs. Richmond of Lowell, Massachusetts.

Poe complained that the *Flag of Our Union* misprinted the lines, for which reason he sent a corrected copy to the *Home Journal.* They seem, however, to have been published simultaneously. Poe sent to Mrs. Richmond a portion of his poem "A Dream Within A Dream," headed "For Annie." In his last revision of this poem he also changed the title, "To ——." and unquestionably addressed the poem to "Annie."

SONNET — TO MY MOTHER

Flag of Our Union, July 7, "To My Mother," 1849; *Richmond Examiner*, October, 1849; *Southern Literary Messenger*, December, 1849; *Leaflets of Memory*, Philadelphia, 1850; Griswold, 1850.

    Text, *Southern Literary Messenger.*

Variations from the text: —

    1. *The angels:* I feel that. F. O. U.; Gr.

    2. *Devoutly singing unto:* The angels whispering to. F. O. U.; Gr.

    3. *Amid:* among. F. O. U.; Gr.

    5. *Sweet:* dear. Gr.

    7. *Filling:* And fill; *God:* Death, F. O. U.; Gr.

    9. *My:* Omit italics. F. O. U.; Gr.

    11. *dead:* one. F. O. U.; Gr.

    12. And thus are dearer than the mother I knew. F. O. U.; Gr.

Notes: This poem refers to his mother-in-law, who was also his aunt — Mrs. Clemm. The *Examiner* text follows the *Southern Literary Messenger.* The *Leaflets of Memory* has one change in punctuation. The sonnet is introduced in the *Southern Literary Messenger* as follows: "One of the most touching of the compositions of poor Poe is the Sonnet to his Mother-in-law. It bears the impress of sincere feeling, and seems

to have been written in his better moments, when his spirit returning
from 'the misty mid-regions of Weir' and the companions of Ghouls, be-
trayed that touch of nature which makes the whole world kin.''

ELDORADO

Flag of Our Union, April 21, 1849; Griswold, 1850.
　　　　　　　Text, *Flag of Our Union.*
Note: The Griswold text shows no changes. A reference is made in
the poem "Dream-Land" to "Eldorado.''

ANNABEL LEE

New York Tribune, October 9, 1849; *Richmond Examiner*, October,
1849; *Southern Literary Messenger*, November, 1849; *Sartain's Union
Magazine*, January, 1850, with sub-title "A Ballad"; Griswold, 1850;
"The Poets and Poetry of America," 1855; Poe MS.
　　　　　　　Text, *Richmond Examiner.*
Variations from the text : —
II. 1. *She . . . I: I . . . She.* T. Gr. MS. and 1850. No italics in
S. U. M.
　5. *Of:* in. T. and Gr. MS.
III. 3. *By night:* chilling. T. Gr. MS. and 1850. S. U. M.
　4. *chilling:* My beautiful. T. Gr. MS. and 1850. S. U. M.
　5. *Kinsman:* S. U. M.; Gr. 1850.
IV. 5. *Chilling:* by night. T. Gr. MS. and 1850. S. U. M.
　6. *And :* chilling. T. Gr. MS. and 1850. S. U. M.
VI. 3. *See :* feel, all others except S. L. M.; S. U. M.; MS., *feel.*
　6. *My life:* omit italics all others.
　7. *Her:* the. Gr. 1850.
　8. *Sounding:* side of. S. L. M.; S. U. M.; R. E.
Note in *Sartain's Union Magazine* with the poem: —
"In the December number of our magazine we announced that we
had another poem of Mr. Poe's in hand, which we would publish in January. We supposed it to be his last, as we had received it from him a
short time before his decease. The sheet containing our announcement
was scarcely dry from the press, before we saw the poem, *which we had
bought and paid for*, going the rounds of the newspaper press, into which
it had found its way through some agency that will perhaps be hereafter

explained. It appeared first, we believe, in the *New York Tribune*. If we are not misinformed, two other Magazines are in the same predicament as ourselves. As the poem is one highly characteristic of the gifted and lamented author, and more particularly, as our copy of it differs in several places from that which has been already published, we have concluded to give it as already announced.''

Notes : Poe's manuscript from which *Sartain's Union Magazine* printed the poem is now in the library of J. Pierpont Morgan, Esq. of New York city. It is written on two sheets of blue glazed paper ruled and pasted together. On the back is written in Professor Hart's hand ''$5 paid.'' ''This was the price paid by *Sartain's Union Magazine* when it was accepted and published in 1850 (J. S. Hart, Editor).'' These comments throw some obscurity upon the previous remarks of the editor of *Sartain's Union Magazine* when the poem was published in January, 1850, wherein it is intimated that they bought and paid Poe himself for the poem. This was an impossibility in 1850 as Poe died in 1849. The statement in *Sartain's Union Magazine* has often been used to reflect on Poe's character, and it now seems unwarranted.

F. W. Thomas, who was conversant with many of Poe's as well as Mrs. Clemm's affairs, states that ''Poe was never paid for the poem by *Sartain's Union Magazine.*'' It seems unlikely that Poe would have parted with the poem for $5. In a letter to Griswold in 1849 (no date) he asks if he cannot sell ''Annabel Lee'' to Graham's or Godey for $50, before same appeared in his book. *Sartain's Union Magazine* acknowledged holding the poem nearly four months, and it now seems doubtful if it was ever accepted or paid for.

The original manuscript also shows that the editor of *Sartain's Union Magazine* did not use Poe's punctuation, italics, or capital letters. Furthermore, that he printed the word ''kinsman'' which reads plainly ''kinsmen.'' The November, 1849, *Southern Literary Messenger* published ''Annabel Lee'' with the statement that the manuscript was handed in by Poe the day before he left Richmond. This manuscript also shows that the *Messenger* failed to follow Poe's punctuation. It has been thought that Griswold used a manuscript of Poe for his text of 1850, but it is now evident that he merely copied from *Sartain's Union Magazine*, following the error there and printing ''kinsman '' for ''kinsmen'' and using ''the'' sepulchre for ''her'' sepulchre as Poe always wrote same in all his manuscripts of the poem. This seems strange when the fact is known that Griswold had at that time a manuscript of the poem in Poe's own hand, which he did not use until later in his "Poets and Poetry of America," and then did not follow the text accurately.

Of the three known manuscript copies of "Annabel Lee," that of the *Southern Literary Messenger* closely follows the text. Poe gave away the Thorne MS. before leaving New York, in June, 1849, the Griswold copy was forwarded by mail in 1849 (no date), and he gave the *Southern Literary Messenger* copy to John R. Thompson the day previous to leaving Richmond, September 27, 1849.

ULALUME — A BALLAD

American Whig Review (" To —— —— ——." " Ulalume ": A Ballad), December, 1847; *Home Journal*, January 1, 1848; *Literary World* (" Ulalume." A Ballad), March 3, 1849; *Richmond Examiner*, October, 1849; Poe MS., 1849; "The Poets and Poetry of America," 1855.

Text, *Richmond Examiner.*

Variations from the text follow : —

II. 4. *Days :* the days. L. W.

VI. 4. *Ah :* Oh. All others except MS.

   5. *Ah :* Oh. All others except MS.

VII. 9. *Surely ;* safely. All others except MS.

VIII. 5. *But :* And. A. W. R.

IX. 9. *Ah :* Oh. A. W. R.; *hath :* has. All others except MS.

  13. *This ;* In the. A. W. R.

X. 7. *Have ;* Had. All others except MS.

Notes : Griswold, 1850, omits " We " in III. 9 and the entire tenth stanza with other slight variations from the text. In his " Poets and Poetry of America," text of 1855 he used the tenth stanza, and follows the *American Whig Review* with the exception of VII. 10, where "Have" is used for "Had" — one of Poe's last corrections.

Poe wrote to the Editor of the *Home Journal*, December 8, 1847, as follows: —

"I send you an *American Review* — the number just issued — in which is a ballad by myself, but published anonymously. It is called ' Ulalume ' — the page is turned down. I do not care to be known as its author just now; but would take it as a great favor if you would copy it in the *H. J.*, with a word of *inquiry* as to who wrote it: — provided always that you think the poem worth the room it would occupy in your paper — a matter about which I am by no means sure."

The poem appeared January 1, 1848, with the following comment: "We do not know how many readers we have who will enjoy, as we do, the following exquisitely piquant and skilful exercise of variety and niceness of language. It is a poem which we find in the *American Review*, full of beauty and oddity in sentiment and versification, but a curiosity (and a delicious one, we think) in philologic flavor. Who is the author?"

Poe wrote E. A. Duyckinck of the *Literary World* February 16, 1849: "Perhaps in the conversation I had with you in your office about 'Ulalume,' I did not make you comprehend precisely what *was* the request I made: so to save trouble I send now the enclosed from the Providence *Daily Journal*. If you will oblige me by copying the slip as it stands, prefacing it by the words 'From the Providence *Journal*' it will make everything straight." The *Literary World* printed the poem March 3, 1849, with the following note: —

"The following fascinating poem, which is from the pen of EDGAR A. POE, has been drifting about the newspapers under anonymous or mistaken imputation of authorship, — having been attributed to N. P. WILLIS. We now restore it to its proper owner. It originally appeared without name in the *American Review*. In peculiarity of versification, and a certain cold moonlight witchery, it has much of the power of the author's 'Raven.'"

In the review of H. B. Hirst (Griswold, 1850), Poe states: "To my face, and in the presence of my friends, Mr. H. has always made a point of praising my own poetical efforts; and, for this reason, I should forgive him, perhaps the amiable weakness of abusing them anonymously. In a late number of 'The Philadelphia *Courier*,' he does me the honor of attributing to my pen a ballad called 'Ulalume,' which has been going the rounds of the press, sometimes with *my* name to it; sometimes with Mr. Willis's, and sometimes with no name at all. Mr. Hirst insists upon it that *I* wrote it, and it is just possible that he knows more about the matter than I do myself. Speaking of a particular passage he says: 'We have spoken of the mystical appearance of Astarte as a fine touch of art. This is borrowed, and from the first canto of Hirst's "Endymion" . . . published years since in the *Southern Literary Messenger*:' —

> 'Slowly Endymion bent, the light Elysian
>   Flooding his figure. Kneeling on one knee,
> He loosed his sandals, lea
>   And lake and woodland glittering on his vision —

>A fairy landscape, bright and beautiful,
>With Venus at her full.' "

Astarte is another name for Venus; and when we remember that Diana is about to descend to Endymion — that the scene which is about to follow is one of love — that Venus is the star of love — and that Hirst, by introducing it as he does, shadows out his story exactly as Mr. Poe introduces his Astarte — the plagiarism of idea becomes evident. Poe quotes the fourth stanza of "Ulalume" and regrets that he finds no resemblance between the two passages in question. He then quotes four lines from "Lenore," which he charges Hirst with using in his "The Penance of Roland," and concludes: "Many a lecture, on literary topics, have I given Mr. H.; and I confess that in general he has adopted my advice so implicitly that his poems, upon the whole, are little more than our conversations done into verse."

Mrs. S. H. Whitman in a letter to the New York *Tribune* dated Providence, September 29, 1875, in answer to F. G. Fairfield's "A Mad Man of Letters," makes the following reference to "Ulalume" : —

"The *gist* of the poem is Venus 'Astarte' — the crescent star of hope and love that, after a night of horror, was seen in the constellation of Leo : —

>'Coming up through the lair of the Lion
>As the star dials hinted of morn.'

The forlorn heart might have been seen hailing it as a harbinger of happiness yet to be, hoping against hope, until, when the planet was seen to be rising over the tomb of a lost love, hope itself rejected as a cruel mockery, and the dark angel conquered. There might also be discerned in this strange and splendid phantasy something of that ethical quality found by an eloquent interpreter of Poe's genius in the July *British Quarterly*. Like the 'Epipsychidion' of Shelley, it is a poem for poets and will not readily give up 'the heart of the mystery.' "

Mrs. Whitman claimed that the last stanza of the poem was suppressed by Poe at her suggestion. This was probably Griswold's authority for leaving out that stanza in the 1850 volume ; but it is to be noted that he afterwards found out his mistake and replaced same in his later publications. All Poe's publications of the poem show the concluding stanza, and in the later revision of the poem he made two corrections in that stanza. There is no evidence to indicate a suppression.

A manuscript copy of the poem, including the last verse written by

Poe in the latter part of the year 1849, is in the library of J. Pierpont Morgan, Esq., of New York city. This manuscript was given by the poet to Miss Susan Ingram at Old Point, Virginia, during September, 1849, with the following letter: "I have transcribed 'Ulalume' with much pleasure, Dear Miss Ingram — as I am sure I would do anything else at your bidding — but I fear you will find the verses scarcely more intelligible to-day in my manuscript than last night in my recitation. I would endeavor to explain to you what I really meant — or what I fancied I meant by the poem, if it were not that I remembered Dr. Johnson's bitter and rather just remark about the folly of explaining what, if worth explanation, would explain itself. He has a happy witticism, too, about some book which he calls 'as obscure as an explanatory note.' Leaving 'Ulalume' to its fate, therefore, and in good hands, I am, yours truly."

In an article by Mrs. Gove-Nichols, published in the *Sixpenny Magazine*, February, 1863, reference is made to a poem sent to Colton, editor of the *American Whig Review*, by Poe prior to the summer of 1846, as follows: —

"We had already read the poem in conclave, and Heaven forgive us, we could not make head or tail to it. It might as well have been in any of the lost languages, for any meaning we could extract from its melodious numbers. I remember saying that I believed it was a hoax that Poe was passing off for poetry, to see how far his name would go in imposing upon people. The poem was paid for and published soon after. I presume it is regarded as genuine poetry in the collected poems of its author."

Her words would seem to apply to "Ulalume," but the poem did not appear in the *Whig Review* until the last of 1847. It may be possible that Mrs. Gove-Nichols had her dates mixed up.

TAMERLANE

1827, 1829, 1831, 1845.
Text, 1845.
Variations of 1829 and 1831 from the text ; —
3. *Deem ;* think. 1831.
26. Insert after: —

> Despair, the fabled vampire bat,
> Hath long upon my bosom sat,

> And I would rave, but that he flings
> A calm from his unearthly wings. 1831.

30. *Fierce :* Omit. 1831.
40. *Have :* Hath. 1831.
57. Was giant-like — so thou my mind. 1829; 1831.
73. *This iron heart :* that as infinite. 1831.
74 *My soul :* so was the weakness in it. 1831.
Insert after : —

> For in those days it was my lot
> To haunt of the wide world a spot
> The which I could not love the less.
> So lovely was the loneliness
> Of a wild lake with black rock bound,
> And the sultan-like pines that tower'd around!
> But when the night had thrown her pall
> Upon that spot as upon all,
> And the black wind murmur'd by,
> In a dirge of melody;
> My infant spirit would awake
> To the terror of that lone lake.
>
> Yet that terror was not fright —
> But a tremulous delight —
> A feeling not the jewell'd mine
> Could ever bribe me to define,
> Nor love, Ada! tho' it were thine.
> How could I from that water bring
> Solace to my imagining ?
> My solitary soul — how make
> An Eden of that dim lake ?
>
> But then a gentler, calmer spell,
> Like moonlight on my spirit fell,
> And O! I have no words to tell. 1831.

77. *Nor would I :* I will not. 1831.
81. *Thus I :* I well. 1831.
82. *Some page :* Pages. 1831,

86. *Oh, she was :* Was she not. 1831.

106. *Throw me on her throbbing :* lean upon her gentle. 1831.

110. *Her :* hers. 1831.

112–115. Omit. 1831.

119. *Its joy — its little lot :* of pleasure or. 1831.

120. *That was new pleasure :* The good, the bad. 1831.

128–138. Omit. 1831.

151. *On her bright :* upon her. 1831.

152. *To become :* fitted for. 1831.

164. *His :* its. 1831.

166–177.

> Say, holy father, breathes there yet
> A rebel or a Bajazet?
> How now! why tremble, man of gloom,
> As if my words were the Simoom!
> Why do the people bow the knee,
> To the young Tamerlane — to me!   1831.

202. *Splendor :* beauty. 1831.

207–212. Omit.

For 213–221 substitute: —

> I reach'd my home — what home? above
> My home — my hope — my early love,
> Lonely, like me, the desert rose,
> Bow'd down with its own glory grows.   1831.

235. *Unpolluted :* undefiled. 1831.

243. Insert after: —

> If my peace hath flown away
> In a night — or in a day —
> In a vision — or in none —
> Is it, therefore, the less gone?
> I was standing 'mid the roar
> Of a wind-beaten shore,
> And I held within my hand
> Some particles of sand —
> How bright! And yet to creep
> Thro' my fingers to the deep!

My early hopes ? no — they
Went gloriously away,
Like lightning from the sky —
Why in the battle did not I ?

The first 1827 version follows: —

TAMERLANE

I

I have sent for thee, holy friar; (¹)
But 't was not with the drunken hope,
Which is but agony of desire
To shun the fate, with which to cope
Is more than crime may dare to dream,
That I have call'd thee at this hour:
Such, father, is not my theme —
Nor am I mad, to deem that power
Of earth may shrive me of the sin
Unearthly pride hath revell'd in —
I would not call thee fool, old man,
But hope is not a gift of thine;
If I *can* hope (O God! I can)
It falls from an eternal shrine.

II

The gay wall of this gaudy tower
Grows dim around me — death is near.
I had not thought, until this hour
When passing from the earth, that ear
Of any, were it not the shade
Of one whom in life I made
All mystery but a simple name,
Might know the secret of a spirit
Bow'd down in sorrow, and in shame. —
Shame, said'st thou?

                    Ay, I did inherit
That hated portion, with the fame,

The worldly glory, which has shown
A demon-light around my throne,
Scorching my sear'd heart with a pain
Not Hell shall make me fear again.

III

I have not always been as now —
The fever'd diadem on my brow
I claim'd and won usurpingly —
Ay — the same heritage hath given
Rome to the Cæsar — this to me;
The heirdom of a kingly mind —
And a proud spirit, which hath striven
Triumphantly with human kind.

In mountain air I first drew life;
The mists of the Taglay have shed ([2])
Nightly their dews on my young head;
And my brain drank their venom then,
When after day of perilous strife
With chamois, I would seize his den
And slumber, in my pride of power,
The infant monarch of the hour —
For, with the mountain dew by night,
My soul imbibed unhallow'd feeling;
And I would feel its essence stealing
In dreams upon me — while the light
Flashing from cloud that hover'd o'er,
Would seem to my half closing eye
The pageantry of monarchy!
And the deep thunder's echoing roar
Came hurriedly upon me, telling
Of war, and tumult, where my voice,
My *own* voice, silly child! was swelling
(O how would my wild heart rejoice
And leap within me at the cry)
The battle-cry of victory!

. . . .

IV

The rain came down upon my head
But barely shelter'd — and the wind
Pass'd quickly o'er me — but my mind
Was maddening — for 't was man that shed
Laurels upon me — and the rush,
The torrent of the chilly air
Gurgled in my pleased ear the crush
Of empires, with the captive's prayer,
The hum of suitors, the mix'd tone
Of flattery round a sovereign's throne.

The storm had ceased — and I awoke —
Its spirit cradled me to sleep,
And as it pass'd me by, there broke
Strange light upon me, tho' it were
My soul in mystery to steep:
For I was not as I had been;
The child of Nature, without care,
Or thought, save of the passing scene. —

V

My passions, from that hapless hour,
Usurp'd a tyranny, which men
Have deem'd, since I have reach'd to power,
My innate nature — be it so:
But, father, there lived one who, then —
Then in my boyhood, when their fire
Burn'd with a still intenser glow;
(For passion must with youth expire)
Even *then*, who deem'd this iron heart
In woman's weakness had a part.

I have no words, alas! to tell
The loveliness of loving well!
Nor would I dare attempt to trace
The breathing beauty of a face,

Which even to *my* impassion'd mind,
Leaves not its memory behind.
In spring of life have ye ne'er dwelt
Some object of delight upon,
With steadfast eye, till ye have felt
The earth reel — and the vision gone ?
And I have held to memory's eye
One object — and but one — until
Its very form hath pass'd me by,
But left its influence with me still.

VI

'T is not to thee that I should name —
Thou canst not — wouldst not dare to think
The magic empire of a flame
Which even upon this perilous brink
Hath fix'd my soul, tho' unforgiven,
By what it lost for passion — Heaven.
I loved — and O, how tenderly!
Yes! she [was] worthy of all love!
Such as in infancy was mine,
Tho' then its *passion* could not be:
'T was such as angels' minds above
Might envy — her young heart the shrine
On which my every hope and thought
Were incense — then a goodly gift —
For they were childish, without sin,
Pure as her young example taught;
Why did I leave it and adrift,
Trust to the fickle star within ?

VII

We grew in age and love together,
Roaming the forest and the wild;
My breast her shield in wintry weather,
And when the friendly sunshine smiled
And she would mark the opening skies,
I saw no Heaven but in her eyes —

Even childhood knows the human heart;
For when, in sunshine and in smiles,
From all our little cares apart,
Laughing at her half silly wiles,
I'd throw me on her throbbing breast,
And pour my spirit out in tears,
She'd look up in my wilder'd eye —
There was no need to speak the rest —
No need to quiet her kind fears —
She did not ask the reason why.

The hallow'd memory of those years
Comes o'er me in these lonely hours,
And, with sweet loveliness, appears
As perfume of strange summer flowers;
Of flowers which we have known before
In infancy, which seen, recall
To mind — not flowers alone — but more,
Our earthly life, and love — and all.

VIII

Yes! she was worthy of all love!
Even such as from the accursed time
My spirit with the tempest strove,
When on the mountain peak alone,
Ambition lent it a new tone,
And bade it first to dream of crime,
My frenzy to her bosom taught:
We still were young: no purer thought
Dwelt in a seraph's breast than *thine ;* ([3])
For passionate love is still divine:
I loved her as an angel might
With ray of the all living light
Which blazes upon Edis' shrine. ([4])
It is not surely sin to name,
With such as mine — that mystic flame,
I had no being but in thee!
The world with all its train of bright
And happy beauty (for to me

All was an undefined delight),
The world — its joy — its share of pain
Which I felt not — its bodied forms   ˎ
Of varied being, which contain
The bodiless spirits of the storms,
The sunshine, and the calm — the ideal
And fleeting vanities of dreams,
Fearfully beautiful! the real
Nothings of mid-day waking life —
Of an enchanted life, which seems,
Now as I look back, the strife
Of some ill demon, with a power
Which left me in an evil hour,
All that I felt, or saw, or thought,
Crowding, confused became
(With thine unearthly beauty fraught)
Thou — and the nothing of a name.

IX

The passionate spirit which hath known,
And deeply felt the silent tone
Of its own self supremacy, —
(I speak thus openly to thee,
'T were folly *now* to veil a thought
With which this aching breast is fraught)
The soul which feels its innate right —
The mystic empire and high power
Given by the energetic might
Of Genius, at its natal hour;
Which knows (believe me at this time,
When falsehood were a tenfold crime,
There *is* a power in the high spirit
To *know* the fate it will inherit)
The soul, which knows such power, will still
Find *Pride* the ruler of his will.

Yes! I was proud — and ye who know
The magic of that meaning word,

So oft perverted, will bestow
Your scorn, perhaps, when ye have heard
That the proud spirit had been broken,
The proud heart burst in agony
At one upbraiding word or token
Of her that heart's idolatry —
I was ambitious — have ye known
Its fiery passion ? — ye have not —
A cottager, I mark'd a throne
Of half the world, as all my own,
And murmur'd at such lowly lot!
But it had pass'd me as a dream
Which, of light step, flies with the dew,
That kindling thought — did not the beam
Of Beauty, which did guide it through
The livelong summer day, oppress
My mind with double loveliness —

 .   .   .   .

x

We walk'd together on the crown
Of a high mountain, which look'd down
Afar from its proud natural towers
Of rock and forest, on the hills —
The dwindled hills, whence amid bowers
Her own fair hand had rear'd around,
Gush'd shoutingly a thousand rills,
Which as it were, in fairy bound
Embraced two hamlets — those our own —
Peacefully happy — yet alone —

 .   .   .   .

I spoke to her of power and pride —
But mystically, in such guise,
That she might deem it nought beside
The moment's converse; in her eyes
I read (perhaps too carelessly)
A mingled feeling with my own;
The flush on her bright cheek to me,
Seem'd to become a queenly throne

Too well, that I should let it be
A light in the dark wild, alone.

XI

There — in that hour — a thought came o'er
My mind, it had not known before —
To leave her while we both were young, —
To follow my high fate among
The strife of nations, and redeem
The idle words, which, as a dream
Now sounded to her heedless ear —
I held no doubt — I knew no fear
Of peril in my wild career;
To gain an empire, and throw down
As nuptial dowry — a queen's crown,
The only feeling which possest,
With her own image, my fond breast —
Who, that had known the secret thought
Of a young peasant's bosom then,
Had deem'd him, in compassion, aught
But one, whom fantasy had led
Astray from reason — Among men
Ambition is chain'd down — nor fed
(As in the desert, where the grand,
The wild, the beautiful, conspire
With their own breath to fan its fire)
With thoughts such feeling can command;
Uncheck'd by sarcasm, and scorn
Of those, who hardly will conceive
That any should become "great," born (⁵)
In their own sphere — will not believe
That they shall stoop in life to one
Whom daily they are wont to see
Familiarly — whom Fortune's sun
Hath ne'er shone dazzlingly upon,
Lowly — and of their own degree —

XII

I pictured to my fancy's eye
Her silent, deep astonishment,
When, a few fleeting years gone by,
(For short the time my high hope lent
To its most desperate intent,)
She might recall in him, whom Fame
Had gilded with a conqueror's name
(With glory — such as might inspire
Perforce, a passing thought of one,
Whom she had deem'd in his own fire
Wither'd and blasted; who had gone
A traitor, violate of the truth
So plighted in his early youth,)
Her own Alexis, who should plight (6)
The love he plighted *then* — again,
And raise his infancy's delight,
The bride and queen of Tamerlane. —

XIII

One noon of a bright summer's day
I pass'd from out the matted bower
Where in a deep, still slumber lay
My Ada. In that peaceful hour,
A silent gaze was my farewell.
I had no other solace — then
To awake her, and a falsehood tell
Of a feign'd journey, were again
To trust the weakness of my heart
To her soft thrilling voice: To part
Thus, haply, while in sleep she dream'd
Of long delight, nor yet had deem'd
Awake, that I had held a thought
Of parting, were with madness fraught;
I knew not woman's heart, alas!
Tho' loved, and loving — let it pass. —

XIV

I went from out the matted bower
And hurried madly on my way:
And felt, with every flying hour,
That bore me from my home, more gay;
There is of earth an agony
Which, ideal, still may be
The worst ill of mortality.
'T is bliss, in its own reality,
Too real, to *his* breast who lives
Not within himself but gives
A portion of his willing soul
To God, and to the great whole —
To him, whose loving spirit will dwell
With Nature, in her wild paths; tell
Of her wondrous ways, and telling bless
Her overpowering loveliness!
A more than agony to him
Whose failing sight will grow dim
With its own living gaze upon
That loveliness around: the sun —
The blue sky — the misty light
Of the pale cloud therein, whose hue
Is grace to its heavenly bed of blue;
Dim! tho' looking on all bright!
O God! when the thoughts that may not pass
Will burst upon him, and alas!
For the flight on Earth to Fancy given,
There are no words — unless of Heaven.

XV

Look round thee now on Samarcand,(⁷)
Is she not queen of earth? her pride
Above all cities? in her hand
Their destinies? with all beside
Of glory, which the world hath known?
Stands she not proudly and alone?

And who her sovereign? Timur, he ([8])
Whom the astonish'd earth hath seen,
With victory, on victory,
Redoubling age! and more, I ween,
The Zinghis' yet re-echoing fame. ([9])
And now what has he? what! a name.
The sound of revelry by night
Comes o'er me, with the mingled voice
Of many with a breast as light
As if 't were not the dying hour
Of one, in whom they did rejoice —
As in a leader, haply — Power
Its venom secretly imparts;
Nothing have I with human hearts.

XVI

When Fortune mark'd me for her own
And my proud hopes had reach'd a throne
(It boots me not, good friar, to tell
A tale the world but knows too well,
How by what hidden deeds of might,
I clamber'd to the tottering height,)
I still was young; and well I ween
My spirit what it e'er had been.
My eyes were still on pomp and power,
My wilder'd heart was far away
In the valleys of the wild Taglay,
In mine own Ada's matted bower.
I dwelt not long in Samarcand
Ere, in a peasant's lowly guise,
I sought my long-abandon'd land;
By sunset did its mountains rise
In dusky grandeur to my eyes:
But as I wander'd on the way
My heart sunk with the sun's ray.
To him, who still would gaze upon
The glory of the summer sun,
There comes, when that sun will from him part,
A sullen hopelessness of heart.

--

That soul will hate the evening mist
So often lovely, and will list
To the sound of the coming darkness (known
To those whose spirits hearken) ([10]) as one
Who in a dream of night *would* fly,
But cannot, from a danger nigh.
What though the moon — the silvery moon —
Shine on his path, in her high noon;
Her smile is chilly, and *her* beam
In that time of dreariness will seem
As the portrait of one after death;
A likeness taken when the breath
Of young life, and the fire o' the eye,
Had lately been, but had pass'd by.
'T is thus when the lovely summer sun
Of our boyhood, his course hath run:
For all we live to know — is known;
And all we seek to keep — hath flown;
With the noon-day beauty, which is all.
Let life, then, as the day-flower, fall —
The transient, passionate day-flower,([11])
Withering at the evening hour.

XVII

I reach'd my home — my home no more —
For all was flown that made it so —
I pass'd from out its mossy door,
In vacant idleness of woe.
There met me on its threshold stone
A mountain hunter, I had known
In childhood, but he knew me not.
Something he spoke of the old cot:
It had seen better days, he said;
There rose a fountain once, and *there*
Full many a fair flower raised its head:
But she who rear'd them was long dead,
And in such follies had no part,
What was there left me *now?* despair —
A kingdom for a broken — heart.

Variations in Poe's MS. from above follows : —

IV. 9. *The mixed tone :* and the tone.

   13. *Dare attempt :* now attempt.

V. 14. *Breathing :* more than.

   15. *My :* this.

   21. *And have :* so have I.

VIII. 2. Such as I taught her from the time.

   7–10. There were no holier thoughts than thine.

   11. *Her :* thee.

   21. *Which I felt not :* Unheeded then.

   30. *Some :* an.

   33. *Confused :* confusedly.

IX. 4–10. Omit.

   11. *Me at this time :* for now on me.

   12. Truth flashes thro eternity.

   15. *Knows :* feels.

   26. *Its :* The.

X. 6. *Own fair :* magic.

   8–10.

> Encircling with a glittering bound
> Of diamond sunshine and sweet spray
> Two mossy huts of the Taglay.

XI. 12–13.

> The undying hope which now opprest.
> A spirit ne'er to be at rest.

   14. *Secret :* silent.

   17. *Led :* thrown.

   18. *Astray from reason :* Her mantle over.

   19. *Ambition :* Lion Ambition: nor fed. Omit.
Insert : —

> And crouches to a keeper's hand.

   20. *As in the desert :* Not so in deserts.

   21. *Beautifies :* terrible.

   22. *Its :* his.

XV. 6. *Proudly :* nobly.

   8. *Earth hath seen :* people saw.

9–11.

> Striding o'er empires haughtily,
> A diademed outlaw,
> More than the Zinghis in his fame.

12. *What:* even.

16. *The dying:* their parting.

17. *Of:* From.

20. *Nothing have I:* And I have naught.

POE'S NOTES TO THE EDITION OF 1827

NOTE 1

I have sent for thee, holy friar.

Of the history of Tamerlane little is known; and with that little I have taken the full liberty of a poet. — That he was descended from the family of Zinghis Khan is more than probable — but he is vulgarly supposed to have been the son of a shepherd, and to have raised himself to the throne by his own address. He died in the year 1405, in the time of Pope Innocent VII.

How I shall account for giving him "a friar" as a death-bed confessor — I cannot exactly determine. He wanted some one to listen to his tale — and why not a friar? It does not pass the bounds of possibility — quite sufficient for my purpose — and I have at least good authority on my side for such innovations.

NOTE 2

The mists of the Taglay have shed, &c.

The mountains of Belur Taglay are a branch of the Imaus, in the southern part of Independent Tartary. They are celebrated for the singular wildness and beauty of their valleys.

NOTE 3

No purer thought
Dwelt in seraph's breast than thine.

I must beg the reader's pardon for making Tamerlane, a Tartar of the fourteenth century, speak in the same language as a Boston gentleman of the nineteenth; but of the Tartar mythology we have little information.

NOTE 4

Which blazes upon Edis' shrine.

A deity presiding over virtuous love, upon whose imaginary altar a sacred fire was continually blazing.

NOTE 5

——— *Who hardly will conceive*
That any should become "great," born
In their own sphere —

Although Tamerlane speaks this, it is not the less true. It is a matter of the greatest difficulty to make the generality of mankind believe that one with whom they are upon terms of intimacy shall be called, in the world, a "great man." The reason is evident. There are few great men. Their actions are consequently viewed by the mass of the people through the medium of distance. The prominent parts of their characters are alone noted; and those properties, which are minute and common to every one, not being observed, seem to have no connection with a great character.

Who ever read the private memorials, correspondence, &c., which have become so common in our time, without wondering that "great men" should act and think "so abominably"?

NOTE 6

Her own Alexis, who should plight, &c.

That Tamerlane acquired his renown under a feigned name is not entirely a fiction.

NOTE 7

Look round thee now on Samarcand.

I believe it was after the battle of Angora that Tamerlane made Samarcand his residence. It became for a time the seat of learning and the arts

NOTE 8

And who her sovereign? Timur, &c.

He was called Timur Bek as well as Tamerlane.

NOTE 9

The Zinghis' yet re-echoing fame.

The conquests of Tamerlane far exceeded those of Zinghis Khan. He boasted to have two-thirds of the world at his command.

NOTE 10

The sound of the coming darkness (known
To those whose spirits hearken).

I have often fancied that I could distinctly hear the sound of the darkness, as it steals over the horizon — a foolish fancy, perhaps, but not more unintelligible than to see music —

"The mind the music breathing from her face."

NOTE 11

Let life then, as the day-flower, fall.

There is a flower (I have never known its botanic name), vulgarly called the day-flower. It blooms beautifully in the daylight, but withers towards evening, and by night its leaves appear totally shrivelled and dead. I have forgotten, however, to mention in the text, that it lives again in the morning. If it will not flourish in Tartary, I must be forgiven for carrying it thither.

SONNET TO SCIENCE

1829; *Philadelphia Casket*, 1830, 1831; *Southern Literary Messenger*, May, 1836; *Graham's Magazine* ("The Island of the Fay," 1841); 1845; *Broadway Journal*, II, 4; *Philadelphia Saturday Museum*, March 4, 1843.
Text, 1845.

Variations from the text: —
1. *True:* meet. 1829; P. C.; 1831; S. L. M.
2. *Peering:* piercing. P. C.
3. *The:* they. P. C.
5. *Should:* shall. P. C.
8. *Soared:* soar. S. L. M.
Insert after 10: —

Hast thou not spoilt a story in each star?
Hast thou not torn the Naiad from her flood?

> The elfin from the grass? — the dainty *fay*
> The witch, the sprite, the goblin — where are they?
>
> Anon.   G. M.

11. *A:* for. P. C.

12. The gentle Naiad from her fountain flood. 1829; S. L. M. *Her.* the. P. C.

13. *Grass:* wood. P. C.

14. *Tamarind tree:* shrubbery. 1831; S. L. M.; P. C. *Summer:* summers. P. C.

AL AARAAF

1829, Poe MS., 1829; 1831, 1845; I. lines 66–67, 70–79, 82–101, 126–129; II. 20–21, 24–27, 52–59, 68–135 appeared in the *Philadelphia Saturday Museum*, March 4, 1843.

Text, 1845.

Variations from the text: —

1–15. Mysterious star!
        Thou wert my dream
        All a long summer night —
        Be now my theme!
        By this clear stream,
        Of thee will I write;
        Meantime from afar
        Bathe me in light!

        Thy world has not the dross of ours,
        Yet all the beauty — all the flowers
        That list our love, or deck our bowers
        In dreamy gardens, where do lie
        Dreamy maidens all the day,
        While the silver winds of Circassy
        On violet couches faint away.
        Little — oh! little dwells in thee
        Like unto what on earth we see:
        Beauty's eye is here the bluest
        In the falsest and untruest —
        On the sweetest air doth float
        The most sad and solemn note —

> If with thee be broken hearts,
> Joy so peacefully departs,
> That its echo still doth dwell,
> Like the murmur in the shell.
> Thou! thy truest type of grief
> Is the gently falling leaf —
> Thou! thy framing is so holy
> Sorrow is not melancholy.   1831.

11. *Oh:* With. 1831. Ah. 1829 MS.

19. *An oasis:* a garden-spot. 1829; 1831.

43. rear. 1831.

88. *Which:* That. S. M.

95. *Red:* Omit 1831.

127. *Merest:* verest. S. M.

128. *All:* Here. 1829; 1831; S. M.

Part II. 33. *Peered:* ventured. 1829.

53. *Cheeks were:* cheeks was. S. M.

56. *That:* this. S. M.

58. *Fairy:* brilliant. S. M.

91. *Wings:* S. M.

92. *Each . . . thing:* All . . . things. S. M.

94. *Would:* will. S. M.

99. *Lead:* hang. 1829; 1831.

117. *A deep dreamy.* S. M.

197. *The orb of the Earth:* one constant star. 1829; 1831.

213. *He:* it. 1829; 1831.

In the *Saturday Museum* transpose II. lines 20–59.

Notes: In *Graham's Magazine*, February, 1845, which was revised by Poe, referring to the lines of "Ligeia" in "Al Aaraaf" it is stated: "In a poem called 'Ligeia' he intended to personify the music of nature." In "The Rationale of Verse" Poe refers to other lines in Part II, beginning: "Dim was its little disk, and angel eyes," and says: "the passages occur in a boyish poem written by myself when a boy. I am referring to the sudden and rapid advent of a star."

Poe evidently derived the name "Al Aaraaf" from Al-Araf, signifying the partition between Paradise and Hell, which is mentioned in the chapter copied from the great gulf of separation mentioned in Scripture. They call it Al-Orf, or more frequently Al Araf — a word derived from the verb Arafa, which signifies to distinguish between things or to part them. See Poe's own "Al Aaraaf" notes.

That he was not satisfied with the name "Al Aaraaf" as taking part in the affairs of the poem is most evident from two changes made by him. The first was made in the copy of the 1829 poems, which he used for the copy of his 1845 poems. In the second part of the poem where it says:

"When first Al Aaraaf knew her course to be" he changed "Al Aaraaf" to read *Tophet*, and when he quoted the passage again late in life in "The Rationale of Verse" he changed it a second time to *The Phantoms*.

In the 1829 volume there are two changes which do not appear elsewhere. In Part II, 38th line, "the" is changed to *thy*; and in the next line following, "Of beautiful Gomorroh!" reads *Too beautiful Gomorroh.*

ROMANCE

Philadelphia Saturday Museum, March 4, 1843; 1845; *Broadway Journal*, II, 8. — *Preface*, 1829; Poe MS., 1829; *Introduction*, 1831.

Text, 1845.

Variations of 1829 from the text: —
12. Heavens. B. J.
14. I scarcely have had time for cares. S. M.
    I have time for no idle cares. 1829 MS.
The 1831 version is as follows: —

INTRODUCTION

Romance, who loves to nod and sing,
With drowsy head and folded wing,
Among the green leaves as they shake,
Far down within some shadowy lake,
   To me a painted paroquet
Hath been — a most familiar bird —
   Taught me my alphabet to say, —
To lisp my very earliest word
While in the wild-wood I did lie
A child — with a most knowing eye
Succeeding years, too wild for song,
Then roll'd like tropic storms along;

Where, tho' the garish lights that fly,
Dying along the troubled sky
Lay bare, thro' vistas thunder-riven,
The blackness of the general Heaven,
That very blackness yet doth fling
Light on the lightning's silver wing.

For, being an idle boy lang syne,
Who read Anacreon, and drank wine,
I early found Anacreon rhymes
Were almost passionate sometimes —
And by strange alchemy of brain
His pleasures always turn'd to pain —
His naivete to wild desire —
His wit to love — his wine to fire —
And so, being young and dipt in folly
I fell in love with melancholy,
And used to throw my earthly rest
And quiet all away in jest —
I could not love except where Death
Was mingling his with Beauty's breath
Or Hymen, Time, and Destiny
Were stalking between her and me.

O, then the eternal Condor years,
So shook the very Heavens on high,
With tumult as they thunder'd by;
I had no time for idle cares,
Thro' gazing on the unquiet sky!
Or if an hour with calmer wing
Its down did on my spirit fling,
That little hour with lyre and rhyme
To while away — forbidden thing!
My heart half fear'd to be a crime
Unless it trembled with the string.
But *now* my soul hath too much room —
Gone are the glory and the gloom —
The black hath mellow'd into grey,
And all the fires are fading away.

> My draught of passion hath been deep —
> I revell'd, and I now would sleep —
> And after-drunkenness of soul
> Succeeds the glories of the bowl —
> An idle longing night and day
> To dream my very life away.
>
> But dreams — of those who dream as I,
> Aspiringly, are damned, and die:
> Yet should I swear I mean alone,
> By notes so very shrilly blown,
> To break upon Time's monotone,
> While yet my vapid joy and grief
> Are tintless of the yellow leaf —
> Why not an imp the graybeard hath
> Will shake his shadow in my path —
> And even the graybeard will o'erlook
> Connivingly my dreaming-book.

Variations from 1829 follow : —

11–34. Omit.

35. *O, then the :* Of late.

36. *Shook the very Heavens :* shake the very air.

37. *Thunder'd :* thunder.

38. I hardly have had time for cares.

40. *Or if . . . wing :* And when . . . wings.

41. *Did on . . . fling :* upon . . . flings.

43. *Things :* thing.

44. *Half-feared :* would feel.

45. *Unless it trembled . . . strings :* Did it not tremble . . . strings.

46–66. Omit.

Notes : The manuscript changes made by Poe in this poem exist in the presentation copy of " Al Aaraaf, Tamerlane and Minor Poems," to his cousin Elizabeth Herring. The date on the title-page of this copy is 1820. The volume was used by Poe while editing the *Broadway Journal* and in printing the 1845 edition of his poems. The changes in this copy indicate that the third draft was made into the *Broadway Journal.*

SONG

"I SAW THEE ON THY BRIDAL DAY"

1827, 1829, Poe MS., 1829; 1845; *Broadway Journal*, II, 11.
Text, 1845.

Variations from the text: —

I. 1. *Thy:* the. 1827.

II. 2. Of young passions free. 1827.

    3. *Aching:* chained. 1827; fetter'd. 1829.

    4. *Could:* might. 1827.

III. 1. *Perhaps:* I ween. 1827.

Notes: The manuscript of this poem in Poe's hand, written about 1829, is in the library of a Chicago collector. It has the additional heading of "In an Album," and on the margin where four lines of the second stanza is omitted is written "4 lines omitted see last page." The last page however is missing. A volume of the *Saturday Evening Post* for 1826 with a few notations in Poe's hand, and coming from the counting house of Ellis & Allan, Richmond, Virginia, where Poe was employed in 1827, has a poem reading: —

> "I saw her on the bridal day,
> In blushing beauty blest,
> Smiles o'er her lips were seen to play
> Like gilded gleams at dawn of day,
> The fairest of the guest."

The changes from 1829 to 1845 are also noted in the 1829 copy of poems with Poe's revision. The word *Though* appears changed throughout from "Tho'."

DREAMS

1827

Text, 1827.

Note: The manuscript of this poem, in Poe's hand, written about 1829, now in the library of J. Pierpont Morgan, Esq., shows the following variations from the text: —

    5. *Cold:* dull.

    6. *Must:* shall.

7. *Still upon the lovely :* ever, on the chilly.
14. *Dreams of living :* dreamy fields of.
15. *Loveliness have left my very :* left unheedingly my.
19. *Only.* In italics.
27. After *tho'* insert *but I have been.* No italics.

SPIRITS OF THE DEAD

Visit of the Dead — 1827; Poe MS.

Spirits of the Dead — 1829; *Burton's Gentleman's Magazine,* July, 1839.

Text, *Burton's Gentleman's Magazine.*

Variations from the text : —

II. 1. *that :* thy. MS.

III. 8. Insert after : —

> But 't will leave thee as each star
> With the dewdrop flies afar. MS.

IV. 4. *Dewdrops :* dewdrop. MS.; 1829; B. G. M.

The 1827 version runs as follows : —

VISIT OF THE DEAD

> Thy soul shall find itself alone —
> Alone of all on earth — unknown
> The cause — but none are near to pry
> Into thy hour of secrecy.
> Be silent in that solitude,
> Which is not loneliness — for then
> The spirits of the dead, who stood
> In life before thee, are again
> In death around thee, and their will
> Shall then o'ershadow thee — be still:
> For the night, tho' clear, shall frown;
> And the stars shall look not down
> From their thrones, in the dark heaven,
> With light like Hope to mortals given,
> But their red orbs, without beam,
> To thy withering heart shall seem

As a burning, and a fever
Which would cling to thee forever.
But 't will leave thee, as each star
In the morning light afar
Will fly thee — and vanish:
— But its *thought* thou canst not banish.
The breath of God will be still;
And the mist upon the hill
By that summer breeze unbroken
Shall charm thee — as a token,
And a symbol which shall be
Secrecy in thee.

EVENING STAR

1827

Text, 1827.

TO ——— (A DREAM WITHIN A DREAM)

Imitation, 1827; To ———, 1829; Tamerlane, 1831; A Dream within
a Dream, *Flag of Our Union*, March 31, 1849; *Richmond Examiner*
(To ———), October, 1849; *Griswold*, 1850.

Text, *Richmond Examiner*.

Variations from the text : —

1. *Thy:* the all others.
4. *To:* Who all others.

The earliest version (1827) is as follows:

IMITATION

A dark unfathom'd tide
Of interminable pride —
A mystery, and a dream,
Should my early life seem;
I say that dream was fraught
With a wild, and waking thought
Of beings that have been,
Which my spirit hath not seen,

Had I let them pass me by,
With a dreaming eye!

Let none of earth inherit
That vision on my spirit;
Those thoughts I would control,
As a spell upon his soul:
For that bright hope at last
And that light time have past,
And my worldly rest hath gone
With a sigh as it pass'd on:
I care not tho' it perish
With a thought I then did cherish.

The 1829 revision is as follows: —

TO ———

Should my early life seem
[As well it might] a dream —
Yet I build no faith upon
The King Napoleon —
I look not up afar
For my destiny in a star:

In parting from you now
Thus much I will avow —
There are beings, and have been
Whom my spirit had not seen
Had I let them pass me by
With a dreaming eye —
If my peace hath fled away
In a night — or in a day —
In a vision — or in none —
Is it therefore the less gone?

I am standing 'mid the roar
Of a weather-beaten shore,

And I hold within my hand
Some particles of sand —
How few ! and how they creep
Thro' my fingers to the deep !
My early hopes ? no — they
Went gloriously away,
Like lightning from the sky
At once — and so will I.

So young ! Ah ! no — not now —
Thou hast not seen my brow,
But they tell thee I am proud —
They lie — they lie aloud —
My bosom beats with shame
At the paltriness of name
With which they dare combine
A feeling such as mine —
Nor Stoic ? I am not:
In the terror of my lot
I laugh to think how poor
That pleasure "to endure !"
What ! shade of Zeno ! — I !
Endure ! — no — no — defy.

Notes : The lines 13–27 appear in " Tamerlane," 1831, revised. In line 18 of "Imitation," the word " sigh " is printed "sight." It is conjectured that Poe's last revision, " To ——," was addressed to "Annie," Mrs. Richmond. In 1849, Poe also sent to Mrs. Richmond all but the first nine lines as a separate poem signed "Edgar," and with the title "For Annie." A facsimile of the manuscript appeared in the London *Bookman* for January, 1909.

Variations in the manuscript are as follows : —

10. *All.* No italics.
19. *O :* Oh.
21. *O :* Oh.
23. *We :* I.

"IN YOUTH HAVE I KNOWN ONE WITH WHOM THE EARTH"

1827

Text, 1827.

Notes: The title "Stanzas" previously used with this poem is the late E. C. Stedman's, and unauthorized. If this was one of the poems written by Poe in 1821–22, he afterwards added the quotation from Byron — "The Island," which was not published until June, 1823.

A DREAM

1827, no title; 1829; 1845; *Broadway Journal,* II. 6.

Text, 1845.

Variations from the text: —
Insert as first stanza: —

> A wilder'd being from my birth,
>   My spirit spurn'd control,
> But now, abroad on the wide earth,
>   Where wanderest thou, my soul ?   1827.

II. 1. *Ah !* And. 1827; 1829.
IV. 1. *Storm and:* misty. 1827.
   2. *Trembled from:* dimly shone. 1827.

"THE HAPPIEST DAY — THE HAPPIEST HOUR"

1827

Text, 1827.

THE LAKE. TO ———

1827, 1829, MS.; 1831 (in "Tamerlane"); 1845; New York, *Missionary Memorial,* 1846.

Text, *Missionary Memorial.*

The 1827 version is as follows: —

THE LAKE

In youth's spring it was my lot
To haunt of the wide earth a spot
'The which I could not love the less;
So lovely was the loneliness
Of a wild lake, with black rock bound,
And the tall pines that tower'd around.
But when the night had thrown her pall
Upon that spot — as upon all,
And the wind would pass me by
In its stilly melody,
My infant spirit would awake
To the terror of the lone lake.
Yet that terror was not fright —
But a tremulous delight,
And a feeling undefined,
Springing from a darken'd mind.
Death was in that poison'd wave
And in its gulf a fitting grave
For him who thence could solace bring
To his dark imagining;
Whose wildering thought could even make
An Eden of that dim lake.

Variations from the text: —

1. *In youth's spring:* In spring of youth. 1845.
9. *ghastly wind went by:* black wind murmured by. 1829.
   Ghastly: mystic. 1845.
10. *In a dirge-like:* In a stilly. MS.; In a dirge of. 1829. *In a dirge-like:* murmuring in. 1845.
11. *Then — ah then:* my boyish. MS.
12. *That:* the. All others.
15-17.   A feeling not the jewell'd mine
          Should ever bribe me to define —
          Nor Love — although the Love be mine.   1829.

19. *Depth:* gulf, all others.

Note: A manuscript copy of this poem in Poe's hand, written about 1829, is now in the library of J. Pierpont Morgan, Esq., of New York city.

TO ———

"THE BOWERS, WHEREAT, IN DREAMS, I SEE"

1829; 1845; *Broadway Journal*, II. 11.

Text, 1845

Variations of 1829 from the text: —

III. 3. *The.* Omit.

4. *Baubles* : trifles.

TO THE RIVER ———

1829; Poe's MS. 1829; *Burton's Gentleman's Magazine*, August, 1839; *Philadelphia Saturday Museum*, March 4, 1843; 1845; *Broadway Journal,* II. 9.

Text, 1845

Variations from the text: —

I. 2. *Crystal wandering:* labyrinth-like. 1829. MS.; B. G. M.

II. 2. In parenthesis. MS.; B. G. M.

4. *Her worshipper:* Thy pretty self. MS.

5. *His:* my. 1829; MS.; B. G. M.; B. J.

6. *Deeply:* lightly. MS.

7. *His:* The. 1829; MS.; B. G. M.; B. J.

8. *Of her soul-searching:* The scrutiny of her. 1829; MS.; B. G. M.

Note: A manuscript copy of this poem in Poe's hand, written about 1829, is in the library of a Chicago collector, and in addition has the title "In an Album."

TO ———

To ———; "I heed not that my earthly lot." Poe MS.; "Alone;" MS. To M———; 1829; Griswold, 1850.

Text, Poe MS.

The earliest 1829 form of the poem is as follows with MS. changes noted below: —

TO M——

O! I care not that my earthly lot
Hath little of Earth in it —
That years of love have been forgot
In the fever of a minute —

I heed not that the desolate
Are happier sweet, than I —
But that *you* meddle with *my* fate
Who am a passer by.

It *is* not that my founts of bliss
Are gushing — strange! with tears —
Or that the thrill of a single kiss
Hath palsied many years —

'T is not that the flowers of twenty springs
Which have wither'd as they rose
Lie dead on my heart-strings
With the weight of an age of snows.

Nor that the grass — O! may it thrive!
On my grave is growing or grown —
But that, while I am dead yet alive
I cannot be, lady, alone.   .

9. *It is not:* I heed not.
10. *Are gushing:* Be gushing, oh!
    Or that the thrill of a single: That the tremor of one.
19. *Yet :* And.
20. *Lady :* love.
Note : The manuscript of this poem in Poe's later-year handwriting is
in the Griswold collection signed E. A. P.

FAIRY–LAND

1829, 1831; *Burton's Gentleman's Magazine*, August, 1839, 1845;
Broadway Journal, II. 13.

Text, 1845

Variations of 1829 from the text : —

13. *kind :* sort.

20. *Over halls :* and rich.

44. *Never contented things :* The unbelieving things.

The 1831 version is as follows: —

FAIRY–LAND

Sit down beside me, Isabel,
Here, dearest, where the moonbeam fell
Just now so fairy-like and well.
Now thou art dress'd for paradise!
I am star-stricken with thine eyes!
My soul is lolling on thy sighs!
Thy hair is lifted by the moon
Like flowers by the low breath of June!
Sit down, sit down — how came we here?
Or is it all but a dream, my dear?

You know that most enormous flower —
That rose — that what d' ye call it — that hung
Up like a dog-star in this bower —
To-day (the wind blew, and) it swung
So impudently in my face,
So like a thing alive you know,
I tore it from its pride of place
And shook it into pieces — so
Be all ingratitude requited.
The winds ran off with it delighted,
And, thro' the opening left, as soon
As she threw off her cloak, yon moon
Has sent a ray down with a tune.

And this ray is a *fairy* ray —
Did you not say so, Isabel?
How fantastically it fell
With a spiral twist and a swell,
And over the wet grass rippled away
With a tinkling like a bell!
In my own country all the way
We can discover a moon ray
Which thro' some tatter'd curtain pries
Into the darkness of a room,
Is by (the very source of gloom)

The motes, and dust, and flies,
On which it trembles and lies
Like joy upon sorrow!
O, *when* will come the morrow?
Isabel, do you not fear
The night and the wonders here?
Dim vales! and shadowy floods!
And cloudy-looking woods
Whose forms we can't discover
For the tears that drip all over!

Huge moons — see! wax and wane
Again — again — again.
Every moment of the night —
Forever changing places!
How they put out the starlight
With the breath from their pale faces!

Lo! one is coming down
With its centre on the crown
Of a mountain's eminence!
Down — still down — and down —
Now deep shall he — O deep!
The passion of our sleep!
For that wide circumference
In easy drapery falls
Drowsily over halls —

Over ruin'd walls —
Over waterfalls,
(Silent waterfalls!)
O'er the strange woods — o'er the sea —
Alas! over the sea!

Notes: In *Burton's Gentleman's Magazine* there was the following note to the poem: "The Fairy-land of our correspondent is not orthodox. His description differs from all received accounts of the country — but our readers will pardon the extravagance for the vigor of the delineation."

In the 1829 edition Poe called attention at the thirty-third line to the following footnote: "Plagiarism. See the works of Thomas Moore — passim."

Poe used the first four lines of this poem, slightly revised, in Dream-Land, lines 9 to 12. See extracts from the *Yankee and Boston Literary Gazette*, page 176.

TO HELEN

1831; *Southern Literary Messenger*, March, 1836; *Graham's Magazine*, September, 1841; February, 1845; *Philadelphia Saturday Museum*, March 4, 1843; 1845.

Text, 1845.

Variations from the text: —

II. 4. *Glory that was:* beauty of fair. 1831; S. L. M.
     5. *That was:* of old. 1831; S. L. M.
III. 1. *Yon brilliant:* that little. 1831; S. L. M.; that shadowy. G. M.
     3. *Agate lamp:* folded scroll. 1831; S. L. M.; G. M.
     4. *Ah!:* A. 1831.

FROM AN ALBUM (ALONE)

Text, *Scribner's Magazine.*

This poem was published in *Scribner's Magazine*, September, 1875, which text is followed.

The poem is signed E. A. Poe, and introduced by a note as follows: "The following verses, which are given in facsimile, were written by Edgar A. Poe shortly before he left West Point in 1829."

Mr. Eugene L. Didier writes that he discovered and cut the poem from the album of a Mrs. Balderstone of Baltimore, Maryland. He further states that the headline "Alone," and the date "Baltimore, March 17, 1829," were not in Poe's hand; also that the account in *Scribner's*, that the poem was written shortly before Poe left West Point, is an error.

SPIRITUAL SONG

Text, Poe MS.

This fragment of a poem, but a most striking fragment, which is written entirely in Poe's well-known later-day hand with all the characteristics of punctuation and heading, was left by him in his desk at the *Southern Literary Messenger* office, Richmond, Virginia. Both the desk and the manuscript are now in my possession. The poem is of special interest, because of the dearth of Poe's new poetry while editing the *Messenger*. It also tends to show how some poetic lines impressed Poe's mind, and with what consummate skill he could improve upon other ideas with his own words.

The poem is written on the reverse side of the following manuscript poem: —

"SACRED SONG

O, Strike the Harp

"O! strike the harp, while yet there lies
In Music's breath the power to please;
And if the tears should fill mine eyes,
They can but give my bosom ease.
But hush the notes of Love and Mirth
Too welcome to my heart before;
For now those airs that breathe of earth
Can charm my pensive soul no more.

"Yes, I have loved the world too well
And roved in Pleasure's train too long;
And I have felt her sweetest spell
In Beauty's smile, and Passion's song.
But now my soul would break her chains,
While yet, perhaps the grace is given;
Then strike the Harp to Zion's strains
And she shall soar at once to heaven."

This is unsigned, and backed "Anonymous composition for the *Messenger*." It is addressed to "Mr. Thomas W. White, Publisher of the *Southern Literary Messenger*, Richmond, Va." and has the postmark "Steam," showing that it came from Norfolk, Virginia, by steamer. The poetry evidently made some impression on Poe's mind, and while he possibly intended to re-write it in his own way and made a good start, yet for some reason he changed his mind, and instead of completing it, hunted up and found the author. On page 554 of the second volume of the *Messenger* for August, 1836, which Poe edited, may be seen the poem printed as written in the manuscript, but headed "by W. Maxwell" and so indexed. The handwriting of the "Sacred Song" is that of William Maxwell, well known as the first Secretary of the Virginia Historical Society; and a poet then residing at Norfolk. He published a volume of poems in Philadelphia which were well received at the time. He afterwards contributed other poetry to the *Messenger* while Poe was the editor. It is also a matter of conjecture, that instead of completing the "Spiritual Song," Poe decided to use "Israfel," as that poem also appeared in the *Messenger* for August, 1836.

In this connection it might be noted that Poe evidently wrote his well-known poem of "The Conqueror Worm " after reading Wallace Cone's "Proud Ladye," which he reviewed for *Burton's Gentleman's Magazine*, June, 1840, in which was the line —

"And let him meet the Conqueror worm."

The idea in the verses "Spiritual Song" is also met with in his poem "The Haunted Palace," fourth verse, fifth line: —

"A troop of echoes, whose sweet duty
   Was to sing
In voices of surpassing beauty
   The wit and wisdom of their king."

ELIZABETH

Text, Poe MS.

This poem has never appeared in Poe's own, nor in the later edited editions of his poetry. It was taken from his cousin Elizabeth Herring's album, and is written on stained and slightly charred paper, and signed "Edgar." The handwriting is probably that of between 1831 and 1834 and approximates later years. It is an acrostic, spelling "Elizabeth

Rebecca." The manuscript was included in the Pierce auction sale at Philadelphia, May 6, 1903. It is now in the collection of an American collector. The text is from a facsimile of the original manuscript.

Miss Herring lived in Baltimore, where Poe visited her.

FROM AN ALBUM

Text, Poe MS.

This poem, like the preceding one, was taken from the album of Elizabeth Herring, and is also an acrostic, spelling "Elizabeth." There is no title to same, and it is signed "E. A. P." It has never appeared in any edition of Poe's poems. The manuscript was also sold at the Pierce auction sale at Philadelphia, May 6, 1903, and is now in the library of an American collector. It too is written on stained and slightly charred paper. Miss Herring stated that Poe wrote her love poetry in the early days. The text is from a facsimile of the original manuscript.

TO SARAH

Text, *Southern Literary Messenger.*

These lines appeared in the *Southern Literary Messenger* for August, 1835, and are signed "Sylvio." In a memorandum left by Poe in the "Duane" copy of the *Messenger*, found by me in Boston, Massachusetts, some years ago, this poem and an unpublished story were both acknowledged by Poe.

The lines were evidently intended for Sarah Elmira Royster, his early sweetheart. They might be read in connection with the early 1829 lines commencing "I care not that my earthly lot —"

THE GREAT MAN

Text, Poe MS.

This poem, entirely in the hand of Poe, is written on paper stamped "Owen & Hurlbut, So. Lee Mass." The oldest employee of the firm wrote that the paper was made and used in the 20's or 30's. The manuscript was found in Poe's desk used by him at the *Southern Literary Messenger* office, Richmond, Virginia. The word " winds" in line fourteen was changed to "breezes " in the manuscript by Poe.

In note 5 to "Tamerlane" Poe wrote: —

> "——— Who hardly will conceive
> That any should become 'great,' born
> In their own sphere —

" Although Tamerlane speaks this, it is not the less true. It is a matter of the greatest difficulty to make the generality of mankind believe that one with whom they are upon terms of intimacy shall be called, in the world, a 'great man.' The reason is evident. There are few great men. Their actions are consequently viewed by the mass of the people through the medium of distance. The prominent parts of their characters are alone noted; and those properties, which are minute and common to every one, not being observed, seem to have no connection with a great character. Who ever read the private memorials, correspondence, &c., which have become so common in our time, without wondering that 'great men' should act and think ' so abominably ' ? "

It is evident that Poe afterwards changed his early views on the subject, or it is a case, as he states in his poem of "Elizabeth," of "innate love of contradiction," which characterized some of his writings. During the later period of his life Poe was known to have written a poem called "The Great, or The Beautiful Physician." Mrs. William Wiley had it from her mother, and is quite confident that the "Physician" manuscript was long in her family, but of late years had gone astray. J. H. Ingram had a note in the January, 1909, New York *Bookman*, in which he gave the particulars of a lost poem by Poe, "The Beautiful Physician," as told to him by Mrs. Shew.

With Poe's known habit of using the early text of his poems in later life, it is not improbable that this early poem was revised and made do duty again as "The Great Physician."

GRATITUDE. TO ———

Text, *The Symposia*.

This poem is signed E. A. P., and was published in "The Symposia," volume i, no. 1, 8vo, pp. 4. Providence, Rhode Island, January 27, 1848.

It was sold at auction in Boston in the spring of 1896. The poem is supposed to have been addressed to Mrs. S. H. Whitman, and was for the benefit of some church or fair in that city.

AN ENIGMA

Text, *Burton's Gentleman's Magazine.*

This appeared in *Burton's Gentleman's Magazine* for May, 1840, and was preceded by the following: —

" PALINDROMES

" A word, a verse, or sentence, that is the same when read backwards or forwards — such as *Madam-eye*, and a few others are palindromes; so that like the *bourgeoise gentilhomme*, who talked prose all his life without knowing it, we repeat extemporary palindromes daily, in utter ignorance of our talent. This is a redeeming quality, by the bye, to conceal any quality we have, when we are so proud of displaying those we have not. Indeed, our talents may be often divided in the same way as some hand-writing I have heard of; *first*, such as nobody can find out; *secondly*, what none but ourselves can discover; and *thirdly*, what our friends can also discern. We subjoin an English palindrome by Taylor, the Water-poet: —

' Lewd did I live, and evil I did dwell.'

And an enigma where all the words required are palindromes; the answers will be easily discovered."

IMPROMPTU

TO KATE CAROL

Text, *Broadway Journal.*

This is printed in the Editorial Miscellany of the *Broadway Journal* of April 26, 1845. In Poe's notices to Correspondents, March 29, in the *Journal* appears "A thousand thanks to Kate Carol." The issue of April 5 contains a poem "The Rivulet's Dream," signed Kate Carol, preceded by the following Poe note: "We might *guess* who is the fair author of the following lines, which have been sent us in a MS. evidently disguised, — but we are not satisfied with guessing, and would give the world to *know*."

Mrs. Frances Sargent Osgood has some verses "Love's Reply," the following week, reading as a response. Strong external evidence indicates that these lines of Poe's were intended for Mrs. Osgood.

STANZAS

Text, *Graham's Magazine*, December, 1845.

In Mrs. Frances Sargent Osgood's own copy of *Graham's Magazine* for December, 1845, she marked these Stanzas to herself, and added Poe's name to the signed initial "P."

The romance between Mrs. Osgood and Poe had then been going on steadily for some months. There were also other previous references to each other in *Graham's Magazine* and the *Broadway Journal*. About the time this poem was written there had arisen some misunderstanding, or Mrs. Osgood's family had interceded in the matter. These lines followed Mrs. Osgood's verses addressed to Poe called "Israfel" in the November *Broadway Journal* and may have been intended as Poe's answer.

THE DIVINE RIGHT OF KINGS

Text, *Graham's Magazine*, August, 1845.

In an old leather-bound copy of *Graham's Magazine* for the years 1845–46, once owned by Mrs. Frances Sargent Osgood, she marked this poem signed "P," as by Poe. The markings of her own writings in the same volume show that the lines were an impromptu reply of Poe's to some words of hers in a story published in the August, 1845, number of *Graham's Magazine*, called "Ida Grey."

The text and additional markings of Mrs. Osgood to this tale make it read like an idealized account of her first meeting with Poe as written in a letter to R. W. Griswold. Her hero, like Poe, "has grey eyes of singular earnestness; manners coldly courteous; with depth to the tone of his voice. His lightning intellect was irresistible." And like Poe he had a wife. In one passage she wrote: "He bids me tell him that I love him, as proudly as if he had a right, an unquestionable, an undoubted, a divine right to demand my love. Ah! With what grand and simple eloquence he writes!"

From this it might be taken that Poe's letters to Mrs. Osgood were equally as interesting and eloquent as those he wrote to Mrs. Whitman and to "Annie."

In some way R. W. Griswold had obtained possession of this volume of Mrs. Osgood's and no doubt the matters made him the more anxious to secure the letters of Mrs. Osgood written to Poe. Mrs. Clemm wrote Mr. Ingram, Poe's English biographer, that Griswold had made her a liberal offer of money for the letters of Mrs. Osgood, but fearing that poverty might force her to give them up, as well as others her "Eddie" had entrusted to her care, she finally destroyed them.

This story of "Ida Grey," with its close references to Poe's romance with Mrs. Osgood, must have been talked about by Poe's contemporaries at the time. While the Mrs. Whitman romance was going on later, as Poe's published letters to Mrs. Whitman show, his "pestilential literary women friends" kept busy sending Mrs. Whitman stories detrimental to Poe's character, while she in turn almost swamped Poe with interrogatories. Among Mrs. Whitman's inquiries to Poe was something about this story of "Ida Grey." It may be recalled that Poe is alleged to have first written to Mrs. Whitman under the assumed name of "Edward S. T. Grey." In reply to Mrs. Whitman's inquiry, Poe merely stated, "Mrs. O.'s 'Ida Grey' is in *Graham's* for August — '45."

THE VITAL STREAM

Text, Poe MS.

A facsimile of this poem entirely in Poe's handwriting is preserved, but the original manuscript seems to be lost. The poem was discovered among the Ellis & Allan papers in the Library of Congress at Washington among a number of other Poe documents. It was written by Poe just after his return from college in 1827, and at a time when his love disappointments with Miss Royster were most keenly felt. This is Poe's earliest known manuscript verse.

"DEEP IN EARTH MY LOVE IS LYING"

Text, Poe MS.

This couplet in faint pencil in Poe's autograph was discovered in the New York Public Library in October, 1914. It is written on the back of an original holograph manuscript of Poe's poem "Eulalie." It was laid in a leatherette-bound copy book used as an autograph album about the period of 1845 to 1850. It is written on light bluish tinted writing paper common to the period in which it was produced, and like Poe used during the latter part of his life. There is pasted on the lower right-hand corner of the poem "Eulalie," on a strip of white paper, "Respt. Yr. Ob. St. Edgar A. Poe"; evidently taken from one of Poe's letters. It is a conjecture that the lines were written in the year 1845, although they may date after the death of Poe's wife in 1847. The couplet is printed in the New York Public Library *Bulletin* for December, 1914, Vol. XVIII. No. 12.

LINES TO JOE LOCKE

Text, *Philadelphia Saturday Museum*, March 4, 1843.

The verses appear in a sketch of Poe's life published in the *Philadelphia Saturday Museum*, March 4, 1843, with many other well-known and fully authenticated poems by Poe.

Joe Locke was an inspector of tactics, and an *ex officio* officer of the barracks, at the West Point Academy while Poe was there in 1830–31. The principal duty of Inspector Locke was to report any violations of instructions. It is said by Poe's contemporaries that No. 28, South Barracks, where Poe sojourned with two other cadets, gave Locke plenty to report.

Poe was hopeful that this lampoon would earn his dismissal, but it was overlooked. The lines eluded the observation of Poe's earlier editors of his poems, but appeared among the "Notes" in the revised Life of Poe by Professor G. E. Woodberry. A cadet who roomed with Poe at West Point has also published one verse erroneously of the poem from memory in *Harper's New Monthly Magazine* for November, 1867. This was copied into the Virginia Poe, Vol. I.

NOTES MAINLY ON CHANGES
AND ADDITIONS IN THE VARIORUM
TEXT OF THE POEMS

Sources of the text for E. A. Poe's poems, page 183. After Griswold's 1850 edition of Poe's poems should follow Griswold's "Gift Leaves of American Poetry." 1849.

The Raven, page 224. The "Raven" first appeared in the *Evening Mirror* of January 29, 1845. This form of the poem was carried over into the *Weekly Mirror* of February 8, 1845, as it is shown by the error in both issues, in the tenth stanza of the poem. In the fifth line the word "he" is repeated.

To One in Paradise, page 252. A holograph manuscript of Poe's, and signed "Edgar Allan Poe," of this poem has been discovered within the past year. It has the heading "To One Departed," which was used once before by Poe to his poem "To F———." published in *Graham's Magazine* for March, 1842. There are only three stanzas, the third stanza as left by Poe in his 1845 revision being cut out. It closely follows the earlier versions of the poem and was probably written prior to 1845. There are a few punctuation changes, and in the last line "eternal streams" is changed to "Elysian streams." The history of the manuscript is not fully traced.

Eulalie — A Song, page 254. A manuscript of this poem in the autograph of Poe was discovered in the New York Public Library in October, 1914. It was laid loose in an autograph album, a part of the collection of R. L. Stuart presented to the library in 1892. It is written on a light bluish tinted paper similar to writing paper used by Poe. On the lower right-hand corner of the poem is pasted "Respt. Yr. Ob. St. Edgar A. Poe"; the salutation and signature of Poe, evidently extracted from a Poe letter. There is written on the back of the manuscript in faint pencil an original couplet by Poe. The poem and lines it is conjectured were written in 1845, although they may date later, or after the death of his wife in 1847. A fac-simile of the poem appears in the New York Public Library *Bulletin* for December, 1914, Vol. XVIII, No. 12.

To F———s S. O———d, page 254. The original manuscript to these verses as first written by Poe have been discovered since the issue of the first edition of this volume. When Miss Herring was married she exchanged albums with a girl friend. Both albums had in them poetry written by Poe. The album of Miss Herring with Poe's verse has been found, but that of her friend, with other Poe matters Miss Herring was known to hold, has so far eluded vigilant search. The lines are entirely in Poe's autograph and were written in the album of his cousin Elizabeth Herring, at Baltimore some time between the years 1832–34. They are signed "E A P." and read as follows: —

TO ELIZABETH

Would'st thou be loved? then let thy heart
From its present pathway part not —
Be everything which now thou art
And nothing which thou art not:

So with the world thy gentle way,
And unassuming beauty
Shall be a constant theme of praise,
And love — a duty.

The Haunted Palace, page 257. This poem was printed by R. W. Griswold in his "Gift Leaves of American Poetry." New York, 1849. The last revised manuscript made by Poe of this poem was sent to Griswold by Poe prior to his death, but it arrived too late, or for some unknown reason Griswold printed and followed the earlier versions of the poem. In the *Aristidean* for October, 1845, is a review of Poe's Tales. The editor, T. D. English, was ill about this time, and it is stated that Poe with a few other friends made up several issues of the magazine. One of the numbers is in the library of a book collector marked in pencil with the names of the contributors of the articles. This handwriting closely approximates Poe's. If Poe did not write the review in the October *Aristidean*, he must surely have inspired many facts therein stated. In the mention of "The Haunted Palace," it is said, "This was originally sent to O'Sullivan, of the *Democratic Review*, and by him rejected, because he found it impossible to comprehend it."

Scenes from "Politian," page 258. The following fragment from the first scene of Act II. of "Politian," was with the original manuscript.

Duke. Why do you laugh?

Castiglione. Indeed

I hardly know myself. Stay! Was it not
On yesterday we were speaking of the Earl?
Of the Earl Politian? Yes! it was yesterday.
Alessandra, you and I, you must remember!
We were walking in the garden.

Duke. Perfectly.

I do remember it — what of it — what then?

Cas. O nothing — nothing at all.

Duke. Nothing at all!

It is most singular that you should laugh
At nothing at all!

Cas. Most singular — singular!

Duke. Look you, Castiglione, be so kind
As to tell me, sir, at once what 't is you mean.
What are you talking of?

Cas. Was it not so?

We differed in opinion touching him.

Duke. Him! — Whom?

Cas. Why, sir, the Earl Politian.

Duke. The Earl of Leicester! Yes! — is it he you mean?

We differed, indeed. If I now recollect
The words you used were that the Earl you knew
Was neither learned nor mirthful.

Cas. Ha! Ha! — now did I?

Duke. That did you, sir, and well I knew at the time
You were wrong, it being not the character
Of the Earl — whom all the world allows to be
A most hilarious man. Be not, my son,
Too positive again.

Cas. 'T is singular!

Most singular! I could not think it possible
So little time could so alter one!
To say the truth about an hour ago,
As I was walking with the Count San Ozzo,
All arm in arm, we met this very man
The Earl — he, with his friend Baldazzar,
Having just arrived in Rome. Ha! Ha! he *is* altered!
Such an account he gave me of his journey!

'T would have made you die with laughter — such tales he told
Of his caprices and his merry freaks
Along the road — such oddity — such humor —
Such wit — such whim — such flashes of wild merriment
Set off too in such full relief by the grave
Demeanour of his friend — who, to speak the truth,
Was gravity itself —

   Duke. Did I not tell you?

   Cas. You did — and yet 't is strange! but true as strange.
How much I was mistaken! I always thought
The Earl a gloomy man.

   Duke. So, so, you see!
Be not too positive. Whom have we here?
It cannot be the Earl?

   Cas. The Earl! Oh no!
'T is not the Earl — but yet it is — and leaning
Upon his friend Baldazzar. Ah! welcome, sir!

              (*Enter Politian and Baldazzar.*)
My lord, a second welcome let me give you
To Rome — his Grace the Duke of Broglio.
Father! this is the Earl Politian, Earl
Of Leicester in Great Britain. (*Politian bows haughtily.*) That, his friend
Baldazzar, Duke of Surrey. The Earl has letters,
So please you, for Your Grace.

   Duke. Ha! ha! Most welcome
To Rome and to our palace, Earl Politian!
And you, most noble Duke! I am glad to see you!
I knew your father well, my Lord Politian.
Castiglione! call your cousin hither,
And let me make the noble Earl acquainted
With your betrothed. You come, sir, at a time
Most seasonable. The wedding —

   Politian. Touching those letters, sir,
Your son made mention of — your son, is he not? —
Touching those letters, sir, I wot not of them.
If such there be, my friend Baldazzar here —
Baldazzar! ah! — my friend Baldazzar here
Will hand them to Your Grace. I would retire.

   Duke. Retire! So soon?

   Cas. What ho! Benito! Rupert!

His lordship's chambers — show his lordship to them!
His lordship is unwell.

(*Enter Benito.*)

Ben. This way, my lord!   (*Exit, followed by Politian.*)
Duke. Retire! Unwell!
Bal. So please you, sir, I fear me
'T is as you say — his lordship is unwell.
The damp air of the evening — the fatigue
Of a long journey — the — indeed I had better
Follow his lordship. He must be unwell.
I will return anon.
    Duke. Return anon!
Now this is strange! Castiglione!
This way, my son, I wish to speak with thee.
You surely were mistaken in what you said
Of the Earl, mirthful, indeed! which of us said
Politian was a melancholy man?   (*Exeunt.*)

In the tale called "William Wilson" Poe mentions the "palazzo of the Neapolitan Duke Di Briglio." In the letter of J. P. Kennedy to T. W. White dated April 13, 1835, mention is made of Poe at work on a tragedy, which was probably "Politian." In Poe's miscellanies called "Pinakidia" he says: "Politian, the poet and scholar, was an admirer of 'Alessandria Scala.'" In this drama Poe has one of his characters named "Alessandria."

The manuscript of the soliloquy spoken by "Politian" alone in the Coliseum, which ended the drama, has recently come to light. It was abstracted from the other manuscript of the drama by Mrs. Lewis, and with a manuscript by Poe of one of her own poems presented by her to an autograph collector many years ago. It will be noted that Poe's verses on "The Coliseum" were evidently made up from this soliloquy which reads in part as follows: —

"Gaunt vestibules, and phantom-peopled aisles,
I feel ye now! I feel ye in your strength!
O spells more sure than e'er Judean king
Taught in the gardens of Gethsemane!
O spells more potent than the rapt Chaldee
Ever drew down from out the quiet stars!
She comes not and the moon is high in Heaven!
Here where the hero fell a column falls,
Here where the mimic eagle glared in gold

A secret vigil holds the swarthy bat,
Here where the dames of Rome their yellow hair
Waved to the wind, now wave the reed and thistle;
Here where on ivory couch the Cæsar sate
On bed of moss lies gloating the foul adder;
Here where on golden throne the monarch lolled
Glides spectre-like into his marble home,
Lit by the wan light of the hornèd moon,
The swift and silent lizard of the stones."

A Valentine, page 270. This poem also appeared in the *New York Evening Mirror* for February 21, 1846. It closely follows the Griswold manuscript version with the exception of "All" in the third line from the last instead of "Ah."

For Annie, page 272. The author's last copy published of this poem was sent to the *Home Journal* by Poe, and appeared April 28, 1849. The introductory note in the *Home Journal* has never been reproduced until now. It was headed "Odd Poem," and continued — "The following exquisite specimen of the *private property in words* has been sent us by a friend, and we are glad to be able to add it to the scrap-book of singularities in literature which so many of our fair readers, doubtless, have upon the table. Poe certainly has that gift of nature, which an abstract man should be most proud of — a type of mind different from all others without being less truthful in its perceptions for that difference; and though (to use two long words) this kind of *idiosyncrasy* is necessarily *idiopathic*, and, from want of sympathy, cannot be largely popular, it is as valuable as rarity in anything else, and to be admired by connoisseurs proportionately. Money (to tell a useless truth) could not be better laid out for the honor of this period of American literature — neither by the government, by a society, nor by an individual — than in giving Edgar Poe a competent annuity, on condition that he should never write except upon impulse, never dilute his thoughts for the magazines, and never publish anything till it had been written a year. And this *because* the threatening dropsy of our country's literature is in copying the *Gregariousness* which prevails in everything else, while Mr. Poe is not only peculiar in himself, but unsusceptible of imitation. We have Bulwers by hundreds, Mrs. Hemanses by thousands, Byrons common as shirt-collars, every kind of writer 'by the lot,' and less of *individualesque genius* than any other country in the world. This extends to other things as well. Horace Greeley is a national jewel (we think) from being humbly yet fearlessly individualesque in politics and conduct. What is commonly understood by *eccentricity* is but a trashy copy of what we mean. The reader's mind will easily pick out instances of the true individualesque, in every walk of life, and, as a mere suggestion, we here leave it — proceeding to give Mr. Poe's verses: — 'FOR ANNIE.'"

Tamerlane, page 279. In Poe's letter to Mrs. S. H. Whitman, dated October 18, 1848, he quoted the following: "I will erect," I said, "a prouder throne than any on which mere monarch ever sat; and on this throne she — *she* shall be my queen." This idea is found in these lines, stanzas XI and XII.

Al Aaraaf, page 298. In connection with Poe's first note to this poem on "Tycho Brahe." His interest in the Swedish astronomer is further shown by a note in the *Broadway Journal*, vol. 2, No. 19, under the heading of "News of Tycho Brahe."

In a letter to John Neal dated December 29, 1829, Poe wrote: "I think the best lines for sound are these in Al Aaraaf,

> There Nature speaks and even ideal things
> Flap shadowy sounds from visionary wings."

Romance, page 300. In a letter to John Neal dated December 29, 1829, Poe wrote: "But the best thing [in every respect] is the small piece headed 'Preface.' I am certain these lines have never been surpassed [Lines 35–39, 1829, quoted] 'It is well to think well of one's self'—so says somebody."

An Enigma, page 319. This appeared anonymously in the Philadelphia *Casket* for May, 1827, and the supposition is that it was among other poetry sent out by Poe before he left Richmond in March, 1827. It constitutes the earliest known published verse of Poe's.

BIBLIOGRAPHY

BIBLIOGRAPHY

[THE following abbreviations are used: — Y. L. G., The Yankee and Boston Literary Gazette; A. C., Atkinson's Philadelphia Casket; B. J., Broadway Journal; S. L. M., Southern Literary Messenger; B. G. M., Burton's Gentleman's Magazine; G. M., Graham's Magazine; S. M., Philadelphia Saturday Museum; Pio., The Pioneer; A. W. R., American Whig Review; S. E. P., Philadelphia Saturday Evening Post; S. M. V., Baltimore Saturday Morning Visiter; A. M., Baltimore American Museum; G. L. B., Godey's Lady's Book; M. M., New York Missionary Memorial; E. M., Evening Mirror; C. M., Columbia Magazine; H. J., Home Journal; S. U. M., Sartain's Union Magazine; U. M., Union Magazine; C., London Critic; N. Y. T., New York Tribune; F. U., Flag of Our Union; Gr. 1842, The Poets and Poetry of America, 1842; Gr. 1855, The Poets and Poetry of America, 1855; L. W., Literary World; W., Richmond Whig; Gr. 1850, Griswold's 1850 Works of E. A. Poe; L. E., Literary Emporium; J. L. G., J. Lorimer Graham copy of 1845, poems with Poe's MS. corrections; MSS. Copy of 1829 poems with Poe's MS. corrections; E., Richmond Examiner. The editions of 1827, 1829, 1831, and 1845 are indicated by dates; MS., Poe's Manuscript.]

1827. 1. The Vital Stream (No title), 1827; MS.
2. An Enigma. Philadelphia *Casket*, May, 1827; B. G. M., May, 1840.
3. Tamerlane. 1827; extracts in Y. L. G., Dec., 1829; 1829; MS. 1829; 1831; 1845.
4. Song (I saw thee on thy bridal day). (To ——), 1827, with same title, and 1829; MS. 1829 (In an Album); B. J., ii. 11; 1845.
5. Dreams. 1827; MS. 1829.
6. Spirits of the Dead. (Visit of the Dead), 1827; 1829; MS. 1829; B. G. M., July, 1839.

7. Evening Star. 1827.

8. A Dream within a Dream. (Imitation), 1827; extract in Y. L. G., Dec., 1829, (To ——), 1829; incorporated in Tamerlane, 1831; For Annie, MS. London *Bookman*, Jan., 1909; (To ——), E., Oct., 1849; F. U., March 31, 1849.

9. (In Youth Have I Known One With Whom The Earth). (No title), 1827. The title "Stanzas" is the late E. C. Stedman's.

10. A Dream. (No title), 1827; 1829; B. J., ii, 6; 1845.

11. (The Happiest Day, The Happiest Hour). (No title), 1827.

12. The Lake, To ——. (The Lake), 1827; 1829; MS. 1829; incorporated in Tamerlane 1831, but not in 1845; 1845; M. M., 1846.

1829. 13. Sonnet — To Science. (No title), 1829; A.C., 1830; 1831; S. L. M., May, 1836; in the Island of the Fay, G. M., June, 1841; B. J., ii, 4; 1845.

14. Al Aaraaf. Extracts in Y. L. G., Dec., 1829; revised in MSS.; 1829; 1831; extracts in S. M., March 4, 1843; 1845; extracts in G. M., Feb., 1845; extracts in S. L. M., Oct., 1848.

15. To ——. (The bowers, whereat, in dreams I see). 1829; B. J., ii. 11; 1845.

16. To the River ——. 1829; MS. 1829, (In an Album); B. G. M., Aug., 1839; S. M., March 4, 1843; B. J., ii, 9; 1845.

17. To ——. (I heed not that my earthly lot). (To M——). 1829; MS. no date, Gr., 1850.

18. Fairy-Land. Extracts in Y. L. G., Sept., 1829; 1829; 1831; B. G. M., Aug., 1839; B. J. ii, 13; 1845.

19. Romance (Preface), 1829; revised in MSS.; (Introduction), 1831; S. M., March 4, 1843; B. J., ii, 8; 1845.

20. Alone. (No title), MS. (From an Album) *Scribner's Magazine*, Sept., 1875. Title E. L. Didier's. Another portion of MS. with title exists, but has some connection with 17.

1831. 21. To Helen. 1831; S. L. M., March, 1836; G. M., Sept., 1841, and Feb., 1845; S. M., March 4, 1843; 1845.

22. Israfel. 1831; S. L. M., Aug., 1836; G. M., Oct., 1841; S. M., March 4, 1843; B. J., ii, 3; 1845; revised in J. L. G.; E., Oct., 1849.

23. The City in the Sea. (The Doomed City), 1831; (The City of Sin), S. L. M., Aug., 1836; A. W. R.; (subtitle, A Prophecy), April, 1845; B. J., ii, 8; 1845; revised in J. L. G.

24. The Sleeper. (Irene), 1831; MS. (Irene the Dead), 1836; S. L. M., May, 1836; Gr., 1842; S. M., March 4, 1843; B. J., i, 18; 1845; extracts in letter to Griswold, April 19, 1845; revised in J. L. G.; E., Oct., 1849.

25. Lenore. (A Pæan), 1831, and with same title, S. L. M., Jan., 1836; Pio., Feb., 1843; S. M., March 4, 1843; B. J., ii, 6; 1845; G. M., Feb., 1845; W., Sept. 18, 1849; revised in J. L. G.; E., Oct., 1849; extracts in S. L. M., May, 1849; Gr., 1850.

26. The Valley of Unrest. (The Valley Nis), 1831; and with same title, S. L. M., Feb., 1836; A. W. R., April, 1845; B. J., ii, 9; 1845.

27. Lines to Joe Locke. MS., S. M., March 4, 1843.

1832. 28. Elizabeth. Written in his cousin Elizabeth Herring's album about 1832.

29. From an Album. From his cousin Elizabeth Herring's album about 1832.

30. To F——s S. O——d. (To Elizabeth), written in his cousin Elizabeth Herring's album about 1832. (Lines written in an Album), S. L. M., Sept., 1835; (To ——), B. G. M., Aug., 1839 (To F——), B. J., ii, 10; 1845.

31. Hymn. (No title), MS. of Morella about 1832–33; S. L. M. (in Morella), April, 1835; and in the same tale, B. G. M., Nov., 1839; Tales, 1840 and B. J., (Catholic Hymn), ii, 6, and with same title, 1845; revised in J. L. G.

32. Scenes from Politian. (Scenes from an Unpublished Drama), MS. about 1831–32; S. L. M., Dec., 1835, Jan., 1836; 1845; extracts in B. J., i, 13; revised in J. L. G. Extracts in The *Southern Magazine*, Nov., 1875; extracts in The "Chandos Classics." London and New York, 1888.

1833. 33. The Coliseum. S. M. V., 1833; S. L. M. (with subtitle A Prize Poem), Aug., 1835; also with subtitle, S. E. P., June 12, 1841; (Coliseum), Gr., 1842; S. M., March 4, 1843; B. J., ii, 1; 1845; extracts from MS. in *The Bibliophile*, London, May, 1909.

1834. 34. To One in Paradise. (No title), G. L. B. (in The Visionary), January, 1834, and S. L. M. (in the same), July, 1835; (To Ianthe in Heaven), B. G. M., July, 1839; Tales (in The Visionary), 1840; S. M., March 4, 1843; MS. prior to 1845, with title "To One Departed," B. J., i, 19; B.

J. (in The Assignation), i, 23; 1845; revised in
J. L. G.; from MS.; London *Spectator*, Jan. 1,
1853; same in L. W., Feb. 5, 1853.

1835. 35. The Great Man. MS. From Poe's Southern
Literary Messenger desk. Written on paper
made prior to 1836.

36. To F——. (To Mary), S. L. M., July, 1835; (To
One Departed), G. M., March, 1842; and with
same title, S. M., March 4, 1843; B. J., i, 17;
1845.

37. To Sarah. S. L. M., Aug., 1835.

1836. 38. Spiritual Song. MS. from Poe's Southern Literary Messenger desk, 1836.

39. Latin Hymn, in tale Four Beasts in One. S. L. M.
title (Epimanes), March, 1836; 1840; B. J., ii,
22.

40. Song of Triumph, in Four Beasts in One. S. L. M.
title (Epimanes), March, 1836; 1840; B. J., ii,
22.

1837. 41. Bridal Ballad, S. L. M., Jan., 1837; (Ballad),
S. E. P., July 31, 1841; (Song of the Newly
Wedded), S. M., March 4, 1843; B. J., ii, 4;
1845; revised in J. L. G.; E., Oct., 1849.

42. Sonnet — To Zante. S. L. M., Jan., 1837; S. M.,
March 4, 1843; MS. 1840; B. J., ii, 2; 1845.

1839. 43. The Haunted Palace. A. M., April, 1839; (No
title), B. G. M.; (in the Fall of the House of
Usher), Sept., 1839, and Tales (in the same),
1840; Gr., 1842; S. M., March 4, 1843 (No title);
G. M., Feb., 1845; revised in J. L. G.; Tales
as before, 1845; MS. about 1849; E., Oct.,
1849.

1840. 44. Silence. (Silence. A Sonnet), B. G. M., April, 1840;

(Sonnet — Silence), S. M., March 4, 1843; and with title, B. J., ii, 3; 1845.

1843. 45. The Conqueror Worm. G. M., Jan., 1843; MS.; S. M., March 4, 1843; B. J. (in Ligeia), ii, 12; revised in J. L. G.; 1845; MS. about 1849; E., Oct., 1849.

1844. 46. Dream-Land. G. M., June, 1844; B. J., i, 26; 1845; revised in J. L. G.; E., Oct. 29, 1849.

1845. 47. The Raven. A. W. R., Feb., 1845; E. M., Jan. 29, 1845; same text in weekly issue Feb. 8, 1845; S. L. M., March, 1845; extracts in Shea MS.; C., June, 1845; extracts in B. J., i, 21; extracts in letter to Griswold, April 19, 1845; L. E., 1845; extracts in G. M., April, 1846; revised in J. L. G.; E., Sept. 25, 1849.

48. The Divine Right of Kings. G. M., Oct., 1845.

49. Stanzas. G. M., Dec., 1845.

50. Impromptu. (To Kate Carol). B. J., i, 17.

51. Eulalie. A. W. R., (subtitle, A Song), July, 1845; MS., no date; also with subtitle, B. J., ii, 5; 1845; revised in J. L. G.

52. Deep in Earth My Love is Lying. MS.

1847. 53. To M. L. S——. MS., Feb., 1847. (To Mrs. M. L. S.); H. J., March 13, 1847. Addressed to Mrs. M. L. Shew.

54. Ulalume. A BALLAD. A. W. R. (subtitle, To —— —— —), December, 1847; H. J., Jan. 1, 1848; L. W., March 3, 1849; E., Oct., 1849; Gr., 1850 and 1855; MS., 1849.

1848. 55. Gratitude. Symposia. Jan., 1848.

56. To —— —— —. C. M., March, 1848, addressed to Mrs. M. L. Shew; MS., (To Marie Louise), 1848.

57. Sonnet, U. M., March, 1848. MS. sent to Mrs. S. A. Lewis, in Nov., 1847; (An Enigma). Gr., 1850.

58. To ———. U. M., Nov., 1848, addressed to Mrs. S. H. Whitman; (To Helen), Gr., 1850. MS. sent to Bayard Taylor, June 15, 1848.

1849. 59. A Valentine. To ———. E. M., Feb. 21, 1846; S. U. M., March, 1849; F. U., March 3, 1849, dated "Valentine Eve, 1849"; MS. 1846 and 1848. Addressed to Mrs. Frances Sargent Osgood.

60. Eldorado, F. U., April 21, 1849; Gr., 1850.

61. For Annie. F. U. and H. J., April 28, 1849, E., Oct., 1849; MS. sent to Mrs. Richmond, 1849; Gr., 1850. Another MS., with same title, sent Mrs. Richmond later, has reference to 8.

62. Sonnet — To My Mother. F. U. (To My Mother), July 7, 1849; E., Oct., 1849; S. L. M., Dec., 1849; Leaflets of Memory, 1850.

63. Annabel Lee. N. Y. T., Oct. 9, 1849; S. L. M., Nov., 1849; S. U. M., Jan., 1850. E., Oct., 1849; MS., 1849; Gr., 1850, and 1855.

64. The Bells. E., Oct., 1849; S. U. M., Nov., 1849; MS., 1849.

INDEXES

INDEX OF FIRST LINES

INDEX OF TITLES

Lightning Source UK Ltd.
Milton Keynes UK
UKOW07f0119181114

241765UK00017B/806/P